"And when in brief moments of achievement he "gets her goin' "—
when he feels his vessel take life and speed ahead with nearly perfect sails and nearly perfect trim and a nearly perfect hull—he comes
pretty close to Heaven."

LEARNING TO RACE

H. A. Calahan

DOVER PUBLICATIONS, INC.
Mineola, New York

Bibliographical Note

This Dover edition, first published in 2000, is an unabridged republica-
tion of the work originally published in 1935 by The Macmillan Company,
New York.

Library of Congress Cataloging-in-Publication Data

Calahan, H. A. (Harold Augustin), b. 1889.
    Learning to race / H.A. Calahan.
        p. cm.
    Reprint. Originally published: New York : Macmillan, 1934.
    ISBN 0-486-40965-1 (pbk.)
    1. Yacht racing. I. Title.

GV826.5 .C3 2000
797.1'4—dc21
                                                                99-056274

Manufactured in the United States of America
Dover Publications, Inc., 31 East 2nd Street, Mineola, N.Y. 11501

To *Julia*—my first command
and to *Jolly Roger, Quad, L'Alouette,
Tiana, Brainstorm, Neaera, Get Busy,
Peedie, Lone Wolf, Wanderlust, Mary
Christmas,* and *Old Timer*—my boats
that taught me all this book contains.

FOREWORD

THE GENEROUS reception which yachtsmen have given to the author's first book, "Learning to Sail," has furnished the courage to attempt a similar work in the related but somewhat advanced field of yacht racing.

I attribute that generous reception to one admirable characteristic of the earlier book—it was written for a carefully defined audience. The concept of a reader who knew nothing about sailing, who had never even grasped a tiller, who knew not the meaning of the words which sailors toss about so glibly, was adhered to rigidly. The thousands of experienced yachtsmen who read "Learning to Sail" were kind enough to remember the true objective of the book and to read it from the point of view of the primary audience.

In "Learning to Race" I have endeavored likewise to conceive and visualize the reader accurately. He has learned to sail. He has not learned to race. He owns a small racing yacht. His financial means are limited. He is interested, not in building a new yacht, but in making his present yacht go.

Yachtsmen who are thoroughly experienced in the game of racing may pick up a few nuggets of wisdom; for no sailor's experience exactly duplicates that of another. But perhaps the book's chief service to the old hand will be expressed as a matter of emphasis. We are, all of us, prone to be careless in our sailing. Things which we know but neglect derive a new importance from the authority of the printed page.

Then, too, the book may perform a service simply by rendering known facts in an orderly manner. Properly marshaled, the axioms of yacht racing align themselves into a system of almost mathematical precision. Of course the actual sailing of a race more nearly resembles the fine arts than the exact sciences; but the experienced skipper is too prone to trust to his skill, too willing to give play to the artistic temperament. He must never forget that he is applying natural forces which move in accordance with fixed laws.

These laws are but imperfectly understood. The conditions under which the yachtsman meets them are invariably complicated. The process through which the phenomena of racing may be isolated and measured and reduced to exact formulæ may never be developed. Perhaps it is to be hoped that the scientists will not be too successful. When the test tube and the slide rule attain ascendency, true sport dies.

No modern book on yacht racing may dare to neglect the recent discoveries in aerodynamics. Yet it is apparent that the science is in its infancy. It is almost certain that many so-called laws discovered to-day will be disproved by the scientist of the future.

It is, therefore, very difficult for the yachtsman to segregate the scientific from the pseudo-scientific.

So this book is written from the practical rather than the theoretical point of view. I deplore the expression, for I realize that scientific development has always had to combat the ignorant opinion of the much-vaunted practical man. I maintain, however, that the scientists and the pseudo-scientists of to-day cannot quarrel with my advice or my conclusions, however much they may scorn my unscientific methods and mannerisms.

The reader is advised to delve deeply into the scientific books on racing, to digest them thoroughly, and to keep an open mind, tempered with a large measure of skepticism. He should be prepared to "try anything once" but to judge by results. The danger lies primarily in the fact that the inexperienced racing man cannot judge the results.

The chapters on racing tactics are strongly tempered by the author's conception of sportsmanship as displayed in American yachting. Yacht racing is a conspicuously clean sport. It is played by gentlemen of generous spirit. There is no excuse for using the weapon of offensive tactics against an unarmed foe.

The first person singular pronoun has crept into this book to a disturbing degree. Yet I have permitted it to do so with the hope that it will not be interpreted as braggadocio. The most blatant of us is forced to modesty in the presence of the sea, and humility is so universal a characteristic of the sailor that it is not even a virtue. The capital "I"s are due to two causes. In the first place, they are necessary in expressing an opinion, as differentiated from established fact—a distinction I have been careful to preserve. In the second place, I have been obliged to illustrate my points by frequent reference to my own races, because those are the only races of which I know the inside story. My task would be easier if more yachtsmen would talk freely of their own cleverness and their own stupidity. It is thus we learn.

Since this book will be used to some extent as a work of reference, I have endeavored as far as possible to make each chapter a complete unit. Necessarily this policy has resulted in repetitions which otherwise I would have preferred to avoid. But I have dared to be tiresome in order to be clear.

Throughout the book, it is assumed that the reader is sailing a small or medium size sloop—the sort of boat in which a beginner would attempt his first racing. The handling of schooners or of other boats of divided rig is not discussed.

A discussion of the relative merits of hull forms, rigs, and the like has been carefully avoided. That is the province of the naval architect. It is amply covered in many excellent works and technical treatises.

After all, this is a book for the beginner in yacht racing just as "Learning to Sail" was written for the beginner in sailing.

CONTENTS

ILLUSTRATIONS

ILLUSTRATIONS

ILLUSTRATIONS

Chapter I

UNVERIFIABLE MATTER

They tell me I could not possibly have remembered this; but it seems so real . . .

The stork dropped me, a little roughly, on the golden pavement near the pearly gates. He groped beneath his breast feathers for a plug of tobacco, bit off a chunk, and started to chew.

"Better pay attention, kid," he admonished kindly. "Here come your good and bad angels with their gifts. They'll play an important part in your life." I was aware of two great shining figures bending over me, so dazzlingly bright I could scarcely look at them.

"I'll make him honest," cried the good angel.

"But poor," added the bad one.

"Why do you guys always begin like that?" moaned the stork. He was obviously bored.

"I'll give him a pleasant smile," continued the good angel.

"And a bad temper."

"I'll give him friends."

"Who will bring him their troubles—not their merriment."

"I give him the love of a woman."

"But only one woman. All the rest will think him a zany."

"Better watch your words," growled the stork.

1

" 'Zany' is good enough in 1889 but by the time he grows up, no one will know what that means."

"All right," answered the bad angel, "I'll say 'flat tire' if that's any better."

The whole thing seemed so unkind, so inexorable, that I started to bawl. Remember, I was very young. The two angels continued but I didn't hear a word they said. After a while I paused and heard the stork say, "Aren't you boys going to give him anything in the line of sport?"

"I'll make him a yachtsman," cried the good angel. "That's the best gift in the whole bag of tricks."

"I've already made him poor," laughed the bad angel. "It takes a lot of money to win races."

"But I'll give him the know-how. He will understand fully the whole theory of the thing."

"That won't help much. He shall sail with a foul bottom and flat or baggy sails, a rubber mast, and poor gear."

"Yet he shall win races."

"But lose more than he wins."

They paused. The stork turned his head and spat a stream of tobacco juice to leeward.

"Between the two of you," he grumbled, "you've made the world's worst duffer. Well, it's too bad, kid, you're sure to have rough going of it. Now it's time we shoved off. I'm going to have a hard beat coming back and I want to catch the tide." He gathered up the ends of the sling in his bill and I felt myself swaying slightly.

Suddenly the good angel cried out, "I'll make him a writer of books. Books on sailing. If he can't win races himself he'll at least help others to win them."

"Not if they read the papers," answered the bad

angel. "The yachting reporters will lay for him. They'll hammer Hell out of an author who writes about racing but can't win races himself. If he wins, they'll call it an upset and a fluky race. If he loses, they'll say, 'Calahan, *as usual,* finished a bad last.' "

Just then the stork hopped off. With a few mighty strokes of his wings, he cleared the pearly gates, then started sailing down hill.

And what a sail that was!

Those great, powerful wings, balanced and poised so perfectly. Silence save for the humming of the wind and an occasional slight rippling of feathers like the rattle of reefing points. I wish Levick and Rosenfeld had been there with their cameras to catch those wings, and Dr. Curry to see the constant adjustment of them as if the stork were trimming his sheets and setting up his shrouds.

I shall never forget their beauty. I lay comfortably enough but a bit precariously as though in a martingale under the bowsprit, looking up at those wonderful sails sharply outlined against the blue of the skies like the blue of the sea.

Then all was dark for a spell. Then I heard someone say, "It's a boy," and I knew the sail was over.

Sometimes I think all yachtsmen try to recapture the thrill and perfection of that first sail. Surely the racing yachtsman remembers subconsciously the power and drive of those great wings against the blue sky.

All his life he tries to reproduce the same results, to recapture those first sensations of perfect sailing. He messes around with a rag and a stick to produce on earth what Heaven alone provides. And when in brief moments of achievement he "gets her goin' "—when he feels his vessel take life and speed ahead with nearly perfect sails and nearly perfect trim and a nearly perfect hull—he comes pretty close to Heaven.

These things are given to the *racing* yachtsman and to him alone. Your cruising man and your day sailor enjoy the beauties of sea and sky and the glory of motion which only a sail boat can give. Your cruising man revels in a quiet anchorage, the huge satisfaction of a voracious appetite, and soul-satisfying sleep to which he is lulled by lapping waves, slapping halliards and the fitful beams of his riding light. He enjoys an indescribable sense of achievement in reaching a distant port. New waters lure him. Old scenes recall fond memories. He has an enviable understanding of comfort and leisure and self-reliance. No one on earth can teach him more than he knows of the meaning of "well-being."

But he misses perfection.

I except, of course, those blithe spirits who race in cruising boats, crossing oceans, racing, driving every step of the way. But the ordinary cruising man is a casual, easy-going sort of person. No profanity makes a blue aura about his craft. If his vessel moves, it is good enough for him. If his helmsman holds his course, he is satisfied. If his sails are clean and free from mildew, his cup of joy is brimming.

Not to him is accorded that quest for perfection which is the urge of the racing yachtsman. Not to him is vouchsafed those exquisite moments when everything is taut and humming, when his craft, heeled down exactly to her sailing lines, is slipping quietly through the water at her very best speed. He has not seen the wings of the stork.

These rare moments of perfect sailing are the supreme reward of the racing man. He may finish in the ruck; but if he has found a brief interval of perfection, he is satisfied. He may finish first and get the consolation· of the winner's gun and a silver cup; but, if he has floundered through a poorly sailed race, there will always be something missing.

The layman and the cruising man do not understand this. They think that because a prize is offered to the winner, he races to gain this prize. They call him a "mug hunter." They conceive it his ambition to fill his home with an infinite number of cups and cigarette boxes and cocktail shakers.

They can never understand. They have not seen the stork.

Chapter II

THE LITTLE THINGS THAT COUNT

Not many years after that sail with the stork, I saw a picture which, to my mind, typifies the racing yachtsman. The picture was in one of the favorite barber shop publications of the day—*Puck* or *Judge* or possibly *Life*. It showed a meeting of two horse-drawn vehicles, one of which was driven by a bewhiskered farmer and the other by a dapper citified feller. It bore the following caption:

City Man (with balky livery horse): "Beg pawdon! But what do you do when your horse balks?"

Farmer: "Trade him. Giddap Dobbin!"

Most yachtsmen are in the position of the city man of the picture. When they ask, "What do you do when your boat won't win?" the answer, "Get a new boat" is obviously inadequate. Only the very rich can go out and get a new boat just like that. Most of us have spent all we can afford on the purchase of our present boat, for if we could have afforded to spend more, we would have bought a larger, finer boat in the first place.

But, even if we could, there would be no assurance that the new boat would travel any faster than the old. Certainly it would require just as much tuning-up, and equally good helmsmanship and strategy. These things must be learned anyway, and an old boat with manifest imperfections makes a good teacher.

Therefore I shall assume that the reader now possesses a racing yacht and that his means and disposition prevent his trading her for a new one. The objective to be determined is not, "Where can I find the fastest boat?" but "How can I win races with the boat I have?"

Races are won or lost by "little things."

No little thing, therefore, is unimportant. I have won a championship race by one second. I have lost by so narrow a margin that neither my opponent nor I knew which was the winner and each congratulated the other. On that occasion the Race Committee reported that my bow crossed the finish line first, but my mast crossed second, and the timing was taken from the masts.

In such a contest, it is easy to find a thousand reasons for losing. On looking back over the race there appear to be so many ways in which a second could have been saved. One says, "I over-stood the weather mark. It was only by a few feet; but those few feet would have saved more than a second." Or, "I should have tacked in-shore earlier. It was blowing harder there and the seas were smoother." Or, "The crew foozled the spinnaker. It wasn't bad, but it might have been better. The upper stop didn't break out for some time. And there was a twist in the head that would have blown out instantly if I had oiled that swivel. And the jib! Why can't those lubbers get that sheet trimmed faster?"

Seconds!

But take another race. You are clearly beaten with a good stretch of open water between your bow and the leading boat. The winner is so far ahead that the name on her transom is illegible. Yet you are traveling fast and you boil across the finish line just two minutes behind. Now the race has taken two hours. You are beaten by only two minutes. If you had been able to sail just one-sixtieth faster, to have saved one minute an hour, one second a minute, you would have earned the gun. A clean bottom would have made that difference. Or a little more strain on the outhaul to make your mainsail set better. Or a little less sag to the jib stay. Such things, or any one of them, could easily have cost ten times two minutes in a two-hour race.

Or you have made a tactical blunder. You tacked on an opponent's wind just too late to blanket him. A heart-beat's hesitation, and his wind was clear. Then your pride perhaps, or possibly your unwillingness to throw away a few more precious seconds in a second tack, made you hang on and take his back wind. You never caught him again. You were beaten right there by a slower boat.

"My for'ard hatch-cover blew off in that squall," explained an old intrepid skipper to me. "I didn't want to lose it. So I reached out for it with green water pouring into the cockpit. The boat came up into the wind, hung in stays, then filled away on the other tack. I got the hatch-cover but I lost the race."

"You lost the race," I answered, "not because you reached for the hatch-cover but because you failed to make that cover fast when you saw the squall approaching." The good old skipper is slightly deaf. He asked me to repeat what I said, but I let it go. He might have asked if my own hatch-cover had been fast that wild day. It wasn't. It will be hereafter, for I have seen a hatch-cover fastening turn first place into third. And that was a race to win—a race of a lifetime.

In the summer of 1932, eighty boats finished at Larchmont within two minutes, to the utter bewilderment of an impotent Race Committee. If it had been possible to take the time of this solidly overlapping fleet, nearly every skipper could have pointed out ways in which his position could have been bettered. Little things.

I recall one race when the entire fleet was becalmed in a bunch off Glen Cove. Beside me, and a trifle ahead, was a competitor I feared. She was very slippery in light airs. As we all bobbed around in that baffling calm, there came the faintest of zephyrs. We were ready for it and gained barely perceptible steerageway. I glanced at my opponent and noticed that her crew were monkeying with the rigging and her skipper was so absorbed with the task that he failed to get her going. That little breeze just kissed that bald spot on the water and went elsewhere. I carried it right to the finish line and won by a very wide margin. But that competitor, with an equal chance, stayed right where I had left him. I beat him by more than an hour. If he had been alert at that one instant, the race would have been his. Now it is certain that at the moment when I was working out that lead that carried me several miles to the finish, my competitor did not realize its importance. Ten minutes before that, he had caught a breath that had worked him into a commanding position. He expected another any minute. But it did not come. That one little breath of air for which he was unprepared was the important little thing in that race.

I cite all these instances to prove what every experienced racing skipper knows: It's the little things that count.

Yet the beginner can never be made to realize it. The beginner sails with a foul bottom and refuses to believe it affects results. Tell him to adjust his leech-lines and he will answer that he can't be bothered. He is blind to windage aloft and to friction below. He disregards trim of hull and of sheets. And his helmsmanship is alert only when he is sailing in close company with a competitor.

He does not realize that winds shift, that currents vary, that lines stretch—and that seconds count.

If this book does no more than make him realize the supreme importance of these little things, it will be worthy of publication.

Let us consider two boats, one admittedly faster than the other. The faster boat has new sails—perfect aerofoils. She has excellent rigging, too, but a poor skipper. The slower boat has old sails, poor rigging, but a good skipper. The good skipper cleans the bottom of his slow boat. He carefully stays and trims his "rubber" mast. He bends his ancient sails as an artist would paint a picture.

The careless skipper gives him fifteen minutes handicap at the start by entering the race with a foul bottom. He throws away the advantage of his wonderful rigging by staying his mast so that no sails could set properly. His perfect sails, badly bent, become actually inferior to the older sails properly bent.

So that right at the start, the experienced skipper of the slow boat enters the race with a faster hull and a faster rig to drive it. The experienced skipper will make no tactical blunders. He will "stay with" his boat, driving it all the way. Barring breaks, the race is his.

We may lay down at the very outset the following rules for winning yacht races:

1. Make your boat—hull, spars, rigging, sails—just as fast as possible.

2. Sail her just as fast as you can every second of the race.

3. Employ racing tactics to improve your own position, to hinder your opponents, and to protect your boat from their attacks.

4. Employ opportunism. Plan to get the breaks and then take advantage of them.

These rules are listed in the order of their importance. If the first rule is disregarded and your boat is conspicuously slow and unmanageable, your skill as a sailor will avail you little.

If the second rule is disregarded, you will have small opportunity to indulge in racing tactics. They count only when the competitors are reasonably well matched.

If the third rule is disregarded, the chances are that you will have little opportunity to take advantage of the breaks.

Let us make here two definitions, which, although they may be inaccurate, will serve the purposes of this book. By "racing tactics" is meant those decisions or maneuvers which are dictated by the position, course, or intention of competitors. By "opportunism" is meant those decisions or maneuvers which are dictated by circumstances over which the racing yachts have no control, such as wind, tide, current, seas, shoals, other vessels, obstructions to sea-room, shifting of marks, etc.

Chapter III

THE RULES AND CONDITIONS OF RACING

Racing between sail boats began on the first day when two boats sailed within sight of one another. That was a long time ago.

It has continued ever since.

In the early days the stakes were often life or death. The weaker vessel fled from the stronger. If she could keep out of striking range until nightfall and then change her course, she lived.

Fishing boats and cargo carriers have always raced. The first boat to reach a market commanded the best price. The tea clippers raced on almost every passage —raced half way round the world.

But modern yacht racing is a game. It is played in accordance with definite rules which the contestants must know and understand.

The first rules to understand are those which endeavor to make racing fair through classification and handicaps. Yachts are classified and handicapped, not on a basis of their actual speed, but on a basis of their potential speed. The maximum speed of a well-designed displacement racing sail boat in knots is approximately equal to the square root of the waterline length multiplied by the constant 1.35. It is evident from this formula that potential maximum speed is proportional to the waterline length. There is a maxim in prize-fighting that a good big man can always beat a good little man. So in yacht racing, a good big boat can always beat a good little boat.

This maximum potential speed was attained many years ago. Despite the advances in naval architecture, it has never been increased. All that the naval architects have succeeded in doing is to produce the same speed with smaller sail area.

Therefore yachts are classified in accordance with their size—yachts of approximately equal maximum potential speed racing together as one class. As a general rule, nowadays, all the yachts in the same class race against one another without time allowance. In some classes, yachts are handicapped in proportion to their racing measurements in accordance with a published time allowance scale of the yacht club sponsoring the race. This scale gives the handicap in seconds of time for each nautical mile of the race. To determine the handicap which one boat must allow another, subtract the smaller allowance from the larger and multiply it by the number of nautical miles stated in the printed circular which announces the course. If the Race Committee has made an error in stating the number of miles in the course, the proper procedure is to call the error to the Committee's attention *before* the race in ample time for the Committee to announce a correction. A protest on this point after the race is usually not honored by the Race Committee, and the length of the course is assumed to be the published length, not the actual length.

This method of handicapping usually applies to squadron runs and other races where yachts of different classes are all combined in a single race. In distance races, it is common practice for the Race

Committee to figure out in advance the time allowances for each yacht for the whole race and to give a copy of this table to each of the contestants.

The measurement rules by which the racing length of a yacht is determined vary with the different clubs. Originally the measurement rule was a simple affair. Yachts were measured from fore to aft along the deck. This rule produced very freakish boats, for, in order to gain waterline length and not be penalized for it, yachts were built with long waterlines and short decks so that the bow often raked forward and downward from the stem-head.

Then the measurement rules shifted to the waterline. This rule, too, produced freaks and brought about unwholesome boats with short waterlines and tremendous overhangs forward and aft. When these boats heeled down to their sailing lines, their overhangs gave them an actual waterline greatly in excess of their measurement waterline. Also there was no penalty on sail area so that these tender, short-waterline boats sprouted long nosepoles, booms extending far outboard, and enormous club topsails.

So sail area crept into the measurement rules and there was inaugurated a very simple rule still in vogue in many waters:

$$L = \frac{LWL + \sqrt{SA}}{2}$$

or, in other words, racing length is equal to half the sum of the load waterline plus the square root of sail area. This rule had the effect of reducing the so-called working sails so that in most boats built to race under this rule the sail area is equal to the square of the waterline length. As a result, the racing measurement under this rule is usually equal to the waterline.

But the long overhangs continued. It was necessary to penalize them. The result was the Universal Rule, a highly complicated formula in which waterline length, sail area, quarter beam length and displacement are all determining factors with penalties for excess draft, insufficient freeboard, etc.

For many years the Universal Rule was the standard measurement rule in the United States. In England and elsewhere another complicated measurement rule known as the International Rule became standard. It attained popularity in this country as well and many yachts have been built to this rule. In it the metric system has been adopted. The six-metre, eight-metre, ten-metre, and twelve-metre classes are all built to the International Rule.

Then the Scandinavian countries began building yachts with no limitations except sail area. The square-metre classes are all built to this rule.

Most rules include scantling restrictions to prevent yachts from being built too lightly to be serviceable.

The Cruising Club of America then developed a special measurement rule for the Bermuda Race. Its primary intention is to bar out mere racing machines and restrict the racing to cruising type yachts. As this book goes to press, a new rule is being formulated for ocean racing, but the objectives will be the same.

Most rules make provision for the greater speed of a sloop or cutter over a yacht with divided rig such as a schooner, ketch, or yawl. Also many rules provide an additional time allowance for yachts carrying a propeller.

It is to be noted that the handicap is a time allowance, not a distance allowance. A yacht may be a mile behind the yacht that finishes first and still win the race. On the very next race, over the self-same course, she may be a few lengths behind the same yacht and yet lose the race if the air is so light that she cannot "save her time." The results of the race are announced in both elapsed time and corrected time. Occasionally there is a prize for the first yacht to finish in a time allowance race, but the real winner is the yacht that shows the shortest corrected time.

Occasionally elapsed time expresses the actual time that elapses between the moment when the mast (or the foremost mast on a yacht with more than one) crosses the starting line and the moment when the mast crosses the finish line. Usually, however, elapsed time commences with the starting gun, regardless of the time the yacht actually starts. Corrected time is elapsed time, minus the time allowance. For a scratch yacht, the elapsed time and the corrected time are identical.

Each yacht club publishes its own racing rules and appoints or elects a Measurer who measures each yacht for a standard fee, presents the owner with a measurement certificate, and files a copy of the certificate with the Race Committee. Remeasurement is usually required every year or every two years. This is made necessary by the fact that a boat improperly stored in the winter may grow longer through hogging or shorter through sagging.

If you are convinced that a measurement is incorrect, the proper procedure is to ask the owner to request a remeasurement. If he refuses and you are still convinced of error, you may protest. If, on the remeasurement your protest is overruled, you must pay the Measurer's fee. If it is sustained, the owner must pay the Measurer's fee. In the event of obvious error and a stubborn owner, it is sometimes good policy for all the captains in the class to protest.

The majority of small boats race in one-design classes. All the boats in the class are built as nearly alike as possible from a single set of plans. Frequently they are the product of one builder and more often than not they are all produced at the same time from the same material. Each one-design class has its own rules which govern the amount of ballast, the number of the crew, the frequency of haul-outs, the equipment which must be carried, the number of suits of sails and the intervals at which they may be bought. The rules may even designate an official sail-maker. They always prohibit changes in hull and in length of spars. If you are racing in a one-design class, it is most essential that you possess a copy of the rules governing the open classes of your yacht club. It is important too that you should know your racing measurement in the event of racing in an open class or in squadron runs.

All these rules of measurement, classification, and handicapping, should not prove discouraging to the skipper. They impose rigid limitations upon the designer and the builder. They are of the utmost importance in the planning and consideration of a new yacht. An understanding of these rules is most necessary for Race Committees who plan and manage regattas. Unless they are understood they are apt to prove confusing to the beginner in racing; but once his classification and handicap are determined, they should not bother the skipper.

A yacht race is sailed over a course. In general,

courses are laid out in accordance with three general ideas. The first is the triangular race. A triangle is laid out in advance in the available waters in such a way that one leg necessitates a hard beat against the prevailing wind, another leg is a reach, and the third leg a run before the wind. Before the race starts the Committee makes careful observations of the wind direction so as to make sure that one leg of the course will furnish a good beat against the wind. If a good beat cannot be obtained from the course as originally laid out, the Committee hoists a predetermined signal fifteen minutes before the preparatory gun, which shows that the course is reversed; that is to say, sailed in the opposite direction from the initial plan. Occasionally, especially in the case of a shifting wind, a race may take such form that there will be no beat. Often it will resolve itself into a beat and two reaches in which the spinnaker cannot be carried to advantage. The triangular race nowadays is by far the most usual.

The second most usual race is to windward and return. The boats cross the starting line on a course directly to windward, round a mark, and return before the wind. It is good practice to specify that the weather mark shall be left on a specified side, to starboard or to port, as the case may be, to avoid the possibility of fouling by boats turning the mark in opposite directions. In the event that the wind is not sufficiently accommodating, the windward and return race resolves itself into a race to leeward and return which gives the same amount of windward work and the same amount of run in the reverse order. This is signaled by the reverse course signal, just as in a triangular race.

The third most common race is the distance race or

squadron run where a start and a finish are indicated and the yachts go from one to the other in the quickest possible time using their own judgment as to course. In most races there are certain requirements or restrictions as to the course sailed. As a rule, yachts are required to pass on the channel side of all government buoys except such as are used as marks of the course and sometimes on distance races certain turning points such as lightships, shoals, or channel buoys must be left on a specified side.

It is important that the skipper shall know his course thoroughly in advance of the race. On Long Island Sound there can be little cause for confusion because the instructions are carefully worded and properly printed and distributed. A reduced size chart with all the marks indicated is sent to every captain a week before the race. The recall signals, postponement signals, starting times, etc., are clearly indicated. Every mark has its distinctive characteristic and cannot be mistaken for any other mark. Compass bearings (magnetic, not true) are given to a quarter point. But this care and accuracy is by no means universal. A typical race circular is shown in Fig. 1, and a more modern but still experimental version in Fig. 2.

In my early days of sailing I lost more races through rounding the wrong mark or otherwise sailing an improper course than from any other cause. It was small consolation to realize that this was not my own fault; that the Race Committee had issued inaccurate instructions and had placed marks that could be confused with fishermen's buoys, eel-pot stakes, and other markers, with which the waters were fairly teeming. A yacht club that does not use specified government buoys as marks should describe the marks clearly. All

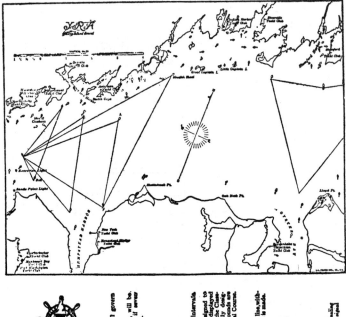

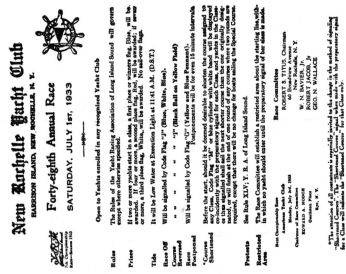

New Rochelle Yacht Club

HARRISON ISLAND, NEW ROCHELLE, N. Y.

Forty-eighth Annual Race

SATURDAY, JULY 1st, 1933

Open to Yachts enrolled in any recognized Yacht Club

Rules
The Rules of the Yacht Racing Association of Long Island Sound will govern except where otherwise specified.

Prizes
If two or more yachts start in a class, a first place or winners flag, Blue, will be awarded. If four or more, a second place flag, Red, will be awarded; if seven or more, a third place flag, White, will be awarded. No sail-over flags.

Tide
It will be Low Water at Execution Light at 11:41 A.M. (D.S.T.)

Race Off
Will be signalled by Code Flag "J" (Blue, White, Blue).

Course Reversed
" " " " " "I" (Black Ball on Yellow Field)

Race Postponed
Will be signalled by Code Flag "G" (Yellow and Blue Pennant).
Postponements will be for even 15 minute intervals.

"Course Shortened
Before the start, should it be deemed desirable to shorten the course assigned to any Class, Code Flag "M" or blue cylinder with white band will be displayed co-incident with the preparatory signal for that Class, and yachts in the Class so signalled shall sail the next shorter course than the one originally designated, or will finish at the end of one round of any courses where two rounds are required, except that there will be no change for boats sailing the Special Course.

Protests
See Rule XLV; Y. R. A. of Long Island Sound.

Restricted Area
The Race Committee will establish a restricted area about the starting line, within which no yacht should enter until the preparatory signal of her class is made.

Next Championship Race
American Yacht Club
Monday, July 3rd, 1933
Chairman of Race Committee
EDWARD A. HODOR
Gaulieon Place
Rye, N.Y.

Race Committee
ROBERT S. TITUS, Chairman
60 Broadview Avenue
New Rochelle, N. Y.
W. N. BAVIER, Jr.
ROBERT JACOB, Jr
GEO. N. WALLACE

*The attention of all contestants is especially invited to the change in the method of signaling "Shortened Courses". The "Shortened Course" signal when made co-incide with the preparatory signal for a Class will indicate the "Shortened Course" for that Class only.

— IMPORTANT —

Attention is invited to the "Special Rule for 1933" which provides:

"That in all Championship Races spinnaker sheets shall be trimmed inside the jibstay and leeward shrouds"

STARTING SIGNALS

DAYLIGHT SAVING TIME

1.50 P. M. **WHITE CYLINDER— WARNING**

1.55 P. M. **BLUE CYLINDER — PREPARATORY**

Course No. 1 15¼ Miles	2.00	2 Red Cylinders	International 12 Meter Class
	2.05	2 White Cylinders	International 10 Meter Class
Course No. 2 11 Miles	2.10	2 Blue Cylinders	N. Y. Y. C. 30-Ft. Class International 8 Meter Class, Open and O. D.
	2.15	1 Red Cylinder	Handicap Class, Division 1
	2.20	1 White Cylinder	"R" Class
	2.25	1 Blue Cylinder	International 6 Meter Class Handicap Class, Division 2
	2.30	2 Red Cylinders	Sound Inter-Club Class
Course No. 3 9 Miles	2.35	2 White Cylinders	Victory Class
	2.40	2 Blue Cylinders	Atlantic Class
	2.45	1 Red Cylinder	Handicap Class, Division 3
	2.50	1 White Cylinder	Star Class
Course No. 4 6 Miles	2.55	1 Blue Cylinder	Handicap Class Division 4, L. I. Sound Junior Class, Pequot Indian Class
Special Course 3 Miles	3.00	2 Red Cylinders	Wee Scots, Larchmont Bullseyes Snipe Class.
	3.05	2 White Cylinders	Dinghy, Meteor, Dories, Canoes and other Small Classes.

RECALL SIGNAL

White Ball with Horizontal Red Band, and one blast of horn or siren for each yacht recalled.

Start and Finish	On line between a White Flag on the Committee Boat and a Mark Boat to the Northward and Eastward of Execution Light, or Red and Black Buoy in absence of Mark Boat.
Course No. 1 15¼ Nautical Miles	From Starting Line N. E. around Blue Fish Shoal Bell Buoy, No. 36, off Port Chester Harbor; thence S. by W. $\frac{1}{2}$ W. around Black Buoy, C. 1, off Weeks Point; thence W. N. W. $\frac{1}{2}$ W. across Finishing Line, leaving all marks to Starboard.
Course No. 2 11 Nautical Miles	From Starting Line N.E. by E. around Black and White Buoy N'A' off Parsonage Point; thence S. $\frac{1}{2}$ E. around Black Buoy, C. 1, off Weeks Point; thence W.N.W. $\frac{1}{2}$ W. across Finishing Line, leaving all marks to Starboard.
Course No. 3 9 Nautical Miles	From Starting Line N.E. $\frac{1}{2}$ N. around Red Gas Buoy 42 off Scotch Caps; thence S. $\frac{1}{2}$ E. around Red Buoy, N. 2, between Motts Point and Prospect Point; thence N.W. by W. across Finishing Line, leaving all marks to Starboard.
Course No. 4 6 Nautical Miles	From Starting Line N.N.E. $\frac{1}{2}$ E. around Black Buoy, C. 1, off Delancey Point; thence S. $\frac{3}{4}$ W. around Bell Buoy 23 off Prospect Point; thence N.W. $\frac{3}{4}$ W. across Finishing Line, leaving all marks to Starboard.
Special Course 3 Miles	From Starting Line to Black and Red Buoy "C" on Hick's Ledge off mouth of Echo Bay, New Rochelle, N.Y. to outer Red Buoy N2 off Hen and Chickens Reef, Larchmont, N.Y. to Black and Red Buoy $\frac{3}{8}$ of a mile N $\frac{3}{4}$ E of Execution Light; thence across Finishing Line, leaving all marks to Starboard.

GOVERNMENT MARKS.

"All Government Marks and Aids to Navigation not used as turning marks shall be passed on the channel side and shall be deemed marks of the course, unless the instructions specify otherwise. When used as turning marks and there is an accompanying buoy, the accompanying buoy may be disregarded and passed on either hand unless the instructions for the race specify otherwise." Rule XXVIII, Yacht Racing Association of Long Island Sound.

A race in any class in which no yacht has finished at 7:00 P. M. (D.S.T.) shall be declared off. Yachts finishing after 7:30 P.M. will take their own time and report it to the Committee.

FIG. 1. Race circular of New Rochelle Yacht Club—standardized for all clubs which start their races off Execution Light

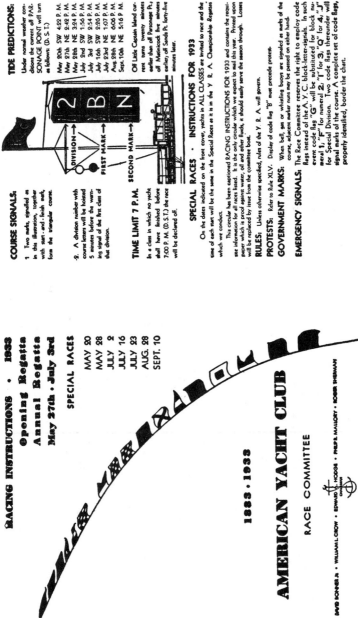

TIDE PREDICTIONS:

Under normal weather conditions the current off PAR-SONAGE POINT will turn as follows: (D. S. T.)

May 20th	SW	4:22 P. M.
May 27th	NE	2:42 P. M.
May 28th	SW	3:24 P. M.
July 2nd	SW	1:50 P. M.
July 3rd	SW	2:54 P. M.
July 16th	SW	2:20 P. M.
July 23rd	NE	1:07 P. M.
Aug. 28th	NE	6:06 P. M.
Sept. 10th	NE	5:16 P. M.

Off Little Captain Island current turns twenty minutes earlier than off Parsonage Pt., off Matinicock five minutes earlier, off Sands Pt. forty-five minutes later.

COURSE SIGNALS:

1 Two marks, signalled as in this illustration, together with start - and - finish mark, form the triangular course.

2. A division number with course letters will be hoisted 5 minutes before the warning signal of the first class of that division.

TIME LIMIT 7 P. M.

In a class in which no yacht shall have finished before 7:00 P. M. (D.S.T.) the race will be declared off.

SPECIAL RACES · INSTRUCTIONS FOR 1933

On the dates indicated on the front cover, yachts in ALL CLASSES are invited to race and the time of each start will be the same as in the Special Races as it is in the Y. R. A. Championship Regatta which we conduct.

This circular has been captioned RACING INSTRUCTIONS FOR 1933 and contains the requisite information for all races listed. It is the only circular which we expect to mail this year. Printed upon paper which is proof against water, oil and other fluids, it should easily serve the season through. Losses will be replaced by issue from the committee boat.

RULES: Unless otherwise specified, rules of the Y. R. A. will govern.

PROTESTS: Refer to Rule XLV. Display of code flag "B" must precede protest.

GOVERNMENT MARKS: When bell, gas or whistling buoys are signaled as marks of the course, adjacent marker nuns may be passed on either hand.

EMERGENCY SIGNALS: The Race Committee reserves the right to employ code flags instead of the A. Y. C. block-letter-signals. In such event code flag "G" will be substituted for block numeral 1; "F" for numeral 2, "I" for 3, "Q" for 4, "J" for Special Division. Two code flags thereunder will signal marks of the course. A complete set of code flags, properly identified, border the chart.

RACING INSTRUCTIONS · 1933

Opening Regatta
Annual Regatta
May 27th · July 3rd

SPECIAL RACES

MAY	20
MAY	28
JULY	2
JULY	16
JULY	23
AUG.	28
SEPT.	10

1883 · 1933

AMERICAN YACHT CLUB

RACE COMMITTEE

DAVID BONES JR. · WILLIAM L. CROW · EDWARD J. HODGE · PHILIP L. MALLORY · ROGER SHERMAN
Chairman

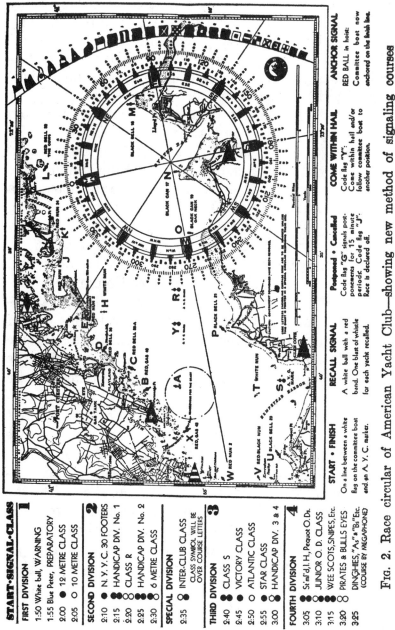

START · SIGNAL · CLASS 1

FIRST DIVISION

1:50 White ball, WARNING

1:55 Blue Peter, PREPARATORY

2:00 ● 12 METRE CLASS

2:05 ○ 10 METRE CLASS

SECOND DIVISION 2

2:10 ● N.Y.C. 30 FOOTERS

2:15 ●●●○○ HANDICAP DIV. No. 1

2:20 ○ CLASS R

2:25 ●●●○○ HANDICAP DIV. No. 2

2:30 ●●●● 6 METRE CLASS

SPECIAL DIVISION

2:35 ○○ INTER-CLUB CLASS

CLASS SYMBOL WILL BE OVER COURSE LETTERS

THIRD DIVISION 3

2:40 ●● CLASS S

2:45 ● VICTORY CLASS

2:50 ○ ATLANTIC CLASS

2:55 ● STAR CLASS

3:00 ●● HANDICAP DIV. 3 & 4

FOURTH DIVISION 4

3:05 ● Sr'mf'd, I. H., Pequot O. Ds.

3:10 ●●○○○○ JUNIOR O. D. CLASS

3:15 WEE SCOTS, SNIPES, Etc.

3:20 ●● PIRATES & BULLS EYES

3:25 ○○ DINGHIES, "A's" & "B's" Etc.
(COURSE BY MEGAPHONE)

START · FINISH

On a line between a white flag on the committee boat and an A. Y. C. marker.

RECALL SIGNAL

A white ball with a red band. One blast of whistle for each yacht recalled.

Postponed · Cancelled

Code flag "G" signals postponements for 15 minute periods. Code flag "J", Race is declared off.

COME WITHIN HAIL

Code flag "V":
Come within hail and/or follow committee boat to another position.

ANCHOR SIGNAL

RED BALL in hoist:
Committee boat now anchored on the finish line.

Fig. 2. Race circular of American Yacht Club—showing new method of signaling courses

the marks should be alike so that competitors, seeing the first mark at the start, will be able to recognize all other marks. The degree of visibility of a mark is important. Low-flying flags, etc., are difficult to distinguish at any distance at all. This is sometimes overcome by the Race Committee placing a marker boat in range with the mark, but many a yacht has mistaken the marker boat for the mark itself, and it is apt to be similarly confusing at the start because most yacht clubs lay out a restricted area around the starting line and it is hard to distinguish between the restricted area buoys and the starting line buoys. Despite my long familiarity with starting line restricted areas, I nearly ruined a start last summer by such confusion.

As a rule the start is laid out between a buoy and the Committee Boat flying the Race Committee's distinctive flag. In some localities a white flag on a separate staff on the Committee Boat marks one end of the starting line. In the absence of such a distinctive signal the mast of the Committee Boat, on which the starting signals are hoisted, is generally taken as one end of the starting line.

The skipper should know not only how to start but how to finish as well. In general there are four methods of finishing. The old, time-honored method is as follows: A triangular race is interpreted as meaning sailing *around* three marks. Therefore, at the finish, the yachts must sail around the last mark and cross the starting line in the same direction as they took at the start. The line should not be crossed in the opposite direction. This is an unsatisfactory way to finish a race and, fortunately, it has largely fallen into disuse.

The second method is to cross the finish line between the Committee Boat and the starting buoy in the opposite direction to the start.

The third method, now most generally in use, is to cross a finish line established between the starting buoy and the Committee Boat. In order to establish this finish line the Committee Boat is shifted, after the start, from her initial anchorage to a new position at right angles to the last leg of the course, on the opposite side of the buoy.

The fourth method, which is becoming increasingly popular, is to place out two buoys on opposite sides of the Committee Boat. The start is taken across the line between the Committee Boat and one of the buoys and the finish line is established between the Committee Boat and the other buoy.

With at least four methods of finishing, you will see the necessity for determining, before the start, just what rules govern the finish of any particular race.

Many regattas are run in classes that are started at intervals of five minutes or three minutes. Two intervals before the start of the first class, a warning signal is hoisted and a gun is fired or whistle blown. At one interval before the start, a preparatory signal is hoisted and attention is called to it by gun or whistle. Thereafter, the races start at the predetermined intervals. The start in each case is given by a visible signal and attention called to it by an audible signal. The visible signal is always the official start. It is unwise to trust to guns or whistles because they are apt to misfire or fail to blow. The starting signal for each class is almost always taken as the preparatory signal for the class that follows. After its preparatory signal, yachts are subject to the racing rules. If you are late and are being towed to the starting line, be sure to cast off the tow lines before the preparatory signal for your class. This rule applies even though your tow boat should be unable to get you to the starting line until long after the race has started.

In the event of bad weather, lack of wind, or other interfering conditions, a postponement signal is hoisted. Races are always postponed for a predetermined time, usually fifteen minutes. The postponement signal remains hoisted until the last class has started. The starting signals usually remain in sight until thirty seconds before the next signal is hoisted. The hauling down of the preparatory signal affords a very valuable check on the time remaining before the starting signal. It must be remembered that in any regatta the different classes are probably sailing different courses—the large boats sailing a long course, the small boats sailing a short course. Sometimes the courses for all boats are laid out around the same marks but the larger boats sail around the course three times; the middle-size boats, twice; and the small boats, once. It is not safe to assume, as too many skippers do, that all you have to do is to follow the class ahead. That class may be sailing a different course and rounding different marks.

In light airs, the Race Committee usually hoists a previously published signal to indicate a shortened course. It is, therefore, necessary for each captain to know not only the normal course but also what the shortened course will be and the signal that will indicate it.

Two other conditions should be mentioned—the entry and the identification.

In every yacht race, every competitor must make an entry. In most races a yacht enters merely by crossing the starting line with proper identification. In others, the captain must fill out an entry blank giving racing measurement, racing number, and other information called for. This blank must be filed with the Race Committee before a stated time. In other races, the entry is made orally at the Club House or at the Committee Boat, usually at least fifteen minutes before the warning gun.

A yacht must always be identified, either throughout the race or at least at the start and finish. The most usual identification is a racing number which is either awarded officially, or accepted officially by the Race Committee. The number shows both the class of the yacht and her individual number. The numbers must be stitched on both sides of the mainsail above the topmost row of reefing points. The best practice today is to place the class letters in a line with the jaws of the gaff of a gaff-headed mainsail and midway between the luff and the leach. On a Marconi mainsail they should be in the corresponding position, if one judged the jib-headed sail as a gaff-headed sail with a topsail. The identifying number is best placed somewhat below and near the leach. The numbers and letters on opposite sides of the sail should not be placed exactly back to back, but one set should be below the other. If they are placed back to back, they are very confusing when the yacht has the sun behind her, as the sun, shining through the sail, makes the two sets of numbers almost equally distinct. Thus, when they overlap, they are very hard to read.

Many yacht clubs require, in addition to the racing number, that a yacht shall fly her owner's private signal from the peak. Every yachtsman is privileged to design his own private signal, with certain restrictions. The signal must be an oblong flag or a swallow-tail. It must indicate the owner—not the yacht. And it must not resemble too closely any other registered private signal. Private signals are registered and published by Lloyd's Register of American Yachts. There is no charge for this service.

Some clubs also insist that the club burgee shall be flown and there are cases on record where yachts have been protested and the protest sustained for failure to observe this rule. Other clubs forbid the display of the burgee during a race.

In races in which cruising boats participate, they are often assigned a letter of the signal code to be hoisted at the starboard spreader as an identification. If the finish is likely to take place in the dark, the competing yachts are assigned colored lights or rockets.

All yachts engaged in a race are subject to the race rules which primarily determine the right-of-way of one boat over another. It is not enough that you should know the ordinary rules of the road at sea. It is necessary that you should get a copy of the racing rules of the yacht club and study them most carefully. Whenever two boats meet, converge, overtake, or are overtaken, the rights of each boat are clearly defined. The boat without right-of-way must yield immediately to the other boat. It is, of course, obvious that a number of boats sailing together in a race around the same course are constantly interfering with one another, and the skipper must always be on the alert to determine whether or not he has right-of-way over his opponent.

Most races must be sailed within predetermined time limits. If one boat in a class finishes within the time limit, it is called a race, even if no other boat should finish within several hours. If the laggards finish after the Race Committee has left the finish line, they take their own time and report it.

Chapter IV

TUNING UP—THE HULL

There is no more expressive phrase in the picturesque language of the yachtsman than "tuning up." He regards his yacht as a musician regards a violin—an exquisite instrument, strung and adjusted to the greatest niceties, and capable of producing harmonious results. The proper tuning up of a yacht is the first step in winning a race. Let us begin our tuning up with the hull.

All motion must overcome resistance and the resistance to the forward motion of a yacht consists of water resistance and air resistance. Air resistance is usually spoken of as windage. Water resistance divides itself into two general classifications, skin friction and wave resistance. The naval architects devote many weary hours in the designing of each yacht to the problem of cutting down, as far as possible, the amount of "wetted surface"; for each square inch of wetted surface means resistance to the water and a hull increasingly difficult to drive. Often by an increase in wetted surface, other factors of form and stability may be achieved which more than balance the increased resistance due to an increased wetted surface; but these terms are given to impress upon the beginner the necessity for keeping his wetted surfaces in such condition as to offer the least possible resistance to forward motion.

The importance of reducing skin friction is far less in strong breezes than in light airs, but no boat can be a good drifter with anything but a very smooth bottom. Yet smoothness is a relative term. A piece of velvet is smooth; yet a velvet covering would make one of the worst possible bottoms on a racing boat. Although velvet is smooth to the hand, it is rough to the water. Every tiny hair catches and drags along particles of water which, in turn, drag other particles adjacent to them and each drop of water sets up friction with the drop next to it.

I remember very well seeing this demonstrated most vividly by looking down the side of a large steamer plowing at high speed through a smooth sea. Ahead, the bow wave curled off and broke. Under the quarter, a long stern wave was forming; but all along the length of the hull perfectly straight for several hundred feet was a path of disturbed water about a yard wide, obviously produced by skin friction. It was as definite and hard-edged as the furrow of an automobile tire on a muddy road.

The smoothness of a racing bottom should be comparable to the smoothness of a fine piece of furniture. It should approach the smoothness of glass. The racing yachtsman should never be satisfied with the smoothness of his bottom if there is any way in which he can get it smoother. Smoothness must be judged when the yacht is hauled out. If there is any sign of a fine scum of marine growth on the boat, it will feel very smooth and slippery to the hand when the boat is afloat, but will present a rough friction surface to the water.

In most racing classes there is a distinct limit to the number and frequency of haul-outs. This is as it should be. If none of the yachts can haul out more frequently than once a month, say, they will all be on equal terms so far as a foul bottom is concerned, and the expense of the haul-out is one of the major expenses of yacht racing. To the owner of a small boat, a haul-out need not represent anything more than hard work. A center-board boat can always be beached and hauled out on rollers. Ways are not necessary. A deep keel boat is generally sailed in water in which there is a large rise and fall of tide, and a moderate size keel boat may be put on the beach and braced up so that her owner can work on her bottom between tides. The best way to do this is beside a stone dock or other strong support. The boat is brought in beside the dock at high water and wide strong timbers are fitted beneath her keel. Her halliards are then run from the top of her mast to the far side of the dock and a strain is kept upon them to cant the boat toward the dock as the tide goes away and leaves her. Presently she will take the bottom. Then the owner, working from a skiff, can start to clean and polish along the waterline and, as the tide goes down, work on her bottom. Great care must be exercised to prevent the boat from being smashed against the dock from the passage of motor boats or from seas kicked up by sudden storms; but if reason-able care is exercised, a boat may be safely cleaned and beached without recourse to the boatyard. If the keel is slanting with the lowest part just forward of the rudder and if the rudder itself extends to the very bottom of the keel, the danger in beaching a boat prob-ably outweighs the saving, and resort must be had to the railway.

It is well, at the outset of the season, to determine the number of haul-outs you can afford and the probable degree of fouling that will occur between haul-outs, for that will determine the kind of bottom paint you should use.

If a boat is to stay in the water most of the season, protection against fouling must be the first considera-tion. If the boat is hauled out at frequent intervals, protection against fouling is a minor consideration and the main purpose to be achieved is the production of a smooth, hard bottom. There is a fundamental dis-tinction between racing boats and cruising boats. Your cruising boat intended to stay in the water for most of the season, uses a strong anti-fouling paint which, by its very nature, is principally rough. Your racing bottom, which needs only incidental protection against fouling, is chosen for its smoothness and hardness; but such a bottom necessitates frequent hauling out.

The preparation should be made when the boat is hauled out in the fall. The thing to do is to clean off every sign and trace of marine growth, particularly the barnacles (and by barnacles is meant *all* the bar-nacles, including the little shell-like stain that they leave behind them). After the bottom is carefully sanded, particular attention must be paid to the seams, the butts, the dowels that cover the fastenings. These must be rubbed down so smoothly that it is impossible to tell where they appear with the fingers. Do not use a sandpaper that is too coarse. Do not be impatient. Take your time and do the job properly.

Seams should be sandpapered first across and then lengthwise. The cross sanding is necessary to reduce the seams to flatness. The lengthwise sanding is to re-move any possible vertical scratches from the cross sandings.

When the bottom planking, wooden keel, and rudder are perfectly smooth, the metal keel should be prepared. An iron keel should be scraped and red-leaded. If there are any inequalities, they should be filled with cement before the red-leading. The red lead coat is then sanded and another coat applied. Three coats of red lead are none too much. To offer its full protection to the iron, the red lead must be freshly prepared and mixed. Do not use red lead that has been standing around in a can. If the keel is of lead, rough spots, bumps and holes can be smoothed out with a hammer and an iron in the manner in which one peens a broken lead pipe. The lead keel does not require red lead and it is better to protect it merely with a bottom paint.

The bottom is then given a thin undercoater. Many yachtsmen prefer an ordinary lead and oil paint for this undercoater. I have changed my opinion on paints many times, but my present inclination is to use a green copper racing bottom paint applied very thinly and allowed to get thoroughly hard before any other work is done to the boat. If the bottom, after sanding, is but poorly protected by paint, it is possibly advisable to put on a second undercoater before the winter sets in. The first undercoater should be sandpapered to perfect smoothness before any more paint is applied. Ordinarily, however, one undercoater will carry the boat through the winter and will give a hard, smooth finish for the work in the spring.

If the boat is to be hauled out very frequently, it is a good idea to use green copper for all the coats. Use three or four coats of copper, keeping them very thin, and rubbing each one down except the last. The last coat should be applied just before launching so that the paint is still wet when the boat takes to the water.

If you cannot afford or cannot arrange for frequent haul-outs, anti-fouling must be your prime consideration. Green copper paint is a poor protection against fouling. Red copper paint is very much better. Brown copper paint is slightly better than red, bronze paint and white mercury paints are the best of all. The mercury paint is very poisonous to marine growth, gives a smooth bottom, and has two further advantages: It is of a color that repels growth and also enables you to see the condition of your bottom. It is strongly advised for fin-keeled boats sailing through seaweed-infested waters, so that the crew can see when there is an accumulation of seaweed on the keel. My personal experience with white mercury paint has been unsatisfactory because of bad blistering, but I think this was probably due to its being used over another kind of paint. Get in touch with the manufacturers and follow their directions. The best bottom paint that I know of for strong anti-fouling characteristics which, at the same time, makes a good racing bottom is put on as follows:

A green copper undercoater in the fall. One or two coats of green copper in the spring, each coat rubbed down and allowed to set. A coat of bronze paint over the copper, allowed to set and then lightly rubbed off with burlap. And a final coat of bronze just before the boat takes to the water. I painted a boat in this way in 1932. She was launched on May 26th. She lay in Mamaroneck Harbor where there is considerable pollution. It is the worst place for marine growth that I have ever known. She was hauled out on the 13th of September and there were no intermediate haul-outs, no under-water scraping, and no care whatever, for, in

FIG. 3. Bronze over copper. *Old Timer's*
bottom after nearly four months in foul
water

FIG. 4. Good racing bottom and topsides; note reflections

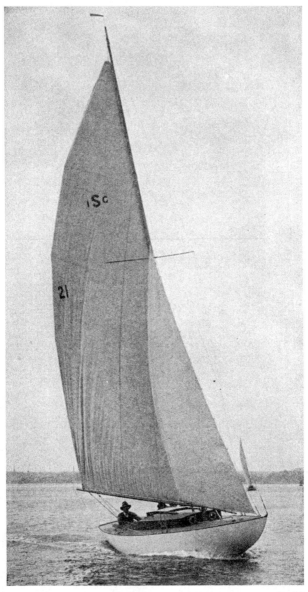

FIG. 7. Retarding wrinkles

that year of the great depression, I was very busy and forced to sail without a proper crew.

When she was hauled out there was not one sign of the bronze paint left. It had all been worn off by the friction of the water and by the fact that it did not adhere to the smooth copper undercoater. But when the paint came off, the slight fuzz of marine growth that had formed on it came off too, so that the bottom, by a constant process of loosing its bronze paint throughout the season, kept itself clean. Fig. 3 shows the condition of the bottom after it had been hauled out. A very slight fuzz of marine growth had formed on the keel in the last two weeks the boat was in the water and there was a slight growth at the waterline, but there was no long dead man's hair, no barnacles, and the yard reported that it was the cleanest boat they had hauled out that summer.

The previous summer I had used nothing but green copper paint and had moored in approximately the same place. Despite my under-water scrubbing, the boat, in a mid-season haul-out was so foul that the yard put her back into the water for a preliminary scrubbing because they were afraid that they could not live in the yard if they had scrubbed her on the ways. With bronze over copper there was still some bronze paint on the boat and not the slightest sign of marine growth until the third week in August. The theory is to have a top coat insecurely stuck to an undercoater so that the paint will not stay on the boat but will come off, taking the growth with it. Perhaps there are better combinations but I know that the green copper and the bronze worked very well. In 1933, I tried the same combination with poor results. Perhaps the undercoater was too hard. Perhaps the bronze paint was of poor quality. This time the bronze paint stuck and the bottom became moderately foul.

While the boat is hauled out, certain other things may be done to reduce skin friction. Some yachtsmen grease their boats. The theory is that grease repels water, that the grease acts as a lubricant to skin friction and is generally more slippery. I believe this theory to be unsound. The slipperiness may be felt by the fingers but not by water. The grease forms little ridges which, in turn, set up eddies of water and a greased boat does not feel so smooth to the water as an ungreased boat, properly prepared.

In the old days, the favorite method of reducing skin friction was to coat the boat with potblack. This has been legislated against in nearly every yacht club. Potblack is nasty, disagreeable stuff to handle but it may possibly have some merit. Certainly all the old timers swear by it. It is my feeling that if it did not have merit, it would have killed itself and there would be no necessity for such legislation. If your club does not forbid the use of potblack on the bottom, it is possibly worth the experiment. I have never tried it because I have never sailed in a club that permitted its use.

The authorities differ on the question of the value of stream lining. Many naval architects maintain that the stream line shape is the one which slips most easily through the water. They support this with many plausible arguments. Others, equally famous, assert that the stream line design is effective only in the air; that the air and water are two different media that react in different ways; and that stream lining is not necessary in under-water parts. It seems to be the consensus of opinion, however, that stream lining does pay. Therefore, while you are hauled out, I would advise that you have the yard stream line your fin keel, the after edge of your centerboard and the after edge of your rudder. The effect claimed for stream lining is that the water leaves the stream lined part smoothly, that no vacuum is formed behind it to hold you back, and that you do not drag the water after you.

Another job that should be done while the boat is in the yard is to clean your centerboard. This is very difficult on the average railway. The hull of the boat must be jacked up so that the board can be lowered or it may even be necessary to pull out the pin and haul the board out of the boat. However difficult this may be, the centerboard should be cleaned and kept clean. It represents a very large part of your "wetted surface" and friction on the centerboard may be a primary reason for losing races. Most yachtsmen neglect this one task. It is very difficult and they seem to think that it is not particularly important. It is, however, worth every bit of trouble and expense it entails. While on the subject of the centerboard, you should study the angle at which you carry it before hauling out so that you may know whether or not a repair is necessary. The ordinary board which pivots about a pin in the lower corner of the forward edge of the trunk, should never be carried so low that the opposite corner sinks below the trunk. If you find it necessary on the wind to carry the board lower to maintain balance, counteract a heavy helm, or keep from sliding off, you should have the top of the centerboard raised by adding a triangular piece of wood. This is necessary for four reasons:

1. If the top of the board descends below the bottom of the trunk, there is a very bad strain put upon the

board and the trunk. The board supported at the forward end of the trunk only is twisted and strained.

2. A board not supported by the after end of the trunk is apt to quiver and vibrate and thus stop the forward motion of the boat.

3. The hole in the trunk sets up water eddies which stop the forward motion of the boat. This hole should be blocked by the centerboard.

4. The centerboard pennant descending below the bottom of the boat offers considerable resistance to forward motion. No part of the pennant should ever be exposed below the bottom of the trunk.

If the boat has not been built for racing, she is probably protected at the deck line by heavy wales. These wales set up a lot of unnecessary skin friction when the boat is held down to her sailing lines. It is advisable to have the wales taken off if the rules of your class permit this.

While working on the hull, be sure to take out any play in the steering gear. It is impossible to feel your boat, as good racing helmsmanship requires, if there is any play whatever in the steering mechanism. Play may occur between the tiller and the rudderhead or between the rudder post and the rudder. Check up, too, on the mast step and chain plates to see that they are solidly fastened to the boat.

There is much discussion among racing men as to the required rigidity of the hull. I have seen racing men pound small boats with an ax in order to make the boat "loose in its joints." They maintain that a boat in which there is some give will adapt herself better to the motion of the waves and weave forward better than a rigidly built boat. This is a school of thought to which I have never been able to subscribe and I would strongly recommend that a boat that gives and weaves too much should be properly strengthened and made rigid as part of the tuning up process.

There are two schools of thought in the preparation of topsides. Some yachtsmen use a dull, chalky paint. They keep it clean by scrubbing it, each time taking off a thin layer of the paint and maintaining a fresh surface beneath. Others use a hard, glossy paint or enamel. When they scrub their boats they remove dirt but not paint. For a racing boat a hard, glossy paint is undoubtedly superior for the reason that it offers less skin friction. When a boat has had too many coats of paint they say that she is "paint sick" and a boat that is paint sick is never very fast. The cure is a burn-off job, getting down to bare wood and building up a fresh coat. Never apply thick coats of paint. Two thin coats are infinitely better than one thick coat. A famous boat builder once expressed himself to me on the paint subject thus: "Paint ain't nothin' to put on a boat, paint's somethin' to take off a boat."

Gleaming topsides and a smooth bottom are shown in Fig. 4. Make sure your own boat reflects the water in this way.

Chapter V

TUNING UP—THE SPARS AND STANDING RIGGING

Most of the subject matter in this chapter has already been covered in "Learning to Sail." Since it is impossible, however, properly to prepare a boat for racing without careful attention to proper tuning up, this information is repeated here. To readers of "Learning to Sail" it will be valuable only as a reminder. The essence of the proper tuning of spars and standing rigging lies in the proper conception of the center of effort of the sails and the center of resistance of the hull. There is a point in every suit of sails around which the work of the wind on those sails balances. The sum total of all the pressure of the wind forward of that point is equal to the sum total of the pressure of the wind aft of the point. Similarly, the sum total of the pressure above the point is equal to the sum total of the pressure below the point. The height of this center of pressure is an important consideration in naval architecture, for it is an important factor in the stability of the boat. To the racing man, however, it is the fore and aft position which is the prime consideration. Inasmuch as this is the case, the center of effort should probably be considered as a vertical line at some point of which line the exact center is located. Locating the center of effort is not, and probably never can be, an exact science because it differs with different degrees of sheet trim, moving forward as the sheets are trimmed in, moving aft as they are started, and then moving forward again as they are started still further.

The center of effort of the sails must be considered in relation to the center of lateral resistance of the hull. There is a point in the hull that corresponds to the center of effort of the sails. The sum total of all the lateral resistance forward of this point is equal to the sum total of all the lateral resistance aft of this point. This, too, is a movable point, moving forward and aft with different angles of heel, different degrees of hull trim, and is noticeably affected in small boats if a single man changes his position a few inches in the boat. A well hung boat is one in which the center of effort is almost directly above the center of resistance. If the center of resistance moves forward at the same time and to the same degree as the center of effort moves forward and moves aft at the same time and to the same degree as the center of effort moves aft, the boat will be perfectly balanced on all points of sailing. The best indication of a properly hung boat is the almost entire freedom from rudder drag. If a strong weather helm is necessary on the wind in moderate airs, the center of effort is too far aft of the center of resistance. If a slight lee helm is necessary in fresh winds, it is a sign that the center of effort is forward of the center of resistance. It is impossible to tune a boat up properly unless she is sailing in varying winds with all her crew and all her ballast on board. This matter of tuning up is often beyond the scope of the naval architect. Very frequently in the most carefully designed boats, the masts have to be moved forward or aft.

Therefore many small boats are now equipped with adjustable steps and adjustable partners. The step is usually more freely adjustable than the partners because it is equipped with a pair of screws placed horizontally, so that the heel of the mast may be slid forward or aft and maintained rigidly in position by turning up these screws. In a boat not equipped with adjustable step and partners much can be done with the wedges in the partners and the wedges in the step. Sometimes moving the mast only one-quarter of an inch will make a very great difference in the performance of the boat. The actual moving of the mast forward or aft really amounts to a major operation and should not be attempted except in the case of a very heavy drag on the rudder. It is better to try raking the mast or moving the position of the jib stay on deck. The adjustments to the mast may be discussed in terms of position, rake, and curve. By position is meant the placing of the mast in the boat, both as to step and partners. By rake is meant the fore or aft slant of the mast from the vertical. When a mast rakes the entire mast from truck to heel slants. By curve is meant a change in direction of the stick itself, not the way it is placed in the boat.

It is quite generally conceded that a mast that carries a gaff-headed rig should rake forward. The degree of this rake is to be determined by the feel of the rudder and by the amount whereby the gaff sags off from the vertical plane in which the boom lies. If the gaff sags off to such a degree that it interferes with efficiency, it is nearly always helpful to rake the mast farther forward.

Similarly, a curved Marconi mast should be raked forward. The curve offsets the rake so that the result may have the effect of a mast slightly raking aft; but a Marconi mast which curves aft should not be raked aft also. The rake should be forward. There is considerable difference of opinion among the experts as to the way a Marconi mast should rake. Many of the experts maintain that a straight Marconi mast should rake aft. Others maintain that it should stand perfectly upright. Still others claim that all masts, including straight Marconi masts, should rake forward. The answer probably lies in three factors: the feel of the helm, the set of the sail, and the twisting or warping of the sail through having the upper part of the leech sag off to leeward. If a Marconi sail has been made for a mast that rakes slightly aft, the whole fit of the sail may be destroyed by changing the rake forward. If you are sailing with a heavy weather helm and a Marconi rig, try first moving the jib stay forward. If this fails, try raking the mast forward. If this remedies the helm but results in a badly fitting sail, restore the mast to its original rake but move both the step and the partners forward so that the position of the mast is forward of its former position. Experimenting with rake should be done cautiously. A difference of a quarter inch in the heel may make a difference of a couple of feet at the truck. It is wise to suspend a plumb-bob from the truck of the mast to the deck. Mark the spot beneath the plumb-bob on the deck. Adjust the mast, then note the new position of the plumb-bob. It is perfectly easy, in that way, to return the mast to its former position in case the change should not prove effective.

There seems to be no difference of opinion as to the rake of a schooner foremast. It must always rake forward.

The only fore and aft curve that should ever be permitted in any mast is the intentional curve in the Marconi mast put in when the mast was built. A mast with a gaff rig must always be straight. It can and should rake forward, but it must not curve. Yet gaff rig masts are often pulled forward by the strain of the jib stay with the result that the mainsail never sets properly. In my catboat sailing days I never knew what it was to have mast trouble. The masts of the old catboats were big enough to carry eight times their spread of sail if properly stayed. These masts never carried stays. They stood up like church towers in the bluff bows of the old catboats. They could be equipped with a head stay which was a handy thing to hold on to when picking up a mooring or making a dock and the head stay also prevented a whip above the jaws of the gaff; but most of the masts were so large and so heavy that they required no stays at all. When carrying a press of sail to windward they would bend slightly to leeward and improve rather than impair the fit of the sail. Nowadays, however, on racing yachts in particular, masts are built very much too light. The idea is to cut down windage and, to a certain extent, this is justifiable, as the lines of flow of wind around the mast blanket parts of the luff of the sail and interfere with its effectiveness. But as will be seen later, the sail is nothing but a wing set up on edge and wings either of birds or of airplanes do not seem to be rendered less effective by presenting a blunt, rounded forward edge. It is, therefore, my opinion that the shaving of a mast has been carried too far and that it is better to have a rigid dependable stick than a stick smaller in diameter but insufficiently rigid and stable. The weight of a large mast, however, does deserve consideration and it pays large dividends to cut down every possible ounce of weight aloft.

The most disturbing curve that a mast can fall heir to is that imposed upon it by the forward thrust of the gaff. If you lie on the deck and sight aloft along a flexible "rubber" mast with a gaff rig you will observe the following curves: From the deck the mast curves forward slightly. Half way up the sail the curve becomes more pronounced, terminating at the point where the jaws of the gaff press against the mast. From that point, the curve runs sharply aft. When a boat with such a mast is jumping in a seaway, the top of the mast begins bowing and nodding in the direction of the gaff. When such a mast breaks, it breaks first at the gaff and second at the deck.

The curve produced by the thrust of the gaff may be counteracted by a jack stay with a short strut running forward from the point where the jaws of the gaff rest when full sail is hoisted. This stay is securely spliced around the mast just below the truck. It runs forward across the strut, then down to the deck where it is spliced around the mast beneath a cleat or saddle. A turnbuckle, let into this stay just above the lower splice, permits it to be set up. This jack stay is set up and adjusted while under sail on the wind. It should be adjusted independently of other stays and shrouds.

The head stay and the back stay should be counted as a single unit and one should not be set up or slacked off without making a counter adjustment of the other. Neither stay should be too tight. These stays, together with the wedges in the step and the partners, determine the rake of the mast. Similarly, the jib stay and the runner should be counted as a unit. It is impossible to adjust the jib stay unless the jib is set and drawing and the weather back stay or runner is properly set up. A jib stay that is too loose may be pulled into position by tightening up the weather runner.

On the other hand, a jib stay that seems perfectly taut may prove to sag annoyingly when the jib is set and drawing. Too taut a head stay may produce a slack jib stay. In fact, in many boats it is impossible to use a head stay effectively because the tension on the head stay makes the jib stay so slack that the jib becomes inefficient. No boat can go to windward at her best if the jib stay sags.

Many Marconi rigged boats have a low fore triangle. In other words, the top of the jib stay joins the mast at about the spot where the jaws of the gaff would rest if she carried a gaff mainsail and topsail instead of a Marconi mainsail. With a low fore triangle, a head stay is usually necessary, but sometimes it can be dispensed with if a short jumper stay is installed from the head of the mast to a point just below the jib stay. The jumper stay increases the rigidity of the top of the mast and takes the down pull of the mainsail and main sheet.

One reason why jumper stays are not more popular is that they are very apt to interfere with the setting of light sails, particularly the spinnaker. This probably must be worked out for every boat; but before deciding to install a jumper stay, it is well to study out the position of your spinnaker, balloon jib, Genoa jib, the location of the halliards and the possibility of fouling either the halliards or the sails.

Just as the stays must be considered in pairs so must the shrouds also. One mistake which the ardent beginner is apt to make is to set up the shrouds too tight. If you will try to picture the sturdy catboat mast that had no shrouds, you will see that it moved slightly to leeward under the pressure of the sails. A mast with shrouds should be permitted to do the same thing. When pressure comes on the mast it must go somewhere. If the mast is not permitted to bend slightly to leeward, it will set up a curve in the form of an "S." This "S" curve is very dangerous and the mast is more apt to break from the strain that produces the "S" curve than from strains that produce a natural bending. The shrouds, therefore, must be slightly slack and tauten under the strain. The way to determine the right tension is to set up the shrouds a little bit too tight, sail until you detect the "S" curve, then slack the shrouds until the "S" curve disappears. Your tension will then be all right. Go about on the other tack and do the same thing. A slight shaking of the shrouds when the boat is at anchor and the sails lowered will tell you whether an equal tension has been set up.

Shrouds frequently come in two sets—upper shrouds and lower shrouds. These are two pairs and lead to two sets of chain plates. The upper shrouds should be made fast to the forward chain plates, the lower shrouds to the after chain plates. If the shrouds are exactly equal in length you may determine whether or not they have been set up properly by counting the threads that show in the turnbuckles. I know a very successful skipper who has figured out the proper tension for his shrouds for varying strengths of wind and adjusts his upper shrouds by setting up or slacking off his turnbuckle until the right number of threads show. It is good practice to sail with slacker shrouds in light airs but not if that practice causes your sails to set badly. You may have two suits of sails for your boat and one suit will behave better if you monkey with the shrouds while the other suit will not. It is only by trial and error that you can determine the advisability of such an adjustment. It is not to be recommended as universal practice.

Many Marconi rigged boats have the upper shrouds returned to the mast to form the so-called diamond rig. (See Fig. 5.) With the diamond rig, the lower shrouds should be somewhat heavier than if the upper shrouds led to chain plates.

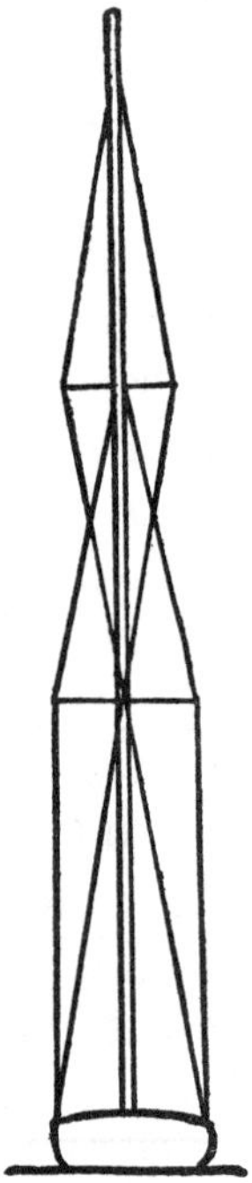

The best material for stays and shrouds is stainless steel wire. The strongest stainless steel wire is the "1x19" type in which there is one single strand of nineteen wires. This is very stiff and very strong but rather difficult to splice. The most commonly used is the "6x7" type in which there are six strands with seven wires to the strand and a hemp or cotton core. A stronger and better form of wire rigging is the "7x7" type in which there are seven strands and seven wires to the strand. The seventh wire takes the place of the hemp or cotton core and this makes the rigging less apt to stretch and adds about 10% to its strength. Flexible wire rigging is inferior for standing rigging purposes because the strands are composed of finer wires.

FIG. 5.
The diamond rig

The spreaders of your shrouds deserve more attention than they ordinarily get. Most spreaders are placed at right angles to the mast. It is better practice to cant the spreaders upward so that they bisect the angle of the shrouds. Spreaders should be provided with spreader lifts running between the spreaders and the mast to keep them from sagging. I have always liked to keep my spreaders as rigid as possible but therein I differ from common practice which seems to prefer freedom of movement forward and aft. To keep the spreaders from swinging too far, however, they may be fastened to one another around the mast. The shrouds should not be made fast to the fork of the spreaders. They should be free to work up and down through them but it is well to serve the shrouds at this point to prevent chafing. Shrouds are generally made fast to the mast by three methods. The most common is by splicing. The second method, employed where there are two lower shrouds to a side, is to pass a single turn of wire up from the chain plate over the spreader, around the mast, and down through the spreader to the other chain plate. This shroud is then seized by a wire seizing close to the mast. This method has the merit of neatness in that only one turn of the wire passes around the mast but this neatness is more than offset by its resulting weakness. If anything should happen to one end of the shroud, the other end will pull through the seizing with the probable loss of the mast. I lost an important night race once owing to a slight accident that carried away a cotter pin on a turnbuckle and my shrouds, seized in this way, pulled through the seizing and put me out of the race. Fortunately the shroud let go with a loud report and the prompt action of the helmsman who luffed immediately was all that saved the mast.

The most modern method of attaching shrouds to masts is by the use of metal tangs which fasten on to the mast and receive the shroud. These tangs are very neat and very efficient and seem to be a great improvement over splicing or seizing. To conclude the subject of the mast and the wire rigging, let me say that all tuning up must be done by the trial and error method. Adjustments must be made under sail and minor adjustments must be made for variations in wind. Only a sensitive helmsman can direct the tuning up. A record should be kept of the number of threads taken up on each turnbuckle. The rake of the mast should be regulated by means of the plumb-bob and the adjustment should continue until the boat herself tells you that she likes it. If your boat has a bowsprit and a bobstay, the tension of the bobstay must be considered in relation to all stays running to the bowsprit. A turn or two on the bobstay turnbuckle may prove more effective that setting up the head stay as the bobstay turnbuckle will not only set up the head stay but may put an equal tension on the jib stay. Similarly in a yawl, the boomkin stay calls for adjustment but this adjustment is usually made in the interest of rigidity alone.

Two other spars call for attention; the boom and the gaff. Ever since the *Enterprise* startled the yachting world with her so-called Park Avenue boom (see Figs. 8 and 9) the boom has called for more attention than ever before. This boom is the invention of Dr. Curry and is useful for two purposes: first, it prevents a downdraft of wind from passing under the sail, and, second, of primary importance, it assures an aerofoil curve extending right down to the foot of the mainsail, a result that is not possible with a straight boom.

The Bigelow boom, an invention of Commodore Paul Bigelow of the Bellport Bay Yacht Club deserves mention in this respect. Commodore Bigelow has equipped his Star boat with a very light, flexible boom, along each side of which he has placed a wire stay similar to a jack stay. A strut extends laterally from each side of this boom. In this strut are three notches. In light airs, the skipper places his foot against the boom and pulls the stay into the outermost notch, thus imparting a pronounced curvature to the boom. When he goes about, he slips the stay out of the notch and pulls the stay on the opposite side of the boom into the corresponding notch.

In moderate airs the stay is pulled to the second notch and in heavy blows to the third notch. This gives

Fig. 6. The Bigelow boom

three degrees of curvature to the sail by a very simple mechanism. A recent ruling in some yacht clubs that the boom must be of such a size as to pass through the diameter of the mast rules out the use of the Park Avenue boom but probably would not prevent the use of the Bigelow boom which is shown in Fig. 6.

The gaff calls for special attention. The fit of many a sail is utterly destroyed by a sagging gaff. The gaff hogs up at the point of attachment of the peak halliard block but sags at the peak itself. This causes hard spots in the sail and a badly fitting leech. It can be remedied by attaching a reënforcing strip along the top of the gaff. To a certain extent it can be remedied by the use of a long wire bridle to distribute the strain of the halliard. The use of the bridle on halliards and sheets should be studied most carefully. Even on jibs, especially if they be large and carry clubs, a bridle for the sheet is often useful.

Chapter VI

A BIT OF AERODYNAMICS

No MODERN book on yachting would be complete without the introduction of the jaw-breaking word, aerodynamics. It lends such a scientific touch, even to a book that does not pretend to be scientific, that one must perforce employ it. Many yachtsmen seem to resent the intrusion of science into their sport and you can hardly blame them. The moment yachting becomes a study it ceases to be a game. The moment it ceases to be a game it becomes a bore and a task and the mad gayety goes out of it. Yet the scientists with their wind tunnels, their tests with down and smoke, and studies of birds' wings and airplanes, have made important contributions to the sport. To them belong the extraordinary developments of the Marconi rig, the conception of the sail as an aerofoil, the discovery of the stream line and other important milestones of progress.

Of the many contributors to the scientific attitude, Dr. Manfred Curry has probably given most, not only by his scientific experiments but by his publication of rigid rules of procedure which have standardized racing tactics and explained phenomena but dimly recognized before his books appeared. To him, in all probability, must be given the credit for the discovery that it is the lee side of the sail that drives a boat to windward; that the power developed on the lee side is three or four times the power developed on the weather side. Until his book appeared, yachtsmen held an almost universal belief that it was the wind blowing on the windward side of the sail that drove their boats. If you have been bewildered by this idea, let me sound one word of caution. The boat is sailed almost identically the same way whether the power comes from the lee or the windward side of the sail. Most yachtsmen, when they read Dr. Curry's discoveries, immediately conclude that they must sail their yachts in a different manner. When I first read Curry's first book I won but two races in the entire summer and I attribute this bad luck solely to the confusion brought about by this amazing discovery. The importance of windage aloft has also been driven home most convincingly by the experts and the scientists. The presence of eddies in the air and their retarding effect have also been proved most conclusively. These are the most important contributions. Yet there are certain dangers in the scientific attitude which may be revealed as time goes on. The analogy between an airplane, a bird's wing, and a sail boat is probably faulty. There are certain differences between an airplane and a sail. The airplane wing function is to hold the plane aloft. The plane is driven by its propeller. The sail, on the other hand, performs the opposite to holding the boat up. The sail performs the function of the airplane's propeller. A sail must work in an average wind of seven knots. The airplane wing operates in an air speed of about 100 knots. No sail could possibly function in a wind of 100 knots. Therefore, wind-tunnel tests, performed in airplane wind tunnels, cannot be trusted as indicative of conditions applying at sailing wind velocities.

Most of our scientific discoveries are too new to be dependable. In all probability, future generations of yachtsmen will laugh at them, just as we laugh to-day at the excessive windage, the inefficiency, and the appalling clumsiness of rigs of the past.

It is desirable in the extreme to keep an open mind on all new developments. But it is equally desirable to preserve a proper degree of skepticism and to accept these discoveries only after they have been definitely proved.

It is hard to distinguish between the scientific and the pseudo-scientific. It is dangerous to jump at conclusions even when a new rig proves superior in actual racing.

For instance: The scientists proved by wind-tunnel tests that the mast breaks up the lines of flow on the luff of the mainsail. They also proved that the twisting of a sail due to the sagging off of the upper part interfered greatly with its efficiency. These two factors condemned the foresail of the schooner rig. The schooner *Advance* then appeared with a new and tricky staysail rig in place of a foresail. These many small sails did not twist. They were spread from stays—not from the foremast except for a short luff on one staysail—so that the windage of the foremast did not interfere with them. They controlled the flow on the leeward side of the mainsail.

And the *Advance* cleaned up. No boat ever had a more brilliant record. The case seemed proved. The next year almost the entire schooner fleet broke out new staysail rigs. But the *Advance* cleaned up again as decisively as ever. Then the men who had paid out their thousands for the new rigs began to wonder whether or not the superiority of the *Advance* lay in her hull and not in her rig. To-day, except in cruising classes, the big schooners have practically disappeared from the racing fleet. Perhaps the staysail rig ruined the schooners, for the rig is undoubtedly expensive and hard to handle. It is still too early to approve or condemn. The acid test of practice has revealed both merits and demerits. Nearly every gain seems compensated by some loss.

Again: A new rig with no sails set on the mast. A boom pivoting about a stay, so that the forward part swung to windward as the after part swung to leeward. A jib set on this so-called jib-boom. The discovery of this new rig was published prematurely, but it was accepted as gospel. The *Rofa,* renamed *Isabella,* put to·sea in the race to Spain with an adaptation of this rig. She proved fast. But she was dismasted at sea, taken in tow by a tanker, and lost. Her skipper still denies that there was anything faulty in the jib-boom idea, and he may be right. It is still too early to say.

One more: The scientists proved that for its area, the jib developed more power than the mainsail. They did not at the time make clear that the reason for this was that the jib increases the power of the mainsail. The *Atrocia,* a 6-Metre, was built with a mast stepped aft, a small mainsail, and a huge jib. The jib had the area usually devoted to the mainsail and vice versa. She was a conspicuous failure.

I realize that I am writing like an old shell-back. But I deplore the present tendency to accept without question anything heralded with the magic words, "Science has proved."

But let us try to glean from the mass of scientific

and pseudo-scientific matter those findings which seem important in the actual winning of races, apart from those which enter into design and rig.

1. A sail is an aerofoil, in many respects resembling the wing of a bird, the wing of an airplane, and the blade of a steam turbine.

2. It should maintain a smooth, arched surface which should be as stiff as possible.

3. The negative pressure or suction of the leeward side of the sail develops three to four times the pressure of the windward side of the sail, while sailing to windward.

4. The sails, spars, rigging, and hull should present as little resistance as possible to the free, uninterrupted flow of the wind.

5. The wind must flow off the sail as well as onto it. Wrinkles, pockets, "hard spots," tight or hollow leeches, set up eddies on both sides of the sail. These eddies break up the flow of the wind and impair efficiency.

6. Inasmuch as it is most important to maintain an uninterrupted flow of wind on the leeward side of the mainsail, the jib must be of such size, and shape, and so trimmed, as to direct this flow as smoothly as possible and increase the wind's velocity.

7. Battens should be as numerous and as long as the class rules allow. They should never be omitted.

8. Wind must never be pocketed in a sail. Only live, moving air drives a boat.

To summarize thus cavalierly the results of the patient research of our scientific seekers must seem crudely inadequate. But the details are all available in the numerous scientific books on yachting, and the little I can add from my own observations of bird flight with slow motion pictures, is not sufficiently established to admit of publication yet.

The yachtsman must summarize these things for himself. He cannot carry a mass of scientific data into a race. When he has read it all and digested it thoroughly, his working knowledge will boil down to a few simple laws as simply stated as the eight precepts I have listed.

CHAPTER VII

TUNING UP—THE SAILS

WHAT IS the proper shape of a sail? We have learned so much about sail design in the past few years that I fear to enter too deeply into any discussion of the matter. It is my firm belief that before this book is very old, we will have a number of brand new ideas on the shapes of sails that will make this book seem antiquated. If it is borne in mind, however, that the purpose of this book is not to discuss design, nor to encroach on the field of the scientist and the naval architect, but merely to guide the sailor in the best use of the sails which he already owns, whatever is here recorded will be justified. I do not propose to enter into a discussion of the relative merits of the gaff or the Marconi rig, of the tall narrow sails versus shorter, broader sails, of the use of full length battens, or of other controversial points. We will assume that you have a boat which has an old suit of sails and it is your problem to get the most out of those sails.

It was not until some years after the discovery of aviation that the sail was conceived as an aerofoil. Essentially the sail performs just about the same function as a bird's wing or an airplane wing. It must therefore have a certain lateral belly; it must not stand flat. To attain this belly, the sail-makers cut roaches along the head, foot, luff, and leech. In other words, these lines are not straight lines, they are curved outward from the center of the sail. When the head is pulled out straight along the gaff, and the foot is pulled out straight along the boom, and the sail is hoisted so that the luff is tight, the sail when filled with wind, develops a pronounced belly. In the purchase of an old boat, one may examine these roaches by pulling the sail out in a straight line between the clews and folding over the edge of the sail. If these roaches are not pronounced and do not form perfectly even curves, the sail will not be a good one. If, on the other hand, these roaches are still pronounced and form curves, it is not an assurance that the sail has not developed hard spots.

Where should the belly come in a sail? Should it be near the luff, amidships, or near the leech? Frankly, I do not know. All I can do is to quote opinions. There are two leading sail-makers in the neighborhood of New York. One claims that the belly should be near the middle of the sail. The other claims that it should be near the luff. This is reported on hearsay and may not be true, but it has been reported so many times that I do not feel the necessity for questioning it. Curry claims that it does not matter so long as the belly is there. After considerable thought on how to present the matter of the belly of a sail, I have concluded that the best way to do it is to show an illustration of the boom of the *Enterprise*. She is probably the fastest and most highly developed boat ever built up to the time this book is written and the curvature of her sails was carefully studied by the most expert yachtsmen in America, and her sails made by one of the greatest of all sail-makers. Furthermore, no expense was spared in the purchase, testing, and development of the fastest possible sails so that the *Enterprise* sails may well be considered a proper model for any yachtsman to follow.

But that is not the point. Toward the end of her trial period, and in the races against the *Shamrock V*, the *Enterprise* was equipped with what was known as the Park Avenue boom. This boom was the invention of Dr. Curry and shows how his ideas were adapted by the leading American yachtsmen with the help of the most expert naval architects and sail-makers. The idea of the Park Avenue boom was this: The foot of the sail was made fast to a strong wire on which sail-slides were arranged so that they could travel forward and aft to allow for stretching the sail. The boom was about three feet wide at its widest part, and on this boom were fastened transverse tracks. The slides were placed on the tracks in such a manner that every time the *Enterprise* went about, the slides glided over to the leeward edge of the boom. The object of this boom was to carry the aerofoil curvature of the mainsail right down to the foot, thus preventing the loss of curvature that resulted with the ordinary boom, which, being perfectly straight, necessarily flattened out the foot of the sail. A study, therefore, of the perimeter of the *Enterprise's* boom would show at a glance exactly the desired belly of the sail that is most efficient. (See Figs. 8 and 9.) You will note that the greatest depth is just about in the middle, not forward, and the relationship of the depth of the belly to the length of the boom can be clearly borne in mind and applied to any sail.

This boom had another feature which is worth noting. There were two rows of holes drilled along the

FIG. 8. The *Enterprise's* Park Avenue boom. Showing the proper
depth of belly to mainsail

FIG. 9. Another view of the *Enterprise's*
boom and mainsail

Fig. 11. A contrast in jibs. Compare the mitred jib in No. 11 with the horizontal cloths in No. 2

Fig. 10. Perfect leeches

sides—the first row, a few inches inside the perimeter, and the second row a few inches farther inside. In strong breezes, pegs were placed in this outer row to make the sails stand somewhat flatter. In still stronger breezes, pegs were placed in the inner row of holes, and when it was blowing so hard that the small mainsail was carried (the equivalent of a reefed large mainsail) the sail was stopped amidships. These rows of holes show clearly the required curvature in a fresh breeze of wind and also in a strong breeze of wind. By studying the illustrations, Figs. 8 and 9, the reader will have a better guide to the proper aerofoil curvature of his sails than I could give him in any other way. This makes clear one other point. In a heavy breeze, a sail should stand somewhat flatter than in light airs. The depth of belly is not so necessary and it is usually conceded that a boat can point somewhat higher with a flat sail than with a bulging sail.

In England, the loose-footed mainsail has a degree of popularity that has never been attained on this side of the Atlantic. But when one of America's leading sail-makers built a boat for his own use, he equipped her with a loose-footed mainsail. The *Gollywog* as she has been called has had such an enviable record that her sails deserve careful contemplation. She is shown in Fig. 11. The curvature of her mainsail is very evident in the photograph. In Fig. 12 is shown a loose-footed mainsail in which the sail is clearly shown to have a miter. A seam bisects the angle of the clew. Below that seam, the cloths run at right angles to the foot; above it, they run at right angles to the leech. Sails made in this manner seem somehow to preserve their curvature, although I have rarely seen a mitered sail that was not loose-footed. Nearly all loose-footed jibs are made with a miter, and I personally prefer my jib mitered even when it is attached to a club. In Fig. 13 it is possible to compare the mitered jib in No. 11 with the jib of horizontal cloths on No. 2.

If you have two jibs of different construction, you must use care in bending them. The adjustment of the outhaul on the club is different with each jib, and in all probability the jib sheet leads will have to be placed differently. With two jibs of different construction, I even go so far as to use two entirely different clubs.

Your attention should always be directed to the leech of the sail. For many years great efforts were made to maintain a deep convex curve along the leech. This is known as the roach. Nowadays less importance is credited to the roach of the leech. It is true that a sail with a wide roach has the benefit of greater area, but it is now known that the leech of the sail develops less power than any other part and this extra area is considered of less importance. But there is a reason for a well-roached sail apart from the extra area thus developed. A sail that is concave along its outer edge is said to be nigger-heeled, and a nigger-heeled sail loses its power because somehow it destroys the proper curvature of the sail and also because it pockets the wind. In stretching and hoisting new sails, therefore, pay attention to the leech and see to it that it preserves the roach and is not nigger-heeled. The roach can be preserved by not stretching the foot of the sail too tight, by not stretching the head of a gaff-rigged sail too tight, and, in a Marconi sail, by paying proper attention to the halliard and its point of fastening to the headboard. New sails, in particular, should not be stretched too tight. Sails are very elastic and rapidly lose their shape. On a small boat the sails should be stretched just "hand tight"—that is to say, just as tight as you can get them by hand without the aid of tackles and without undue muscular effort. On a day when the sails are likely to be wet, allowance must be made for shrinkage. It must be borne in mind that the most frequent cause of wet sails is spray. Sailors who are very careful about the effect of rain on their sails may utterly disregard spray and dew, yet both spray and dew have both precisely the same effect as rain.

Care must be taken at all times to prevent vertical wrinkles in the sails. Wrinkles usually originate at the lacing lines or from slides that are not free to move along the track. They can also be caused by lazyjacks, topping lifts, or unusual stretching. Wrinkles impede the flow of wind along the sail and set up annoying little eddies that interfere seriously with its power. (See Fig. 7.) The leech must be studied not only for nigger-heeling, which is improper curvature in a fore and aft direction, but also for pocketing, which is improper curvature in a lateral direction. If the very edge of the leech curves over to windward, the wind is caught and pocketed in it so that it cannot flow freely off the sail. Pocketing is avoided, first, by proper battens; second, by adjustment of the leech line; third, by proper hoisting.

The battens should fit loosely in the batten pockets. They should never fit tight. A tight fit will cause wrinkles and hard spots in the sail. They should be tied firmly into the grommets in the leech and should never touch the forward ends of the pockets. The leech line should be adjusted after the sail is hoisted and, preferably, under way. It should be adjusted several times in the course of every race. The leech line is like the whisky which an old Kentucky Colonel gave to his colored servant and which the servant declared was just right. "If dat whisky, Kunnel, had been any bettah, I wouldn' ha' got it, and if it had been any wo'se, I couldn' ha' drunk it." If the leech line is too tight, a pocket develops; if it is too lose, the leech of the sail shakes. It must be adjusted between the two extremes so that there is no pocket and no shaking. The leech line of the jib deserves special attention because a pocket in the leech of the jib not only interferes with its efficiency but also back-winds the mainsail and somehow the leech of the jib is usually more prone to shake than the leech of the mainsail. The mainsail is properly hoisted only when the luff and the leech are stretched tight enough, but not too tight. Serious deficiencies in a gaff-headed mainsail may often be cured by hoisting the peak higher. Thus a pocket in the leech may be stretched out or if the cure is not effected in this way, it may sometimes be remedied by lowering the peak an inch or two. In the same manner, the leech of a Marconi mainsail may be adjusted by placing the halliards in the proper hole in the headboard. As a rule, there are three holes in the headboard for the attachment of the halliard. Try hoisting your sail with the halliard attached to the center hole.

If the leech is too tight, lower your sail and move the halliard to the forward hole. If the leech is too loose, move the halliard to the after hole. The correct height to which the peak of a gaff-headed mainsail should be hoisted is determined by the wrinkles in the sail. If the wrinkles are parallel to a line from the throat to the clew, the peak is not hoisted high enough. If the wrinkles are parallel to a line from the peak to the tack, the peak is hoisted high enough. The proper depth of these wrinkles must be determined by the trial and error method. The most common error is to fail to hoist the peak high enough. The proper wrinkles in a Marconi mainsail should lie parallel to and fairly close to the mast. The wrinkles mentioned in this paragraph are discernible only when the boat is headed into the wind. They disappear as soon as she has filled away. A distinction should be made between these proper wrinkles and the improper ones that remain in the sail after it is filled with wind.

Hard spots in a sail are most difficult to overcome. You can detect hard spots by sighting along the sail and seeing whether or not the curvature of the belly is uniform. Wherever the curvature is not uniform there is a hard spot. Frequently, by looking up at the windward side of the sail, you will see the curve flatten out into a plane and then continue as a curve beyond it. Unless the cure for these hard spots can be discovered, the sail should be abandoned for a new one. Occasionally the sail can be saved by re-cutting, in which case the seams are opened up and sewed together again after tiny strips have been cut off at each seam. But frequently hard spots are caused not by the sails but by the spars. A mast that develops strange curves under strain will work hard spots into the sails. A gaff that sags or a boom that bends unduly are frequently guilty. Improper curvature in a mast may be remedied by slacking the shrouds, or tightening the jack stay, or setting up the runners, etc. It is all a matter of trial and error. In general, the business of tuning up the sails consists of the following operations: 1. Obtain a sail with the proper aerodynamic curvature with sufficient continuity and depth of belly. 2. Secure proper lacing and stretching. 3. Avoid nigger-heels and pockets in the leech. 4. Hoist properly with special attention to height of peak and correct placing of halliard in Marconi headboard. 5. Eliminate hard spots.

Do not give up as hopeless a sail that performs badly. Sails possess great powers of recovery. If hoisted in the warm sun and allowed to shiver and shake in a light breeze, a badly stretched sail, full of hard spots, will often recover. The best of sails, improperly bent and improperly hoisted will prove a poor power plant. A poor sail properly tuned up will often yield surprisingly good results.

Chapter VIII

BOATSWAINISM

An apology is in order for the use of a manufactured term. I know of no word that describes the constant attention and tuning and adjusting that is a necessary part of every race. On a big ship in a long passage, this duty falls upon the boatswain and for that reason I have manufactured the term "boatswainism."

No matter how carefully a boat may be prepared for a race, with sails carefully hoisted and everything shipshape and Bristol fashion, there is almost certain to occur some loss of tuning which must be compensated for if the boat is to proceed at her best speed. Sometimes tuning is lost through natural causes such as stretching and shrinking; sometimes through accidents, such as chafing, unlacing, and the breaking of shackles, blocks, etc., tears in sails, or breaking or losing battens; sometimes it comes from sheer carelessness, such as loss of efficiency through permitting a topping-lift to cut into the belly of the sail. Whatever the cause, it must have prompt and immediate attention.

I recall vividly our preparations for the Block Island race of 1931. It must have rained during the night, or the dew had been exceptionally heavy, for the sails were wet even under their covers. I recall vividly the care with which we hoisted sail that morning. I even got out in the dinghy and sculled some distance abeam of the boat to study the wrinkles in the mainsail, the tightness of the luff, the curvature of the leech, the angle to which the peak had been hoisted. I studied it for about five minutes, shouting back instructions to the rest of the crew. I did not desist until I was absolutely satisfied that the mainsail was hoisted perfectly. There was a good drying wind from the Northwest that morning and the day was blisteringly hot. We sailed down to Execution Light and while we were jockeying for the start, Rosenfeld, the seagoin' photographer, cruised alongside and snapped a picture. When the proof arrived during the following week, I was appalled at the loss of tuning which the boat had suffered in the three or four miles between Mamaroneck Harbor and Execution Light. First of all, the halliards had stretched, dropping the sail noticeably. The outhaul on boom and gaff had also given way a bit so that there were long disheartening wrinkles running vertically across the mainsail. The jib had developed a terrible bag on the foot just forward of the club, and instead of a reasonably powerful piece of machinery, the boat was now about as efficient as a very old and badly-cared-for coasting schooner. Fig. 14 shows the picture just as I saw it. It makes an interesting contrast with Fig. 15 in which we see the same boat and the same sails. In this illustration, the sails are a year older and they have undergone terrible punishment. They have stretched and mildewed; they have been sailed by day and by night, in storms and in calms, they have had more neglect than care. But here they are properly hoisted and kept properly set up and are much more efficient than they

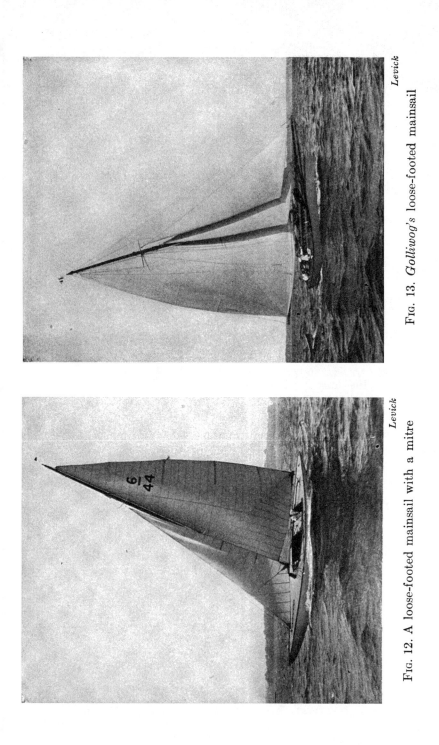

FIG. 13. *Golliwog's* loose-footed mainsail

FIG. 12. A loose-footed mainsail with a mitre

Rosenfeld

FIG. 14. *Old Timer's* sails at start of Block Island race in 1931. Halliards and lace lines have stretched since hoisting

Rotofotos

FIG. 15. *Old Timer* winning in Knickerbocker Yacht Club Regatta in 1932. The same sails, much the worse for wear, but now properly bent and hoisted

were the year before when they had lost their careful tuning through drying out.

Stretch must be watched for at all times, particularly if you are using rope halliards or if you are sailing under conditions that are progressively drier.

If you have wire halliards and wire luff lines, their stretching becomes unimportant, but with rope, stretch is always a factor to be reckoned with. An alert crew is constantly setting up on its halliards. Similarly, the lacing lines at the head and foot of the sail and the outhauls on boom and gaff must be watched for stretching. It is always wise to stretch any cotton line by means of hard pulling or possibly even by the use of a winch before using it to bend a sail. Even then, under the constant pressure from the sail, these lines are likely to stretch. The canvas itself is elastic and is apt to grow loose and bag through stretching, especially in a hard breeze and a long sail. To pull stretched canvas still tighter is sometimes disastrous, but it is the only way to restore the proper tuning lost from this cause. I have known the tackle of a backstay or runner to stretch to such an extent that the mast would whip around. There is not much line in such a tackle.

The reverse of stretching is shrinking. Lines and sails will shrink when they are wet from any cause. They may become thoroughly soaked from rain, spray, fog, or even dew. Nearly all racing boats have their boom outhauls lead pretty far forward to a cleat that will be inboard regardless of the trim of the sheet. The wise skipper slacks this outhaul whenever the sail is wet. Of course, on a small boat it may be necessary to adjust the outhaul several times in the course of a race. There may be two long hard windward legs in which the spray is flying and everything is soaked. These will be followed by a reach and a run in which there is no spray but a good hot sun and a strong drying breeze. On the windward leg, the wise skipper will be forced to slack his outhaul as his sails become wet. Somewhere along the reach or the run it may be necessary to set up on the outhaul once or even twice. If there is a second lap to the race, these processes must be repeated all over again. In sailing in a night race, it is necessary to make constant adjustments after nightfall if there is a heavy dew and to set up on the lines again in the morning if the boat dries out.

In short races in sheltered waters, there is very little danger from chafing. At sea, however, in ocean races, the danger from chafing is very great indeed, and great care must be observed to prevent it at all times. Nevertheless, even in sheltered waters I have occasionally parted a halliard through some unsuspected chafing aloft. Great care should be exercised to observe whether the halliard blocks have been twisted in unshackling them and shackling them again when removing a sail cover. If the lines cross one another up aloft, they may chafe through. Chafing is not confined to heavy weather. It is far more apt to occur in a flat calm, especially if there are motor boats about, churning up the waters with their wakes and making the racing boats flop around without the quieting effect of a breeze. I remember losing one race through having the lacing line of the head of the mainsail chafe at the throat. Again Rosenfeld was on the job. In Fig. 16 you will see that the lacing line has let go at the throat and the head of the sail is held to the gaff merely through friction. A few minutes later the entire head of the sail tore away and we had to send a

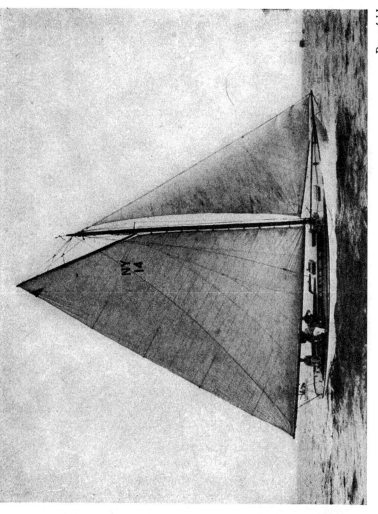

Rosenfeld

Fig. 16. The lacing line on the head of the mainsail has chafed through near the throat

FIG. 17. The runner cutting into the mainsail

FIG. 18. The throat halliard has stretched

man aloft to patch things up. On this occasion there had been a heavy shower after the sail was hoisted. Probably shrinkage of the line was one of the causes of its parting.

Occasionally a line will unlay under a strain. I have known this to happen particularly with spinnaker halliards where a ballbearing swivel hook was used. The swivel turned so freely that the strain on the halliard served merely to spin the line around and unlaid it for a distance of several feet up aloft.

Under the strain of sailing it is surprising how many pieces of hardware will break, or otherwise fail. My own particular problem is that of keeping jib sheet fair leaders on my deck. In every real blow in which I race I seem to lose a fair leader. I have tried bolts, screws, and everything, but I continue to scatter them over Long Island Sound. Perhaps blocks fail more frequently than anything else. They should constantly be examined and a questionable block should never be used.

One of the most annoying things that can happen is to tear your sails. In a short race it is usually wise to continue sailing even though a bad tear has developed. In Douglas Fairbanks's old motion picture, "The Black Pirate," the hero stopped the pirate vessel by thrusting his sword successively into the sails near the head and tearing them to the foot. It was a spectacular stunt but it would not stop a ship from moving. A torn sail is better than none and will continue to drive you provided it still stays in the bolt ropes. In a long race, however, it is wise to mend a sail just as soon as a tear develops, otherwise the tear is apt to go clear across the sail, making it impracticable for you to continue and causing you a much greater loss of time than if you stopped at once, made the repair, and then sailed on. Needless to say, no boat should enter a race without needle, sail twine, beeswax, and sail-maker's palm.

Most of us have great trouble with the loss of battens. Battens are easily broken, are most apt to tear the sails at the inboard ends of the pockets, and they are also likely to break their lashings, whip out of the pockets, and be lost. Nearly every racing boat carries spare battens. I go further than that. I keep a saw and draw knife on board and carry a neat lumber pile of dressed white ash in the bow. I have found that I lose or break a batten about once in every three races. Battens should be made shorter than their pockets; they should be lashed firmly in the grommets in the leech in such a way that they will not whip out and not touch the forward ends of the pockets. Great care should be used in hoisting and lowering sail to see that they do not catch under topping-lifts or lazyjacks.

A very serious loss of tuning occurs when a screw in a turnbuckle turns under stress. (For the sake of English readers it should be stated that by "turnbuckles" I mean "rigging screws.") Turnbuckles will not loosen up if they are properly fitted with cotter pins. Unfortunately, cotter pins seem to be scarcer than hen's teeth aboard most boats so that nails, hairpins, bits of wire and even match-sticks are sometimes used to take their place. Iron cotter pins rust out quickly and can never be depended upon. If you have ever lost a shroud and thereby lost a race through the failure of a cotter pin, you will make it a practice to check up on them constantly before and during every race.

One of the most dangerous things that can happen is the loss of the staying qualities of a shroud through the sagging of a spreader. On small boats very few spreaders are provided with spreader lifts. On larger boats spreader lifts are essential, but inasmuch as they are usually made of very light wire, they are apt to part. Even when a boat is re-rigged completely, the spreader lifts are apt to be neglected. The sagging of a spreader may cost you your mast.

Lines that need constant attention during a race are the leech lines in jib and mainsail. They are more vitally important in the jib than in the mainsail because too tight a leech line will kill the efficiency of the jib and cause it to back-wind the mainsail. Furthermore, the leech line in the jib is exposed to spray from the bow and is very apt to shrink and grow too tight. On the other hand, the leech lines may be so loose that jib or mainsail will flap along the leech, thus setting up eddies which are very disturbing to the flow of wind across the sails.

Perhaps the most usual function of "boatswainism" is to watch the topping-lifts, quarter-lifts, lazyjacks, runners, and backstays to see that they do not interfere by cutting into the belly of the sails. It is a good plan to appoint one member of the crew to observe these lines at all times and make it his duty to see that the perfect aerofoil curvature of the sails is never disturbed by these lines. This is pretty elementary, but the lines may shrink, they may catch on a cleat or a screw eye, or otherwise be tautened up so that they will ruin your performance. In light airs I have known a loosened lee backstay repeatedly to knock all the wind out of the mainsail. The heavy block at the bottom of the stay, flopping back and forth as the boat rolls, will cause the backstay to whip against the mainsail as though it were beating the dust out of a rug. When a backstay does this, carry it forward to the shroud and seize it there with a couple of turns of sail twine. If you should need it, one pull on the tackle will break the twine and your backstay is ready for immediate use.

Many a race has been lost by under-water obstructions. I have heard tales of boats picking up eel pots, lobster pots, moorings, cables, and all sorts of flotsam. Perhaps the most usual is seaweed, floating in big sticky masses. Seaweed will gather on keel, centerboard, scag, rudder, and propeller and stop the boat almost as much as a sea anchor would. One year on Great South Bay the seaweed was particularly bad. In the Star class every boat was equipped with some form of hook or pitchfork to pull or push the seaweed off the keel.

A necessary part of boatswainism is to watch out for unnecessary windage. A loose, flapping line will stop a boat very much more than a tightly trimmed line. The windage of a coil of halliards hung too high on a pin is worth considering. In small boats, certainly, the windage of a crew sitting upright is considerably more than the windage of the same crew lying flat on deck, or snugly stowed in the cockpit. Apart from windage, the careful coiling down of halliards and other running rigging is a necessary function of boatswainism. Personally, I abhor coiled halliards, and in some of my boats I have built in drawers under the forward deck in which I dropped the halliards just as they came from my hand. With this arrangement the line "takes its natural lay" and is far less apt to foul than when coiled. But the use of some such device, or coiling, is necessary to cut down windage, to have the line ready to pay out instantly, and to keep the line from going overboard. Dragging lines are a serious hindrance to the progress of any boat. The chief offender is usually the spinnaker guy. Necessarily, it must pass outside shrouds and backstays and, therefore, if it is not carefully watched is apt to get overboard. Large ships, running before heavy gales at sea, have often been known to hold the stern to the wind, simply by trailing a couple of cables overboard. This fact will give you some notion of the retarding power of a line that is dragging in the water.

A necessary phase of boatswainism is to keep down the water in the bilge. If the boat leaks, she must be pumped several times in the course of the race. If she is perfectly tight, but there is spray flying, or water comes in over the cockpit, she must be pumped promptly and pumped dry. Even with a perfectly tight boat, sailing in light airs, the pump should be tried out occasionally. In the Block Island race of 1933 we were careless in this respect and did not realize that we were down several inches below our normal sailing lines due to an enormous amount of water in the boat. A corroded pipe in the toilet spurted water into the boat until it was above the floor boards of the cabin, and only then was the leak discovered and fixed.

In the excitement of a race one rarely thinks of what is going on in the cabin. Nevertheless, there should be an occasional policing below. We are sailing, let us say, before the wind and the boat is proceeding calmly on an even keel. We round a mark and trim sheets, then we hear below a crash of china. There is a more ominous sound of rolling tinware, and another crash. We find the muriatic acid with which we have been cleaning brass has spilled into the ice box. A can of varnish has been dropped on the spinnaker. The dishes from which we have eaten lunch are in a frightful and fragmentary mess on the cabin floor. All these are caused by improper policing and possibly by the presence on board of some green hands who do not know that things on a boat must not be laid down but wedged in. Boatswainism, therefore, must be observed at all times, alow and aloft, on deck and below deck, and even under the bottom.

Chapter IX

THE CREW AND EQUIPMENT

IN MOST classes the number of men in the crew is
limited by the rules. Sometimes these rules limit the
number of persons on board, at other times they limit
merely the number of men or boys actually taking part
in the sailing. Ladies sailing as guests may or may not
be counted in the crew. No rule should be ambiguous
in this matter and, in case of doubt, it is always wise
to get a decision from the Race Committee before the
race. If there are no crew restrictions, your success may
be governed by the number of men you carry. In light
airs it is wise to travel light. In heavy airs you may
be able, particularly in a small boat, to load her down
with live ballast so as to have a distinct advantage
over your opponents. In the very small classes it is frequently wise to judge your crew by their avoirdupois.
In fact, in regions where boats are small, where crews
are limited in number, and where the wind is strong,
everybody loves a fat man. In the old days of the
sandbaggers, crews were selected primarily by their
weight and strength, and each man was given the
largest sandbag he could possibly handle. Crew and
sandbags were constantly shifted to the windward
side of the boat and cases are on record where boats,
suddenly having their wind cut off, were capsized to
windward by the weight of the crew and the shiftable

ballast. As a general rule to-day, a dead weight may not be shifted in any boat after sunset of the previous evening, and in most cases no ballast may be added to or subtracted from the boat after she has been measured by the official Measurer.

Unless the weight of the crew is vitally necessary for stability as in the case of small centerboard boats in heavy winds, it is usually wise to travel light with the smallest possible crew which the rules allow. I have raced a 43-foot boat, single-handed, but that is not to be recommended as a practice. On that same boat I carry five men when it is blowing hard and four men when the air is light. Even in light airs it takes four men to jibe the boat smartly, and in a blow it is necessary to have an extra man on the boat to trim for a jibe. The number of men necessary to jibe the boat is the main consideration in the minimum number of crew. Every other job can be handled by such a crew with men to spare.

A very necessary qualification for any good crew is that all hands should be perfectly congenial. One crab, or one bore, is enough to spoil not merely the pleasure of the race, but the entire efficiency of the crew. In a long race the members of the crew are very apt to get on one another's nerves and great care must be taken in their selection with this thought in mind.

Some day, if I live long enough, I hope to set sail with a crew all of whom have good tough hands. The dainty, lily-white hands of the average office worker are totally unadapted to the business of hauling on a line, or stopping a sheet that is smoking through his fingers. When issuing invitations to a crew to accompany me on a long race, I invariably beg of them to harden up their hands. The following methods are recommended to a landsman: Tie a line to the bumper of your car and pull it, preferably up a slight grade; work in the garden; use a sledge-hammer or ax. If you live in a city apartment, use a hammer and drive a lot of nails in a plank. While sitting at your desk, pound the palms of your hands on the arms of your chair. Do anything and everything to get your hands hard. No sailor is any better than his hands. If his hands are too tender to trim on a line when the boat is putting up a fight, he might better be ashore.

The most important member of the crew is the skipper. Above and beyond all knowledge of sailing a boat, he must have one important qualification—he must be the boss. There can be only one skipper; there can be only one boss. Let him listen to the advice of his crew, but let him make his own decisions. Right or wrong, when he has made those decisions, let him act upon them. He should quench criticism firmly and instantly. When he gives an order, he should see to it that it is obeyed cheerfully and with alacrity. He should apologize at the outset for his cussing and then should cuss like a longshoreman if necessary to make his crew hop. Like every leader, a good skipper is constantly tempted to sacrifice his own comfort for the comfort of his crew. He will not send a man into a dangerous situation in which he would not go himself. He will be the last to be fed and, if the cigarettes or the water are running low, he will discover that he does not want to smoke or that he is not thirsty. This can be carried too far, however. Since the skipper is easily the most important man aboard, he should look after his own comfort and spare himself unnecessary fatigue for the good of the crew and for the fulfillment of the supreme purpose for which he is sailing—the winning of the race.

In addition to the skipper, every crew should have at least one helmsman. This relief helmsman should be selected in advance and he should be designated to take the stick at any time when the skipper feels that he can no longer stay with his boat. Sailing a boat at her best speed is highly fatiguing. No one should ever hold the helm for more than two hours and frequently a five-minute rest for the skipper may mean a minute's better performance over the course.

The worst crew in the world is the seasick crew. The skipper should be a judge not merely of character, congeniality, or toughness of hands; he must also be a judge of the toughness of stomachs. If a man is seasick, handle him considerately, avoid giving him any unnecessary work, and then stop talking about it. Expressions of sympathy will do him no good, but they are quite likely to infect the rest of the crew with his malady. If he is demonstrably sick, quarantine him out of sight of the rest of the men on board, but do not on his account abandon the race.

A most necessary characteristic for a good crew is keenness. The crew must be in the race heart and soul to win it. Even if they are way down at the end of the fleet, they should be anxious to overtake the boat ahead as if it were the primary end in life. They should be willing to sacrifice their comfort, their ease, and their laziness to win the race. No amount of tinkering or monkeying with sails or gear should be too much for them. If a man lapses back into a daydream after each trimming of the spinnaker sheet and guy, get rid of him; he does not belong in a race. The fellow who says, "Oh, what's the use!" or expresses that attitude if only by the way he hunches his shoulders does not belong on the boat. The man who makes a date for a dance on the evening of the race and complains when you are becalmed does not belong in your crew. He is better off at the dance. The man who sings eternally the same song until you are sick of him is more than a nuisance. Soon the whole crew will have the song running through their heads and will be hating him and themselves and one another. All of these considerations point out the difficulty of obtaining a good crew. It is certain that some of the crew at least should know how to sail a boat, but to my mind character, keenness, and fitness are more important than any actual knowledge of sailing.

If there are one or more green hands in the crew, it is very necessary that they be given a quick course of training before the race. Their duties should be definitely delegated and they should be trained in those duties and in none other. In a race in the summer of 1933 I had one of the best and most efficient crews I ever sailed with. Here was the line-up: skipper, I myself; mate, an old hand who knew sailing, knew the boat, knew my peculiarities, loved the sport and was particularly keen. The rest of the crew were the following: (1) A youth from Kentucky who had been on the water just once before in his life. (2) An old man, over sixty, slow, clumsy, and heavy. (3) The fifteen-year-old son of the mate, light and under-developed and sailing on his first sail.

It seems impossible that such a crew could be characterized as one of the best I ever sailed with. How was this miracle achieved? First, I explained to the entire crew the difference between the windward and leeward sides of the boat. I made them shift back and forth from the windward side to the leeward; I made them realize that the leeward side was always down and the windward side was always up. The most difficult job on board was trimming the jib sheet. That job was assigned to the mate. On rounding marks, or altering course except by tacking, he took his station at the main sheet, but on the wind his job was at the lee jib sheet. To the old man was assigned the job of casting off the jib sheet; to the youth from Kentucky who fortunately had hands, was given the job of trimming the weather backstay; to the fifteen-year-old boy was assigned the job of casting off the lee backstay. Each one, individually, was taught just how to trim or to cast off one single line—that, and that only. Each one was also taught to call out the accomplishment of his particular task. We started sailing on the port tack. The skipper cried, "Ready about." The youth from Kentucky trimmed the backstay that would be the weather backstay when we went about. When it was on the cleat, he called, "Backstay down." Then I called, "Hard alee" and put the boat about. Immediately the old man cast off the jib sheet and called out, "Jib sheet's away." The fifteen-year-old boy cast off the backstay and cried, "Backstay away." The mate trimmed the jib sheet and when it was cleated cried, "Jib sheet down." As the boat filled away on the other tack, the old man immediately overhauled the jig on his jib sheet so that it would be ready for trimming on the other tack and announced, "Jig overhauled." It went reasonably smoothly the first time we tried it, but it took a long time to go about. Then I cried, "At your stations." The entire crew shifted position, as it was easier for them to shift positions than to shift jobs. Again, we went through the same routine, this time tacking from starboard to port. In that practice spin we went about eight times and the last five times the handling of the boat was as smooth and perfect as could be desired. I found that I was able to keep my eyes on the boat and on my opponents without watching my crew because I compelled them to call out on the completion of their jobs.

This is the way to train a green crew. Do not teach any green hand too much, but give him a few definite jobs and train him to do those jobs perfectly.

It is always well to have a substitute for any member of the crew who fails to show up at the last minute. If a boat is reasonably successful, the skipper is quite apt to be able to attract a worthwhile crew, but on any boat it is usually best to have a young boy or girl in reserve who is anxious to sail and is not offended if left ashore through the substitution of an adult.

Most small boats are sailed with strictly amateur crews. The question of amateur or professional differs in different localities. The generally accepted definition of an amateur or Corinthian is as follows: "No person who follows the sea as a means of livelihood or who has accepted remuneration for services in handling or serving on a yacht shall be considered a Corinthian yachtsman." Where this rule is in force, it is generally specified that an officer or sailor in the U. S. Navy is not considered a professional. Similarly, naval architects, yacht brokers, editors of yachting magazines, authors, and others who may make incidental gain from the sport are not considered professionals. In some localities even a more rigid definition is applied. A man who receives money, or other valuable consideration "for sailing on a boat in a race" is held to be a professional, and everyone else is held to be an amateur. The intent of the rules is clear. The man who follows the sport for the love of it is an amateur. The man who sails in a race because he is paid for it is a professional.

The rules governing professionals differ in different classes and in different localities. It is important to determine the limitations placed on professional sailors in the class and the club in which you sail. It may be that you are allowed no professionals at all. It may also be that you may have a limited number of professionals. In some classes you may carry one, in others, two, and in the big classes the number may even be unrestricted. In most cases the rules require that the helmsman must always be an amateur. In such cases it does not ordinarily disqualify a boat if a professional takes the helm for a momentary relief while the helmsman is lighting a cigarette, wiping his glasses, or putting on an oilskin. In some cases it is required that the man who sails the boat to windward must be an amateur, but a professional may take the helm when sailing free. It is considered generally desirable to restrict the use of professionals in all classes that can be comfortably sailed without their help. In the large classes where the handling of sail is burdensome, the use of professionals is usually allowed. The idea of the rule is to keep the fun of the sailing in the hands of the owner so that he will not be forced by competition to pay for the maintenance of the boat, give the fun of sailing her to a paid servant, and then pay that servant. Most restrictions in yachting are designed to hold down costs and make the competition one of skill rather than one of expenditure. I feel incompetent to give advice on the question of the professional crew, primarily because I have never had a paid hand who was worth his keep. My own experience leads me to the conclusion that I can keep the boat better and sail her better without professional aid. Yet, I realize that this conclusion should not apply generally and that a good paid hand is worth his weight in gold. My one advice, however, is to be captain of your own ship and to keep your professionals as foremast hands rather than as sailing masters. Even if you should get a competent sailing master, you will have more fun if you sail your own ship and do not follow blindly the advice of your professional, even though he should be competent to give good advice, otherwise he will be sailing the ship even though you may have your hand on the tiller, and you will miss the supreme reward of racing—the thrill of making the boat go yourself.

A boat is sailed not only by her crew but also by the equipment which is on board. Most racing boats are chiseled down in equipment to a point that is ridiculous. In a well-planned racing class, the list is completely specified so that all boats will be required to carry what is necessary and it will be illegal for any boat to gain an advantage over her competitors by leaving ashore the things which it is wise for all of the boats to carry. When the New York Yacht Club Thirty-foot Class was launched in 1905, Nathaniel Herreshoff, the designer and builder, was approached by one of his assistants with a proposed list of equipment. Mr. Herreshoff glanced at the list and then exclaimed, "Make it whatever you like, but if I were doing it, I would carry only a corkscrew and a can-opener." Yet the famous "30"s can be disqualified if they fail to carry such things as a mirror, a water bottle and glass, a stove, oil can, all lights and light screens, an anchor of specified weight, a cable of specified weight and length, life preservers, cushions, blankets, pillows, and everything else that came with the boat originally. A mirror and an oil can are not particularly necessary in winning a race, but certain other equipment is most necessary and should be on board any well-found racing yacht.

The question of battens has already been discussed. Certainly extra battens for jib and mainsail are most necessary. No boat should attempt to race without a pump. The pump should be in good order and should be of such a nature that it can be used on either tack and whether the boat is sailing on an even keel or heeled-down to her cockpit coaming. On shoal draft centerboard boats it is particularly necessary that the pump shall be of such a nature that it can be used in the bilge as well as beside the keelson. I have known of shoal draft open boats to take along a couple of coal scoops to bail out the water in heavy going. An anchor and cable should always be carried even if the rules do not require it. They may be the means of winning a race. In water where there is a strong tidal current it is not unusual to see a boat that has anchored in a light wind and a foul tide pass several of her competitors. In shoal waters a "settin' pole" is most necessary to free a boat that has gone aground. In deep waters the pole is both unnecessary and useless. In most of the smaller classes, carrying a compass is not required. Yet I have won many races in small classes simply through carrying a compass and being able to find marks in a fog. It is strange that in the years in which I sailed on Great South Bay I knew of no other boat that carried a compass even though racing in waters in which fog occurred frequently.

It is always wise to provide means for taking compass bearings. They are very helpful in being able to determine the course which you can lay, for determining whether you are gaining on or losing to an opponent, for getting an accurate fix if thick weather is closing in, for determining the angle of the starting line, and for many other uses. An elaborate azimuth-ring is not necessary, provided the compass is so mounted that across it you can get a clear unobstructed view of the object of which you are taking a bearing. With a compass so mounted, you can erect a shadow pin in the middle by means of a wooden toothpick and a stick of gum. This device is so useful that my own boat always carries a package of chewing gum and a package of toothpicks as part of her regular equipment. The necessary sail twine, beeswax, sail needles (at least two of them), and sail-maker's palm should be kept all together in a canvas fetch-bag or box. The needles should be coated with vaseline to keep them from rusting; a piece of fine sandpaper or emery paper will be useful in removing rust if it should once start. A small kit of tools should be on board, containing several knives, at least one marline-spike, a hammer, pliers, screwdriver and a Stillson wrench for setting up turnbuckles. A ball of marline is worth its weight in gold. There should also be plenty of extra line, preferably light cotton line to use as outhauls and hold-downs in reefing, to patch or repair if a lacing line gives way, to make fast things that get adrift below or in the cockpit, and for countless other uses. The race circular should be on board and should be held down by thumb tacks to a small piece of plank so that it will not be blown overboard. If plank and all go overboard before the start of the race, the circular can usually be recovered. A worthwhile gadget is a small triangular prism cut out of soft wood on which the skipper may write the compass bearings of each mark. It is very easy to forget such complicated bearings as WSW¼W, but if this prism is placed beside the compass, with one side facing the helmsman on which the directions for that leg are printed, it is always easy to refresh a confused memory.

A lead and line may lie in its locker all summer, but in case a fog descends in just one race, it will prove worth while to have carried it for the entire season. It may save you from running aground. It may give you a definite fix from which you can find the next mark and keep the course. It may enable you to run closer to shore, thus taking advantage of an off-shore wind. As a rule, the lead and line is neglected because the courses we sail are so familiar that we deem sounding unnecessary, but in a fog the waters are never familiar and even in clear daylight we may be tempted to run nearer to the shore than we have ever run before. If the shore is free from bowlders or sudden shoalings, the sounding lead may well enable you to run in close and thereby win the race.

In some localities the use of a protest flag is not required by the rules or, if required, is omitted by mutual consent. This is not good practice. In the event of an alleged foul, the skipper should be required to give immediate notice of his intention to protest by hoisting the red code flag "B" to his starboard spreader. If more than one boat is involved in a foul, or injured by a foul in which she is not involved, it is only fair that the intentions of the most closely interested boats should be proclaimed.

Binoculars are a very necessary part of a boat's

equipment. With them it is easy to pick up a mark long before it can be seen by the naked eye, and the course corrected accordingly. But binoculars serve other purposes as well. On calm days the approach of wind can often be seen through binoculars long before the little ripples on the water would appear to the naked eye. Signals on a Committee Boat can be studied at a great distance, such as the postponement signal when you are becalmed and struggling frantically to get to the starting line in time; the signal calling off the race, and similar visual notices. Do not use too strong a glass. A 10-power glass is almost useless in a small boat. An 8-power is helpful only when there is very little motion. A 6-power is about the limit to be recommended. The small, new type glasses which magnify only three diameters, but which may be worn on the face like spectacles, are very much to be recommended. It is possible for the skipper himself to wear a pair of these glasses while studying distant objects and yet look over them or around them at the luff of his sail and at the same time keep one hand on the tiller and one on the main sheet.

The use of a fly on the truck of the mast needs no elaboration. Flies are usually made of dark blue bunting. For night use I have had a white fly made which shows up clearly in the light of a flashlight and is very much better than the usual dark blue gadget. Most yachtsmen like to tie strips of baby ribbon to the shrouds as an indication of wind direction. This is very helpful if you will remember that it indicates the apparent wind only and that the direction of the wind is somewhat turned by the sail and also by the motion of the boat. If there is wind enough to move the fly, it is a better indication. The fly is affected only by the wind and the direction of the boat, but on a gaff-headed rig, with a high peak, it may also be affected by the peak.

A few spare parts may mean the winning or losing of a race. A turnbuckle, extra fairleaders, shackles, cotter pins, blocks, thimbles, snap hooks, and sail slides are certain to be used at some time or other during the season. A good assortment of nails, brass screws, threaded bolts and nuts will also prove invaluable.

Do not forget your personal comforts for they may mean much to you in a long hard race. Wet gear for every member of the crew, sweaters, food, water, tobacco, are all of the utmost importance. Particularly water is necessary. On a calm day in the hot sun one's suffering from thirst may be intense. It is always well to have on board a small first-aid kit with a disinfectant for cuts, a remedy for burns, some bandage roll, and adhesive tape. There is scarcely a race in which some member of the crew does not return home with a cut or a splinter, or a broken blister, or even a bad case of sunburn. These little ailments are rarely serious but they should have proper attention. On Long Island Sound all the racing boats carry life preservers for every member of the crew, and at least two life preservers must be carried on deck or in the cockpit at all times. This provision is less necessary in shoal waters with lightly ballasted boats that will float even when capsized and filled, but it is a wise rule for any boat to carry life preservers for every member of the crew. In thirty-six years of sailing (and here I knock wood) I have never had to resort to them, except to use them as fenders or to buoy an anchor, but once I was glad to wear them on deck; and I think there have been many occasions when I have driven my boat harder because they were aboard. Yachting is a dangerous sport only to the foolhardy. It is the mark of a good seaman to provide for the unforeseen and to be equal to any emergency in matters of equipment as well as in matters of skill.

CHAPTER X

BEFORE THE START

THE PREPARATION for a race should begin promptly with the end of the last previous race. The way the boat is put to bed has an important bearing on her condition for her next contest. All this will be covered subsequently, but at the end of any race the skipper should make certain that there are entered in his little note-book all missing items of equipment, all material taken ashore for drying out, repairs, or other purposes, all the equipment which is not on board when it should be, and the little tuning up jobs that should be done before the next race.

If the boat is one that is not sailed daily, the skipper should make it a point always to visit his boat on the evening before the race. It is surprising to see how many things may happen when a boat is lying at anchor. She may have been run into by another boat, halliards or other gear may have gotten loose and become tangled aloft. The centerboard pennant may have broken; she may have started a leak and require an hour's pumping. Any or all of these things will seriously affect your time schedule the next day, and it is important that the boat be surveyed carefully to determine the things that must be done before the start of the next race. I have missed more races from a failure to observe this rule than from any other cause.

On the day of the race, an early start will prove to be most important. I remember asking a group of well-known sailors how often they had arrived at the starting line with ample time and with everything in perfect condition, entirely ready to race, and the almost unanimous opinion was "Never." There is always some little last minute job that, if done on time, may save some of those precious seconds which mean the difference between winning and losing. Especially if your boat is moored some distance from the starting line, it is well to allow plenty of time. If you must sail to the starting line, you may have foul and light winds or a foul tide. If you tow to the starting line, your motor may not be in condition. The best procedure is to make ready to race at your mooring, then sail or tow to the start. If you are late, however, you can tow and prepare as you go, or sail under jib and spinnaker while getting the mainsail ready.

On the day of the start the skipper's note-book should be consulted. Such items as "Replace broken batten," "Tighten tiller," "Serve jib halliard," "Binoculars," "New cotter pins for jack stay" will serve to remind the skipper to bring all necessary equipment on board.

In most parts of the country a separate entry is necessary for every yacht race. In the races held under the auspices of the Long Island Sound Yacht Racing Association, a single entry for all the championship races is made in writing for the entire season; but where an entry must be made for every race, the skipper should see to it personally that the Race Committee is informed orally, or in writing, as the rules may require, of the name, class and racing measurement of the yacht, and the name and address of her owner.

Having made the entry, the yacht should get out under way and start sailing. If there is plenty of wind, if the crew is used to the boat and well trained, if everything on board is in perfect order, some skippers prefer to lie at the yacht club dock, or at a mooring until shortly before the preparatory gun for their class. This is probably a wise procedure, for it is frequently disturbing to the nerves and the morale of the crew to jockey back and forth in a huge fleet of competing boats. The fewer the boats near the starting line the better the opportunity of the early classes to make a good start. Furthermore, there is always the danger of a collision before the start of the race, and by remaining at anchor this danger is largely avoided. There are few boats, however, that are not benefited by a practice sail. If the boat is put through her paces and the crew shakes down in its proper stations and has an opportunity to practice its various jobs, the start is likely to be a good one. During the practice sail, count your competitors. Figure out how many are going to try to hit the starting line at the gun. Note what sail they are carrying, or if they are reefed; which boats are completely under control and on which there seems to reign confusion.

In this practice sail, study the starting line and select the better end. The rules for selecting the correct end will be given in later chapters. Outline the general policy of the race. At this time figure when the tide will turn, try to guess whether or not the wind will increase or decrease in volume, and whether it will change direction. Plan your race accordingly.

Give each member of the crew a definite station, let

each one get acquainted with the lines which he must handle, the cleats to which he must make fast, the clearance of the boom, the quickness or slowness of the boat in stays, and the other little adjustments which they must make to be keen and efficient. On small boats that I raced, I have even outlined a definite order in which the crew climbed from the leeward to the windward side when the boat went about. The crew, observing this order, never stumbled over one another in the usual mad scurry to climb to the weather side. During the preliminary jockey and during the course of the whole race, the skipper should appoint one man to act as lookout. The lookout should be responsible for all boats on the opposite side to the skipper. If the skipper sits to leeward and steers with his eye on the jib, he should be responsible for boats to leeward, while the lookout is responsible for boats to windward. If, on the other hand, the skipper sits to windward and steers by the luff of the mainsail, the lookout should be responsible for boats to leeward that would be cut off from the skipper's view by the sails. Before the race the circular of instructions should be studied carefully. The course, the time of the start, the starting signals, the shortened course, postponement, and recall signals should all be memorized carefully. During the practice sail the crew should be made acquainted with all of these points, and care should be taken to keep the circular dry and secure from falling overboard. One man should be told off to keep his eye on the Committee Boat and watch for any signals that may be shown.

Timing the start should be done with two watches. The first watch should be carried by the skipper, or better still, strapped to his wrist; the second watch, a stop-watch, should be given to the timer. The reason for two watches is this: the timer may miss the preparatory signal, the stop-watch may not function, it may run down or stop, or fall overboard. With all of these things likely to happen, it is wise to have the skipper's watch as a check on the stop-watch. Furthermore, the stop-watch must be started at the flash of the preparatory gun. The skipper's watch, on the other hand, is timed from any of the preceding guns so that he can do his own timing before the preparatory gun and can know just when to warn the timer to be on the alert for the preparatory signal. The timer should be instructed in the use of the stop-watch and should be taught to call out the time exactly as the skipper wishes it called.

With all these preparations the boat should now engage in trial starts. Inasmuch as the starting line must be kept clear for the early starting classes, it is wise to practice the starts on an extension of the starting line carried beyond the mark. These trial starts present an opportunity for the skipper to judge pace and distance. A block of wood, or a crumpled piece of newspaper thrown overboard will enable the skipper to see just how far he can sail with or against the tide in a period of a half minute, or a minute. Inasmuch as pace differs with varying strength of wind, and inasmuch as it is different for all stages of tidal current, this practice is important for even the most skillful helmsman. While these trial starts are being made the skipper must note the trim of the sails, the angle of the helm, the interference by wave action, the length of time necessary to come about or jibe, and every other phase of the boat's activity. The lookout keeps alert for other boats and will warn the skipper not merely of danger of collision but of possible interference with a trial start that is about to be undertaken. The man who is to watch the Committee Boat will report all signals that are hoisted. The current especially should be studied and its strength and direction noted carefully. In light airs the current is particularly important. If the current is fair for the start and the wind is light, the skipper will do well to forget his trial starts and other maneuvers and devote all his effort to remaining behind the starting line. Many a start is spoiled by boats without steerage way being carried beyond the starting line and being unable to return in time for the gun.

Trial starts should be made as far as possible before the warning gun for the entire regatta. After that the skipper should note the starts of the early classes. If, in the first class, five boats hit the line with the gun and a few minutes later the leeward boat is several lengths ahead of the others, he should seriously consider the leeward end of the line. If the Committee Boat is on the windward end of the line and boats starting under her lee are blanketed by her, it will point out a danger to be avoided. If half an hour or so elapses between the start of the first class and the start of the class you are sailing in, you should study the course and relative positions of the boats in the first class. Has the boat which stood under the shore climbed out ahead? Has the boat that tacked and stood out away from the shore gained anything thereby? Where is the wind strongest a mile from the starting line? Does it pay to carry a spinnaker on this leg? These are questions that can be answered by watching the early classes. In your study of the circular you noted that your class follows the 10-Metres, or the Interclubs, or whatever class it is. You noted also the second preceding class. When the second preceding class crosses the line, that is your own warning signal. Your preparatory signal will come at the expiration of the next starting interval. At your warning signal, note the second on the skipper's watch and be sure that the minute hand previously set by the guns has been set correctly.

Command silence after your warning gun; do not permit any general conversation on the boat. This is important. Orders come in rapid fire succession after the warning gun. It should not be necessary to interrupt conversation to command attention. Every member of the crew should be alert and at his station. The skipper is watching his competitors, noting his pace and distance, counting seconds, perhaps changing his plan at the last minute, and must not have his calculations interrupted by questions or by general conversation. Then comes the preparatory gun. In nine cases out of ten the boat should have gone about near the mark and be reaching away from the starting line as the gun goes off. From now on the duties of the timer are most important. He should take his time from the flash of the gun, not from the report. If the boat is at some distance from the Committee Boat, several seconds may elapse between the flash and the report. If the timer fumbles in starting his watch, he should note the amount of the fumble and report to the skipper that he has the time correctly. If, for instance, he is two seconds late in starting his watch, he should calculate mentally the addition of two seconds on all his reports to the skipper. He should never report that he didn't get it, that he isn't quite sure, or otherwise disturb the skipper in his calculations. From this time on the timer should report the elapsed and the remaining time in a low calm voice to the skipper as follows: half minute gone, four and one-half to go; one minute gone, four to go; one and one-half gone, three and one-half to go, etc., thus reporting at one-half minute intervals. If the skipper is planning the usual start of reaching away from the line and then reaching back again, he is entitled to ask the timer for the time at any point in between these half-minute reports, and the timer should be prepared to give it instantly. When the timer reports four minutes gone, one to go, he should then announce the remaining time at ten-second intervals.

Some skippers prefer that these intervals be announced by the time elapsed, others by the time remaining. Thus the timer may report "Ten, Twenty, Thirty," etc., or he may report "Fifty, Forty, Thirty," etc. In a start at a five-minute interval when four minutes and fifty seconds have elapsed, the timer should give the time in seconds, thus: Ten, nine, eight, seven, six, five, four, three, two, one, gun. If he does a perfect job, the word "gun" will be drowned in the roar of the starting gun; but for some unknown reason, not one timer in a hundred can call the time correctly. A timer should be trained to call those seconds at exactly one-second intervals. It seems an easy thing to do, yet very seldom does the word "gun" coincide with the report of the starter's gun. If the skipper is obviously late, he may command the timer to shut up and thereby spare his nerves; but if he can stand it, it is good practice to let the timer call the seconds right up to the gun, even though the boat may be a minute or two behind the line. If the air is calm and you are crossing close to the Committee Boat, it is usually possible to hear the time called on the Committee Boat.

In that event, stop your own timer and take the official time as it is being called by the Committee timer to the signal man.

In many clubs it is the practice to leave each starting signal hoisted until thirty seconds before the next signal. If anything happens to the timer or to the record of the time, the stop-watch should be stopped and snapped back to zero and the time taken again from the lowering of this signal of the class ahead. Thus, a last half-minute reprieve is given. It may seem silly to devote so much attention to the simple problem of noting and reporting the exact time, but it is essential in any start and is one of the principal rocks on which good starts are wrecked.

It must be borne in mind that the official signal for the start is always visual, never audible. The flag or cone or ball that is hoisted is the starting signal. The gun that is fired or the whistle that is blown is not the official signal but merely calls attention to it. The distinction is usually not important because the visual signal and the audible signal coincide; but sometimes a gun misses fire or a whistle fails to blow, so the time must be taken from the visual signal. I have never known an audible signal to precede a visual signal, but have frequently known it to follow the visual signal. Therefore, if you are running up to the line and hear the gun, you may safely assume that the visual signal is hoisted. If, on the other hand, you are running to the line and fail to hear the gun when you expect it, look for the visual signal. If it is climbing the signal mast, go ahead.

Chapter XI

THE REACHING START

INASMUCH AS the proper start of a yacht race is different under different conditions of beating, reaching, and running, they will be considered under those three divisions. Let us consider first the reaching start. By that is meant any start that is not made close-hauled and is not made running before the wind or nearly so. The importance of a good start cannot be stressed too strongly. More races are won at the start than at any other point in the race. The reasons are partly physical, partly psychological, and partly chronological. The physical reason is that a boat ahead has many defenses which she can erect against the boats that follow. It is always easier to keep a boat behind you than to catch a boat ahead of you. For the greater part of any race the boat ahead can blanket or back-wind an overtaking boat and interfere with her by means of the broken water of her wake.

The psychological reasons are nearly as important. A boat that is ahead is sailed joyously, freely, lightly. A boat thus sailed moves faster, behaves better, responds to her helm. A pursuing boat is being driven hard, her skipper presses, and pressing is as bad in yacht racing as in golf. Soon the failure to overtake the leading boat becomes a conviction that she cannot be overtaken. All of these things, for some unknown reason, slow down a following boat.

The chronological reason is also important. The boat that is two seconds late at the start may find that those two seconds are all that is necessary to win the race. I cannot stress too often the value of seconds. Furthermore, the boat that makes a good start chooses her position well in relation to the other boats and is able to take advantage of that position through the first leg and possibly throughout the entire race.

In general, the starting line on a reaching start is laid out at right angles to the first leg of the course. Some Committees slant the starting line so as to make the leeward end slightly nearer the first mark than the windward end, but starting lines are frequently laid out carelessly, and as frequently affected by changes of wind, by the dragging of the anchor of the Committee Boat, or by the swinging of the Committee Boat around her anchor so that the starting line may be slewed around, thus making the buoy end or the Committee Boat end nearer to the first mark. If the skipper has been alert in his practice sailing, he will take a careful compass bearing of the starting line and figure which end, if either, is nearer to the first mark. If the leeward end is nearer, that may possibly be the better end to start; if the windward end is nearer, it is almost certainly the better end to start.

The windward end offers certain notable advantages. In the first place the boat that crosses the line next to the mark will have its wind free. It will sail a slightly freer course to the first mark. This is an advantage only on a close reach; on a broad reach it may be a disadvantage. If the boat at the windward end of the line is up with the gun, there is a very good chance that she may blanket and slow down her opponents who would have to sail through her lee. These are important considerations. The following disadvantages, however, must also be considered. If the Committee Boat is at the windward end of the line, the danger of being blanketed by her hull and superstructure is very serious. It is a particularly serious danger for small boats. There is also a threat of a jam at that part of the line —it is the popular end. Most of the boats in the class will make for it. If the class is small, this is not a serious question; if it is a large class with a dozen or more starters, it is a very serious question. The boat that starts at the windward end must be absolutely on time. If such a boat is early, there is no escape. She cannot waste time by sailing up along the line. She cannot bear away because of the other boats under her lee, and lacking an overlap she may be obliged to pass on the wrong side of the mark, come about, and start over again. If, on the other hand, she is late and other boats are ahead of her, she is in a bad position because she suffers from their back wind.

Consider now the advantage of the leeward end. At this end of the line there are probably few competitors —there may be none. While all the other boats of the class are struggling in a thick mass at the windward end, the boat at the leeward end has her wind free, plenty of room to maneuver, freedom from danger of a foul, and a very good chance to sail her own race. If the line is long and the boats are small and most of the boats are clustered about the windward end of the line, the lone boat at the leeward end will probably have her wind entirely free. If the leeward end of the line, however, is not so far advanced as the windward end, the danger of being blanketed is greatly increased.

The boat at the leeward end of the line can afford to be too early. If she sails up to the line before the gun, she can trim her sheets and sail to windward up the line and have right-of-way over all converging boats because she will be pointed closer to the wind and holding a better course. A boat thus sailed is under better control than a boat that is slowed down but sailing free. When she straightens out on her course she will travel faster. From the leeward position the chance to back-wind one's opponents is very good indeed. She also has a chance of sailing faster, especially if the first leg of the course is a broad reach. With these considerations in mind, I find that in my own sailing at least two-thirds of my reaching starts are made at the leeward end of the line.

The problem of making a perfect start may be expressed thus: Pick the proper part of the line, hit the line with the gun, moving fast, with the wind free. The test of a start is made thirty seconds after the gun fires. It is not important where you are when the gun goes off; it is very important where you are thirty seconds after the gun. A boat that is on the line with the gun but is blanketed or interfered with by some other boat has made a poor start. A boat that is standing still or moving slowly when the gun goes off will be behind a boat that is not up to the line with the gun but is moving so fast that she will overtake and pass her within the next half minute. The way which a boat carries to the line is important. It is more important with a large heavy boat than with a small light boat.

To make this clear let us cite the analogy of motor cars at a traffic light. Consider four cars: Car "A" has come to the crossing and stopped, car "B" has come up behind car "A" and stopped, car "C" is in the next lane beside car "B" and still rolling along slowly, car "D" is half a block away traveling at thirty-five miles an hour. The light changes. Cars "A" and "B" shift to first speed and struggle away; car "C", moving slowly, shifts to second and bobs on ahead; car "D", although half a block behind, is traveling fast, stays in high speed and overtakes and passes all three. Let us apply the analogy to boats. Boat "A" is like car "A", on the line but not moving; boat "B" is behind boat "A", not on the line, not moving; boat "C" is too early and is wasting time, killing her way, luffing along but maintaining some steerage way. She is not up to boat "A", but because she is already moving she will pass "B" and "A" before they can gain steerage way. Boat "D", behind them all is racing for the line with a rap full, sheets trimmed exactly right, crew at their stations, traveling fast. Thirty seconds after the gun, boat "D" will be ahead, boat "C" will be next, boat "A" will be a poor third, and boat "B" will still be at the starting line. It is more important to maintain full headway than to be up to the line at the gun, but the perfect start is made when the boat is both up and moving fast. At this point it is well to stress a rule which some yachtsmen have never learned. In nearly all racing rules, time is taken at the start and the finish from the moment the mast of the sloop, or the foremost mast of the yacht carrying two or more masts, crosses the line. Timing is not done from the bow.

The standard start is made by reaching away from the line, tacking or jibing, and reaching back again. In the absence of current, it takes the same length of time to sail away from the line as to sail back. Allowance must be made for the length of time it takes to jibe or to go about. Making that allowance, the remaining time is divided in half. In the *Enterprise's* defense of the *America's* cup, this was reduced to a mathematical formula which may be expressed as follows: $\dfrac{TR+TAB}{2}$ = TIME TO ALTER COURSE. In this formula, TR means time remaining, TAB means time to go about, or to jibe. Let us apply this formula. Assume that your boat is at the starting line headed away from the line on a reaching course at the time of the preparatory gun, with the starting interval of five minutes. Let us assume also that you plan to go about and sail back to the starting line, and that you know from previous timing that it takes forty seconds to go about. Your time remaining is therefore five minutes, which expressed in seconds, is 300. Your time to go about is 40 seconds. Therefore, $\dfrac{TR+TAB}{2} = \dfrac{300+40}{2} = 170$. 170 seconds = 2 minutes and 50 seconds. Therefore, when two minutes and 10 seconds have elapsed and 2 minutes and 50 seconds are remaining, the helmsman puts his boat about, trying to use just 40 seconds in the maneuver, then sails back to the starting line, endeavoring to maintain the same pace as when sailing away from the line. If this is done perfectly, and current is not a factor, he will hit the line on the gun, moving at top speed. Let us apply the formula again. Suppose the boat starts sailing away from the line 50 seconds after the preparatory gun. The time remaining is now 4 minutes and 10 seconds, or 250 seconds. Suppose it is planned to jibe the boat and not to bring her about, and that the skipper knows that 30 seconds are necessary for jibing. We have from the formula $\dfrac{250+30}{2} = 140 = 2$ minutes and 20 seconds remaining time in which to start to jibe. Thus the boat with only 4 minutes and 10 seconds remaining will sail away until 2 minutes and 20 seconds remain or, in other words, will sail away for 1 minute and fifty seconds. She will then jibe in 30 seconds, sail back in 1 minute and 50 seconds, and hit the line on the gun.

This formula is very helpful to the skipper who plans his start by calling the remaining time. This is the logical way and the most usual way to start a race. Stop-watches made for yachtsmen are designed to register remaining time and not elapsed time. There are many other stop-watches, however, that give the seconds beginning with 0 and ending with 60, not as in a yachtsman's stop-watch beginning with 60 and ending with 0. Most timers, working with such watches, become confused when called upon to announce the remaining time, so the skipper who works from elapsed time rather than remaining time must apply another formula. In this case he figures his time remaining when he is on the starting line, reaching away from the line. Then, instead of adding the time to go about, or the time to jibe, he subtracts it, divides the remainder by two, and tells the timer to let him know when half of this remainder has elapsed. Let us apply this new formula to the conditions of the first case outlined above:

The boat is on the line reaching away from it at the preparatory gun. There are five minutes to go—it takes 40 seconds to go about. Therefore, 300 seconds minus 40 seconds equals 260 seconds. Divide that by two and you will get 130 seconds. "Let me know at two minutes and ten seconds," says the skipper to the timer. The timer calls, "One-half minute, one minute, minute and a half, two minutes." "Ready, about," says the helmsman. "Ten seconds," cries the timer. "Hard alee," cries the helmsman and puts the boat about in 40 seconds and sails back with 2 minutes and 10 seconds remaining.

It will be perceived that these two formulæ are essentially the same in their application, but if the timer calls the elapsed time and is one of those dumb fools who cannot think in remaining time, the second formula will prove more helpful.

To the sailor in a large class these formulæ are useful as indicating a principle. They are far less valuable as an instance of actual practice, for conditions at a crowded starting line are usually so involved that the best laid plans are upset by the other boats in the race. One is often forced to go about long before the predetermined time by other boats holding right-of-way. Often, instead of sailing away on a good reach with a beam wind, conditions are so crowded that one must point up to windward or bear away to leeward. In any strong tideway, the formula must be modified to such an extent that it is usually easier to depend solely upon one's judgment of pace and timing. In small classes, however, with negligible currents, the formula offers the best method of hitting the line with the gun, under full way.

In starting in light airs, it is usually wise to forget that there is any such thing as a formula. Usually the best policy is to stay as close to the starting line as one possibly can and drift across with the gun. If the air is light and the tide is foul, it will pay to stay on the wrong side of the line and let the tide carry you to the right side of the line just before the gun. If the air is light and the tide is fair, it will pay to stay a long way behind the line even before the preparatory gun, thus taking no chance of being swept across the line before the starting gun and being unable to work back against the tide.

If you are late at the line, there is only one remedy, to sail as fast as you can. If you are early, however, it is very necessary to kill time before getting to the starting line. You can kill time by heading up into the wind, by starting your sheets, or by alternately luffing and bearing away with the rudder hard across the boat. Kill time early enough and some distance behind the starting line. Do not wait until you get to the line for the following reasons: First, you may be caught in a jam by other boats; second, you will lose all way and will be a dead boat when the gun goes off, at which time you will be passed by the boats that are behind you, but moving with full way. One of the very best starts I ever made was a reaching start in a night race when I got to the line too early. Inasmuch as most of the boats were very large, a long line had been established by the Committee and the beam of a search-light played from the Committee Boat on the starting buoy, thus marking the line distinctly. Through an error of timing, we hit the line with a minute to go, close to the Committee Boat. Fortunately, all the other boats were making a very bad start and were at least a hundred yards away. We bore away and sailed down the line just on the safe side of the search-light beam, anxiously counting the seconds. With three seconds remaining, we bore up almost at the buoy and the gun went off a heart-beat before the beam of the searchlight played on the mast.

Very frequently, through an error in timing, or failure of the timer to start his stop-watch at the preparatory gun, it is impossible to know the exact time to the second. In such circumstances, I have frequently made an excellent start simply by watching my competitors and at times I have even disregarded what I suspected to be inaccurate timing by swinging about alongside a competitor who customarily made good starts and sailing through the line with my heart in my mouth and my faith in his judgment. I remember one occasion when we arrived late for the start of a night race. It was just dusk. We could see no signals on the Committee Boat and we had heard no gun. I thought we had time but I noticed that, instead of the aimless jockeying that usually precedes a race, all of the boats were heading for the starting line in a bunch on the same tack. Suspecting that the next gun was the starting gun and feeling reasonably certain that most of the skippers in a distance race were a little gun-shy, I put my boat about in front of the fleet and headed for the starting line. I hit it with the gun and got off to a good lead in the most careless start any yachtsman could possibly make.

CHAPTER XII

THE START TO WINDWARD

PROBABLY MORE races are started on the wind than on any other course and most yachtsmen would rather start on the windward leg than in any other way. Such a race has an advantage over a race with a reaching start because the Committee can usually plan a windward leg better if it is laid out from the start rather than from the first or second mark. It is much to be preferred to the leeward start because boats sailing before the wind take up so much room at the starting line and because on a leeward start most skippers are gun-shy. Whereas, a reaching or running starting line is always laid out as nearly as possible at right angles to the first leg of the course, on a windward start, the best practice seems to be to lay out the line at an angle of 12° from a right angle. Mr. Edward A. Hodge, the hard working Chairman of the Race Committee of the American Yacht Club has experimented widely with starting lines at various angles and from close observation and careful records has come to the conclusion that the fairest windward start is attained with this 12° angle to the starting line. The line is laid out in such a manner that if all boats should start on the starboard tack, the leeward boat would be as much ahead of the windward boats as the windward boats would be to windward. With this line, too, a boat on the port tack starting near the Committee Boat end of the line would be able to cross a boat on the starboard tack starting at the buoy end of the line, provided both were sailing with equal speed and both arrived at the starting line at the same instant.

Despite the slight advantage of a port tack start on a line of this character, it is my contention that all boats in a windward start should start on the starboard tack only. There are only three occasions when a port tack is ever justified: The first is when the line is laid out in such a way that a starboard tack is obviously inferior, so inferior in fact, that every boat starts on the port tack. The second exception is when a boat is so late at the line that there is no possibility of a foul. The third exception occurs when there is a long line and only two or three boats are starting in the race. With all boats starting on the starboard tack, the question of right-of-way is simple and it is always easy to avoid a foul. With some boats starting on the port tack, however, and some on the starboard tack, the advantage of right-of-way rests so strongly with the boat holding the starboard tack that the boats on the port tack are at a decided disadvantage.

When the port tack is obviously the better, and most of the boats are holding it, one frequently sees a boat on the starboard tack sailing down the line, hogging it—colliding with boats on the port tack and thus disqualifying them. If it is possible to cross the line on the starboard tack this maneuver is perhaps justified, but it is often seen even when it is impossible to cross the line on the starboard tack. Thus a boat closehauled on the starboard tack will sail the whole length of the line and will be unable to cross without tacking. This is known as "hogging the line" and while it may be perfectly justified under the rules, it is everywhere recognized as the height of bad sportsmanship. The good sportsman never tries intentionally to disqualify a competitor. He prefers to beat him in a race, not in a debate before the Race Committee. There can be small satisfaction in disqualifying all your opponents at the start of the race and then sailing the course alone. Trophies so won do not deserve an honorable place in any trophy cabinet. Let us assume then that we will start on the starboard tack, across a starting line properly laid out. The question immediately presents itself: Shall we start at the windward or the leeward end of the line? The advantages of the windward end of the line are as follows: First, there is the opportunity of blanketing the opponents that are on the leeward end. Second, there is the greater advantage of being able to keep your own wind clear. Third, and more important still, is the fact that the farther you are to windward, the farther you are ahead of your opponents that are to leeward. Of course, if the line is laid out in such a way that the leeward end stretches nearer the·first mark, your opponents may be able to make up your advantage to windward by being farther ahead on the course. If they reach the line at the same instant you reach it, they will be clear of your blanketing and may be able to give you an uncomfortable dose of back wind. In such a case the leeward end of the line would possess these advantages: First, the boats at the leeward end would be as far ahead as their opponents are to windward and possibly more so. Second, they would be free from blanketing and be able to back-wind their opponents. Third, if they are at the extreme leeward end of the line they would be free from the danger of being back-winded.

Another consideration that enters into the better end of the line is the question of crowding. As a rule the windward end of the line is the favorite end. Boats are generally massed in a great bunch there, all involving danger of a foul, and even if that danger is avoided, seriously interfering with one another for a considerable portion of the first leg. In general then, the leeward end of the line seems to be the preferred position provided the leeward end is at all nearer the first mark than the windward end. If the line is at right angles to the first leg of the course, or if the windward end is nearer to the first mark, then the windward end would seem to be better.

In Fig. 19 the illustration shows a start in the Star class several years ago. In Fig. 19A we see six boats crossing the line on the port tack. They are Nos. 1, 148, 11, 194, 12, and the boat which lies between 194 and 12. In the next picture, Fig. 19B, we see what has happened a moment later. Boat No. 11 having been back-winded has lost steerage way and has filled away hard on the port tack fouling 148 and 194. The boat between cannot be found. Perhaps she is in the mess, and perhaps she has escaped. No. 12 has escaped miraculously. No. 1 has managed to come about and gain steerage way on the starboard tack. From this picture we may draw two lessons. First, the error of starting the race on the port tack and, second, the error of being caught in a bunch like that at the starting line. You will note that, although No. 1 has escaped from the mess, the other boats shown in Fig. 19A to be on the starboard tack have sailed right out of the picture. They are 40, 190, 27, and 24, and 1 has been passed by 222, 50, 60, and 26.

In Fig. 20A we see a start of the Interclubs in a

Levick

40   190   27   50   24   1   148   11   194   12   61

FIG. 19A

Levick

223   50   60   1   33   37   12   11   148   194   63

FIG. 19B

FIG. 19. A start in the Star Class

27 7   9   19 26   *Levick*

FIG. 20A

7 27   9   19 26   *Levick*

FIG. 20B

7   27 9 19 26 *Levick*

FIG. 20C

FIG. 20. A start in the Interclub Class

regatta of the Huguenot Yacht Club. Note particularly
the positions of 27, 7 and 26. You will note that 19 and
26 are crossing so close to the Committee Boat that
they are forced to luff up and lose their headway,
whereas Nos. 7 and 27 are crossing with plenty of room
to spare. Fig. 20B was taken a few moments later. No.
19 has sailed out of the picture but it is evident now
that No. 7 had a commanding lead over 26 and she is
giving such a dose of back wind to 27 that she has
pushed her distinctly behind her, although 27 is still
to windward. Fig. 20C shows the same group of boats
a few minutes later. No. 26 has been interfered with
by the boat on her weather and, although she may not
be blanketed by her, she is certainly getting enough
broken water from her bow wave to be held back. No.
27 has fallen way back and has lost her weather berth.
No. 7 has drawn ahead to a clear lead. Go back now
and compare the positions of 7 and 27 in Fig. 20A.

One of the most important considerations in the
choice of the proper end of the starting line is the
question of the policy of the race. For instance, assume
the first leg of the course to be laid out along the shore.
It is your experience that the southwest wind which
is blowing on the day of the race draws most strongly
off that shore. That shore is on the windward end of
the line. If you cross the starting line on the port tack,
it would direct you into the shore where you would get
better wind than the boats on the starboard tack. This
consideration might not justify starting on the port
tack; but it would justify your choosing the windward
end of the line so that, having crossed on the starboard
tack you would soon be able to go about and sail on
the port tack into the stronger path of the wind along
the shore. Now, if you were to start at the leeward

end of the line, you would be obliged to come about and sail through all the boats between you and the shore. These boats would all have right-of-way and you would engage in an endless number of dog fights, in each one of which the boat with right-of-way would hold a slight advantage. The policy of the race, therefore, would dictate that in these circumstances it is wise to choose the windward end of the line even though other considerations might make the leeward end preferable.

In Fig. 21A the starting line is laid out in such a manner as to make it exceedingly difficult to cross on the starboard tack. The boats have to round the stern of a very large Committee Boat on a very windy day and even then seem to find difficulty in crossing the line close-hauled. In Fig. 21B, we see the same boats a minute later. K-12, the leech of whose mainsail appears just behind the leech of K-20 in Fig. 21A has managed to luff up to the line so as to be in the best possible starting position. K-6 evidently arrived at the line too soon and has had to slack her sheet to lose her way. 8, footing up close to the Committee Boat, has hit the line fast with a rap full. K-20 looks as if she would not be able to cross without going about. On a start like this a boat would be justified in starting on the port tack provided she came up behind the boats on the starboard tack and, crossing their sterns, managed to keep clear. But in a case like this it takes a good prophet and a very good judge of racing conditions to realize that the boats on the starboard tack would be in such a mess at the starting line.

The best form of jockeying for a windward start is precisely that described in the previous chapter on the reaching start—reaching away from the line, reaching

3 K20 K12 K1   8   *Levick*

Fig. 21A

K12   8   3   K20   *Levick*

Fig. 21B

Fig. 21. A start in the Six Metre class

Levick

FIG. 22. Stop at head of spinnaker has
failed to break

Levick

9

FIG. 23. A leeward start among the Interclubs. No. 9 has preserved
maneuverability by keeping her spinnaker in stops until crossing
the line.

back to the line, and as you approach it getting your sheets trimmed. This system of starting is better than a run and a beat for the obvious reason that it is much easier to time. Furthermore, your boat is in hand at all times and is approaching the line at so much greater speed that even if you are late in getting your sheet trimmed your way will carry you over the starting line and possibly a long distance to windward. When you hit the line you should be close-hauled on the proper tack. With a good crew it is possible to get your sheets trimmed while you are still reaching toward the line and before you lay her full and by.

In light airs of course, it is a pretty good plan to stay close to the starting line. If the air is light and you have a strong fair tide you can frequently make a good start by luffing right into the wind, letting the tide carry you to the line and filling away just as the gun goes off. In jockeying in a strong foul tide it may be necessary to sail the boat hard, right at the line and cross when you get a little extra puff or the current relents somewhat. I recall to mind two memorable starts, one at East Chop off Vineyard Haven and the other at Larchmont. At East Chop we were towed to the line by a power boat and then cast off. Instantly I was aware of the fact that I would have to devote my greatest effort to staying on the right side of the starting line. The wind was light and the tide wanted to swerve me over the line. For the five minutes between the preparatory and starting guns, it was a question of whether we could possibly hold our position. Just as the starting gun went off, we were swept over the line by the tide. On that day the *Vanitie* never did get across the starting line. She was cast off from her tender on the wrong side of the line and after a long struggle just kept going. That day at Larchmont we were right on the starting line at the gun. We crossed it an hour and four minutes later. What little air there was was not sufficient to enable us to overcome the strong tidal current. It is very easy to underestimate the strength of the tide. Its strength and direction may be fairly determined by a close study of the starting buoy. The way the buoy leans may be governed by either the wind or the tide, but the action of the water around the buoy will show the strength and direction of the tidal current. A buoy in a tideway leaves a wake as if it were being towed through the water in a direction opposite to the direction of the tidal current.

After a start on the wind, it is necessary to size up your situation and that of your opponents very promptly. The first question to determine is what damage is being done to you by the other boats. The second question is what damage are you able to inflict upon them. First beware of blanketing; determine if there is any boat to windward of you that is likely to cut off your wind. Even if your wind may be free, if another boat is overtaking you very fast on the windward side within five lengths of her mast she is apt to get your wind. Next, look out for back-winding. Boats immediately ahead of you, or boats to leeward of you and slightly ahead or abeam will be stopping you with their back wind. Back wind is more dangerous than blanketing because it is less apparent. If you are blanketed, you know it at once. If you are back-winded you may not detect it unless you are on the alert for it. Therefore, size up the situation quickly. If you are in the wake of any boat or being blanketed by her or getting a strong dose of back wind, tack at once and free your wind. If, on the other hand, you are in a tight mess and are giving one boat as bad treatment as another boat is giving you, wait a few minutes and see what will happen. The boat that you are maltreating will probably go about and will leave you free to go about. In general, however, it is wise to get out of a bad situation as promptly as you can. It is right there that many a race is lost. If you tack to free your wind, do not hesitate to tack back again as soon as your wind is free. If you stand as good a chance as the other boats or if perhaps your boat is a trifle faster or you are a little better sailor, sail in general the same course as your most dangerous opponents. Stay with them so that they will not get the advantage of any breaks that you are not getting too. If on the other hand, you are being beaten, then split tacks and take a chance on getting better conditions. But don't split tacks too soon. Split only to free your wind but tack back again to stay with your opponents.

Chapter XIII

THE RUNNING START

ON ANY course dead before the wind, cross the line with your main boom over your port side. The reason for this is that then you are technically on the starboard tack and have right-of-way over boats on the port tack.

Let us consider, however, that the wind is somewhat over your starboard quarter so that you are sailing almost before the wind but not quite. The port end of the line may fairly be called the leeward end. That leeward end of the line offers very decided advantages. In the first place, if you are about to sail your course from that end you will sail not quite so directly before the wind as a boat crossing at the other end. This means that you will sail a little faster. Try to hold that position at that side of the fleet. If you can do so, you will sail the entire leg just a little bit faster than the boat that starts at the windward end and is sailing more directly before the wind. If you are able to cross the line at the leeward end and another boat comes up behind you to blanket you, you can trim your sheets, sail up the.line and have plenty of room to cross. At the same time every boat on your starboard hand will have to yield to you because you have the right-of-way· as a converging boat holding a better course. If you should be thus blanketed at the windward end of the line you would have to stand and take it. The third advantage is that at the leeward end of the line no other boat can converge upon you with superior right-of-way.

In preparation for a leeward start you should have your light sails hoisted in stops. For stops use light cotton thread—basting thread is the best. Do not use fish line, sail twine, or other heavy cord. To stop the spinnaker, lay it out on deck or down below in the following manner: Place the luff and the leech together, pull out the rest of the sail and roll it into a very tight small roll alongside the luff and leech. Then pass a single turn of the thread about the sail and tie it. Repeat this at intervals of three or four feet down to the very foot of the sail. At the foot it is permissible to take two turns of the thread. If it is blowing hard, the bottom stop may be made with three turns of thread and the next two or three stops above it with two turns. In light airs, however, only one turn of the thread should be used throughout. Do not stop a spinnaker within six or eight feet of the head. That is always the stop that refuses to break. (See Fig. 22.)

The balloon jib may be stopped in the same manner and both ballooner and spinnaker may be hoisted but should not be broken out until after you have crossed the line. The reason for this is evident. Until you have started you are always in danger of fouling another boat. Your one protection against a foul is to preserve maneuverability and you will not be able to trim your main sheet and sail up to windward with the spinnaker in place. I have always made it a rule to be a little slow in breaking out the spinnaker. At the other end of the running leg I invariably carry it to the last possible minute but at the start of a run I like my spinnaker hoisted and in stops so that the operation of breaking it out will be of as short duration as possible. In this way I am frequently able to start breaking out my spinnaker much later than my opponents, thus preserving maneuverability to the last and despite this fact having my spinnaker set and drawing about as soon as any of them.

In Fig. 23, we see a running start among the Interclubs. You will note that No. 9 is ready to break out her spinnaker with one jerk of the sheet; but her position is bad and she has delayed in order to be able to jibe or to work to windward as opportunity offers.

Once more, I recommend jockeying on a reach instead of beating away from the line, then running down upon it. Not only is your timing better but you will be traveling faster when you hit the line. Approach the line on a reach, then bear away gradually. It must be borne in mind that on a running start the dangers of a crowded starting line are greatly aggravated. On a reaching or windward start the boats take up no more room than their combined beams. On a running start, however, they advance like troops in extended order with their main booms off to one side and their spinnaker booms off to the other. In this way each boat takes up nearly five times as much of the starting line as on any other start. The question of room at the line in a large class is usually acute on any running start.

While timing is essential on any start, it is perhaps more important on a running start. In this of all starts it is most dangerous to be early. It is far better to be late if you cannot be sure of hitting the line with the gun. The first reason for this is that there is often very little that you can do to waste time. On a start to windward, you can always luff up. On a reaching start, you can pay out your sheet. But on a running start, you are borne inevitably to the line and if you have no sea-room you are apt to get into trouble or to cross before the gun. On a start to windward, if you are recalled for crossing too early, the penalty is not very great. You merely pay off, wear around, jibe, and cross the line again, making certain to keep clear of all other boats because by your early start you give right-of-way to every other boat. On a running start, however, you must beat back while your opponents with a fair wind are romping away down the course.

If you are late at the starting line on a windward or reaching start, the penalty is severe, for you are not only behind but are in danger of being stopped by blanketing, back-winding, and broken water. If you are late on a running start, however, you have a very good opportunity to blanket the boats ahead and thus perhaps sail into a commanding position. Taken all in all, the penalty for being late is a very slight one indeed, while the penalty for being early is severe.

If in a running start a boat comes up behind you and threatens to take your wind, be slow to engage in a luffing match. These luffing matches always seem to work out to the advantage of the overtaking boat. If your spinnaker has not been broken out, delay for a minute or two. If your overtaking opponent breaks out his spinnaker, you can jibe and escape immediately. Your opponent, handicapped by his spinnaker, cannot follow in time to catch you. Then, when your wind is clear you can jibe back with almost no perceptible loss of time and continue on your course.

Chapter XIV

GETTIN' HER GOIN'

RACES ARE won by making the boat go faster than the other boats. Getting the best possible speed out of your boat for every part of the course will win races. A good start, good work in the pinches, good work at the marks, the offensive and defensive tactics of blanketing, back-winding, and the like, are all valuable, but except in the very largest classes, nine-tenths of the time a race is sailed with no other competitors within the Zone of Interference, and the boat that travels the fastest nine-tenths of the time will win the race.

There are two prime requisites for a successful skipper: The first requisite is the ability to determine whether or not his boat is traveling at her best pace; the second requisite is the ability to speed up that pace.

There is a sixth sense of pace, and a most complicated sense it is, for the skipper must be able to detect the difference between real speed and apparent speed; between speed over the bottom and speed through the water. He must be able to judge his speed in relation to the favorable factor of wind and the unfavorable factors of waves and current. He must know how to compromise between pointing and footing, and he must be quick to recognize the sometimes barely perceptible changes in the factors that make for success.

For instance, in the class of small sloops in which I sailed for many years the boats perceptibly slowed down the minute the edge of the rail got under water. This was probably due to the shape of the bilges and not to the slight extra resistance of the water along the lee deck. The experienced skippers in that class immediately luffed up to bring the rail out of water and kept their boats footing fast, while the less experienced skippers were unable to recognize the change of pace and concluded that the more the boat heeled the faster she was footing. In most boats extreme heeling is coincident with fast footing, and the more a boat heels, the faster she is traveling. Particularly is this true with boats with good bearings that rapidly increase the waterline length as they are heeled down. Boats with a pronounced tumble-home will also increase in speed as they are heeled over, for the tumble-home keeps the rail and the deck fairly clear of water. With other boats, however, there is a distinct point in heeling beyond which speed is not increased and may even be decreased.

On very windy days when the boat is carrying too much sail her speed may often be increased by pointing high into the wind and letting the sail luff even though with a rap full she would heel more and apparently foot faster while thus held down.

This sense of pace must be acquired by long practice, by close observation of the water and the shore, and particularly by sailing in close company with a competitor. The skipper should form a habit of watching the bubbles along the lee rail. It is easy to see by their action whether the boat is really going forward fast or merely bobbing up and down and creating a disturbance in the water. In a foul tide a boat may be sailing through the water very fast, yet making no progress whatsoever over the bottom, whereas if she were sailing a course a few hundred yards distant from her position she might be traveling less swiftly through the water but going over the bottom at a greater speed.

One of the most valuable tests of pace is to sail in close company with a competitor. At such times the crew of every boat is constantly making small adjustments calculated to increase speed. A boat apparently is doing her best, there seems to be nothing that can be done to get greater speed out of her. Then a competitor tacks and comes alongside. When the two boats are sailing side by side, the skippers order little adjustments until one or the other begins to pull away. It is at those times that a boat sails at her best.

This story was related to me by one of the men who sailed on *Teal* in one of the Bermuda races. They thought they were getting their best out of *Teal* during a night of hard sailing. When day broke they found the *Malabar* sailing alongside, a few hundred yards to leeward. Then they started monkeying with *Teal*. They set up the runners, trimmed the fore sheet, slacked the main sheet, set up on the halliards, played with the outhauls. The two boats continued sailing side by side. Then one of the men pressed his foot against the clew of the ballooner and *Teal* seemed to travel a little faster. That gave him an idea. He poked the point of the boat hook into the clew cringle of the ballooner and pushed it out so as to increase the draft on the lee side of the foresail. Instantly *Teal* started to pull ahead and by sundown *Malabar* was hull down astern. The crew of *Teal* might never have discovered how to get this extra power out of the balloon jib if *Malabar* had not presented herself as a trial horse.

Another story: *Old Timer* was sailing on the windward leg of a course on Long Island Sound on a very rough day. She pointed high and seemed to be doing well. Nevertheless, in spite of her good start, all other boats but one in the class had managed to pull out ahead. I was at the helm and I could not understand the difficulty. The tiller was amidships, the helm light. There was a pronounced absence of rudder drag. Jib sheet and main sheet were trimmed to the points where I knew from long experience they worked best. The leeches were flat; the sails set well; yet it was evident from the way the other boats were sailing, *Old Timer* was not at her best. I took my eye from the luff and began watching the bubbles. Then it became evident to me that the boat was stamping up and down but not going ahead at the speed which the strength of wind would warrant. The problem was how to cure the stamping. It was only then that it became evident to me that the mast—a very limber stick—was whipping in such a way as to throw the boat out of her stride. I put two men on the weather runner, luffed, and let them set it up. They gained perhaps half an inch. It did not stop the stamping. The boat was going but not going ahead. The wind was blowing harder, the seas were increasing. Then we set up the lee runner. It was against all the laws of good sailing to do so, for the runner cut into the belly of the mainsail and thus decreased its efficiency; but immediately the stamping stopped. It was evident from the bubbles that the boat was getting right down to work, plowing through the seas instead of being stopped by them. By that time we had only about a quarter of a mile to go to the next mark, and in that short distance we overtook three boats. In this instance, a sense of pace made evident by the action of competitors showed that something was wrong. The bubbles confirmed the impression and led directly to the seat of the difficulty—an improperly stayed, whippy mast. In Fig. 24, Nos. 24 and K-28 are stamping badly. In such conditions a whippy mast will kill headway.

The fact that the pace of a yacht can be judged only by sailing in company with another yacht is well recognized. When *Shamrock V* came over to race against *Enterprise,* the New York Yacht Club graciously offered Sir Thomas Lipton the use of the old defender *Resolute* to act as a trial horse. One famous yachtsman of my acquaintance, who is better provided than most of us with this world's goods, never buys one boat in a class. He buys two and uses the second boat as a trial horse to get the first boat in the best possible condition and to learn all her idiosyncrasies.

The measure of your speed in relation to another boat is determined by two methods: By bearings and by "making land." If the other boat is at the beam or nearly so, take a beam bearing and see where it strikes the other boat. If you have a cabin, sight along the two edges of the companionway. If the edge of the deck makes a straight line, thwartships across the after end of the cockpit, sight along that line. Thus you will be able to see whether the bearing creeps ahead or drops behind. If your compass is so located that you can take compass bearings, take them at intervals and note them down.

The other method is by "making land." Sight across the bow of the other boat and note some land mark. If you are gaining on the other boat, the land mark will move out ahead and the land will seem to be sailing along with you. If the other boat is gaining, the land mark will disappear behind her jib and the land will seem to be going backward. I remember once racing into Newport in company with another boat. The wind hauled aft but we were more interested in dinner than in setting the spinnaker. I was not aware of her in the darkness until she was abeam. Then we broke out the spinnaker and pulled ahead. A long row of lights on the Narragansett shore began to appear in regular procession in front of the dark shadow of her jib and we knew we were regaining our old position. These lights at regular intervals marked our steady gaining as accurately as a piece of machinery until we finished at Brenton Reef Lightship.

There is no better school for the development of a sense of pace than night racing. When you are racing at night and cannot see your competitors, when the panorama of the shore is wiped out, when the set of your sails and condition of your rigging can be revealed only in the fitful gleam of a flashlight, when you cannot see but can merely hear the water rushing past the hull, you must attune your perceptions very finely and be keenly alert to the slight changes in wind direction and velocity that seem constantly to be occurring. I have frequently been ship-mate with a man whose sense of pace was extra keen at night. When off watch he would sleep in the forecastle where the bow waves growling along the planking made sweet music in his ears. If, for any reason, the boat lost pace he would bob up through the fore hatch and rush aft yelling, "Come on, let's get her goin'." From his position below he was able to judge pace more keenly than we could judge it on deck.

It is hard to define the elements that enter into a sense of pace. Most important is a feeling of the boat and a knowledge of what she can do. You feel it by your grip on the helm, by the way you brace your legs, by the angle of your body, by the wind in your hair, and by your sense of rhythm. Perhaps the most important seat of this sense is, strangely enough, in the seat of your trousers, for when you are sitting down you are maintaining a firm contact with the boat and you sense her behavior in much the same manner that a good horseman can sense the performance of his horse through his seat, his thighs, and his stirrups. The good helmsman can readily distinguish between the stamping, ineffectual struggles of a boat that has lost pace and the headlong rushing surge of the boat that is doing her best. The eyes and ears next enter into it. The eyes to perceive the water and the passing shore; the ears to listen for the swishing of the waves, the humming of the rigging and other little indications of rapid forward progress. Perhaps the ears are less important than they seem, for one of the best helmsmen of my acquaintance is a deaf mute; but it is perhaps his lack of hearing that has made his kinæsthetic perception so extraordinarily keen.

Coextensive with the feeling for pace is the feeling for trim. A large boat is trimmed by the trial and error method and once trimmed properly is not thereafter disturbed. A small boat must be trimmed constantly, for by moving members of the crew forward or aft, to windward or to leeward, a very great difference in performance can be noted instantly. I have often walked away from competitors by moving one member of the crew a few inches and have doubtless often been defeated by failing to make such slight adjustments. Most skippers who know their boats have favorite stations for their crew for every course and for varying conditions of wind and weather, but the men who trim a boat best are those whose perception of pace is so keen that they can perceive the slightest variation that accompanies the shifting of live weight. In a small boat the perception is easy because the shifting weight makes such a pronounced difference. In a large boat it is much harder to perceive.

A boat that is doing her best responds with a powerful rhythm that is absent in the boat that is fighting ineffectually. The rhythm is induced partly by the waves and partly by the adjustment which the boat makes to the waves. The good helmsman quickly perceives any interruption to this rhythm; the poor helmsman never recognizes that such a thing as rhythm exists.

It is perhaps presumptuous to attempt to teach helmsmanship through the pages of a printed book, for good helmsmanship can only be attained by a lifetime of earnest practice. Certain precepts may be laid down, however, and they should prove invaluable to the beginner. A helm at all times should be light. A properly hung boat sailed to windward in moderate airs should have a helm that is barely perceptible. If, under these conditions of going, you cannot sail your boat with thumb and finger there is something the matter with you or with the boat. As the wind increases the helm becomes heavier. As your course is changed to bring the wind abaft the beam, the weight of the helm increases. By bearing these changing conditions in mind, the helm should never seem to be heavy. The helm is moved in tune with the rhythm of the boat, not too hard, not too violently, never more than necessary, never too soon, and never too late. It is this perception of the rhythm and the helmsman's subliminal adjustment to it that makes good helmsmanship. In other words, the good helmsman *times* his tiller work just as a golf player or a tennis player times his strokes.

The helmsman must always learn to "stay with" his boat. Many a man is a good helmsman for an hour; after that he becomes careless, slovenly, and out of time. It is then that his sailing becomes ragged. He wanders from his course, or even worse, he fights his boat. Your good skipper can tell instantly when a poor helmsman takes the tiller. He can feel the loss of rhythm. He will know it whether he is on deck watching the progress of the race, or below in his bunk. He will also know when a good helmsman gets tired and will change helmsmen immediately. On long night races I make it a rule never to hold the stick for more than two hours at a time and never permit anyone else to hold it for even that period. In very light airs it is more difficult to be a good helmsman than in heavy blows. It is more difficult to produce good helmsmanship when there are no real competitors than when you are sailing in close hard competition with another boat.

To a certain extent, the good helmsman gives the boat her head just as a good horseman rides with light hands. Any good boat will almost sail herself, with just a touch now and then to bring her back before she gets out of hand. The good helmsman recognizes this and knows that when he is not imposing his will upon the boat he gets glorious bursts of speed out of her. He will proceed with one burst of speed after another, gently bringing her back to her course and meanwhile letting her sail herself.

When on the wind, the skipper must constantly

make the decision between good pointing and good footing. There is a critical point beyond which it does not pay to point closer to the wind. There is a critical point beyond which it does not pay to trim the sheets. When you flatten the boat down too hard you kill her, when you point her too close you kill her likewise. On the wind, the good helmsman never pinches, never luffs so as to lose headway and, on the other hand, never bears away a fraction of a point more than necessary to keep the boat going at her best.

And there are other compromises as well. In sailing free, the skipper may know that by trimming his jib sheet he can reduce his rudder drag. On the other hand, by starting his jib sheet he may increase his rudder drag but, despite that fact, increase the speed of the boat. Here too a sense of pace is all important. In these circumstances it is perhaps well to turn the helm over to another member of the crew and judge pace without feeling the tiller. I remember one race in which I was second and was rapidly being overtaken by another boat. I was sailing a broad reach, the helm was light, the boat lively, yet I was rapidly losing my position and a nice silver mug that was waiting a mile or so ahead. In despair I turned the tiller over to another man and then, and not until then, perceived that the jib sheet was far too flat. I started it at once. The new helmsman raised a howl. It had increased the rudder drag, yet the boat seemed to be moving faster. I felt the helm. The rudder drag had increased perceptibly, but the boat that had been overtaking us was now dropping behind and we had gained a little on the leader. I kept her as she was and we finished a good second with plenty of open water between us and the third boat.

Getting the boat into her groove, finding where she does her best, how she likes her sails trimmed, can only be determined by this sense of pace.

One more warning. When you get your boat moving, leave her alone unless there is some very definite reason for interfering with her again. I recall vividly a race last summer in which we were doing very poorly. The air was very light. We were flopping along with spinnaker set and all sails drooping rather sadly. Most of the fleet were out ahead. Then what little air there was seemed to come from a new direction. We guyed the spinnaker forward, trimmed the main sheet, and she seemed to go a little faster. For five or ten minutes we gained perceptibly on all the other boats. It was then that an observant member of my crew suggested, "Skipper, do you realize that we are trimmed flatter than any of the other boats? Look at them. Every one has the spinnaker guyed further aft and the main sheet started more than ours." To which I replied, "Perhaps that is why we are gaining on them. When we were trimmed as they are, we were dropping back." The moral of this is, "Do not disturb your boat when you once get her goin'."

One final word: Yacht racing is a game—not a business. To excel in any game, you must play at it—not work at it. The minute racing becomes deadly serious, the boat slows down. The fast boat is sailed joyously. The joyously sailed boat is fast.

CHAPTER XV

SAILING TO WINDWARD

IN THE next three chapters I am going to assume that you are sailing your boat alone and that no competitors are anywhere near you. The conduct of a boat in a race divides itself into two distinct classifications: When two boats are sailing in close company, they are able to interfere with one another by cutting off or altering the direction of the wind and by breaking the water through which the other boat sails. This business of fighting your opponent with wind and water is discussed under the chapters on racing tactics. Racing tactics in the strict sense of the word is applicable only within your Zone of Interference. Outside that Zone of Interference the ability of one boat to interfere with another becomes negligible. In large classes, boats sail in the Zone of Interference of other boats for a very large part of each race. In the smaller classes, however, in which there may be only six or eight boats contending, the opportunities for racing tactics are distinctly limited, and for the greater part of the race boats may be sailing without paying much attention to the matter of interference. For this reason, if for no other, it is most important to be able to get the greatest possible speed out of your boat on sailing any course. These three chapters will be devoted to that matter of getting speed out of the boat.

On the wind, the first question to be determined is the trim of the sheets. Let us begin with the main sheet. Nearly every main sheet is rigged to a traveler. To the beginner the traveler is an inexplicable piece of machinery for he concludes that if it were not for the traveler he would be able to trim his main sheet flat. I know one skipper who has put hooks into the deck on the sides of his traveler and is very proud of the fact that he can lead his main sheet under the hooks and trim his main boom flat amidships and even, by straining a point, get it up to windward. The traveler is placed there for the very purpose of preventing that sort of trimming, because that trimming does not enable the boat to point high or sail faster but results in the most serious handicap—that of a twisted sail. A boat that is properly designed by a good naval architect has a traveler of exactly the right length. When the main sheet is trimmed properly the boom is trimmed down toward the end of the traveler, but not in toward the middle of the boat.

This trimming down is the correct way to trim the main sheet. If the sheet should be trimmed amidships owing to the absence of a traveler or a change in the traveler, the result would be that the upper half of the sail would sag off to leeward resulting in a sail that is twisted instead of a true aerofoil. With a gaff-headed rig this twisting is most pronounced because it can readily be seen that the gaff does not lie in the same plane as the boom. With a Marconi mainsail the twisting is less apparent but is probably more pronounced because of the long leech of the sail. The first question of trim, therefore, is to trim down to the end of the traveler and not attempt to trim too flat amidships.

If the traveler should be too long and if it should be possible to get better results by trimming the boom in somewhat, it is best to set small blocks of wood under the ends of the traveler, thus shortening it a bit. In general, however, it is inadvisable to trim the sheet too flat. It is easy to determine where the point of too great flatness is reached. The boat becomes dead and logy and does not point perceptibly higher into the wind.

A twisted mainsail or sagging gaff may be a signal that your traveler is not long enough. It may, however, be the fault of the cut of the sail itself. A sagging sail is usually very much pronounced in the foresail of a schooner, and in both the mainsail and the mizzen of a gaff-headed yawl. The reason for this is that the gaff is too long in relation to the boom. In general, a gaff-headed mainsail should be trimmed in so that it crosses the transom at the point where the counter joins the side of the boat. A Marconi mainsail may be trimmed a trifle flatter. The way to determine the trim of the main sheet, however, is by the trial and error method. Trim it right in flat and see how fast she goes. If you are sailing in company with another boat, you can soon determine the point beyond which flattening the main sheet results merely in killing headway.

You should be guided by three considerations. Ask yourself these questions: 1. Will trimming the sheet beyond this point make the boat point higher or only seem to point higher? 2. Will starting the sheet make the boat go faster without causing her to point more to leeward? 3. If by pointing to leeward I will travel faster, do I gain or lose by that procedure? In explanation of these questions, let me state that there is a point beyond which trimming the sheet will not enable

you to point any higher. To determine whether you
gain or lose by sailing freer is also a matter of trial and
error. Perhaps an artillery man or a good mathematician can figure it out mathematically.

The theory of it is something like this: A mil, with
which mathematicians and artillery men are familiar,
is an angle which, at a distance of 1,000 yards, subtends a chord of 1 yard. If you sail one mil freer,
therefore, you must travel 1,001 yards in the time that
you would have traveled 1,000 yards on the closer
course. If you sail two mils freer, you will have to sail
1,002 yards in the time it would have taken you to sail
1,000 yards on the first course, and so on. But mathematics really does not tell the story for the following
reasons: If you are pointing close to the wind and there
is a heavy sea, the seas will stop you more on the close
course than on the freer course. You will also make
more leeway. Thus, so many elements enter into the
calculation, the only way to determine the best way
for your particular boat is to try to sail her on several
courses, with every angle of trim of the main sheet,
in company with another boat until you can determine
just how close you dare to trim the main sheet.

The trim of the jib sheet offers another problem best
determined by trial and error. Like the main sheet, the
jib sheet should be trimmed down and not in. If there
is a single jib sheet, it should work on a traveler. The
fall should lead forward to a deck block close to the
bow and then lead aft to the cockpit. If there is a
double-ended jib sheet passing through a block on the
jib club, the traveler may be dispensed with but the
location of the fairleaders through which the sheet is
led aft should be studied carefully. The location of
these fairleaders determines the point to which the jib

is trimmed down and thus they take the place of the traveler. If there are two jib sheets, the leeward one is always trimmed and the weather sheet is usually left free. On some boats, however, I have found it advisable to trim both the lee and the weather jib sheets, using the lee sheet to trim down and the weather sheet to trim in. The use of the two sheets affords a fine adjustment.

On a loose-footed jib, whether an ordinary jib or an overlapping Genoa jib, the jib sheet is made fast to a cringle in the clew and is always trimmed to leeward. With a jib of this character the lead of the sheet from the clew to the first fairleader is most important and will reward the closest study. In general, it may be stated that if the jib sheet were continued across the sail in a straight line from the clew to the luff, it would bisect the angle of the clew and intersect the luff at right angles. If the jib is made with a miter so that some of the cloths are sewed in at right angles to the leech and the others are sewed in at right angles to the foot, the jib sheet should lead away from the clew in a prolongation of the miter. With this lead of the jib sheet, the pull is exerted evenly over the entire surface of the jib and neither the foot nor the leech is stretched too tight so that the other side of the sail sags off. If the jib sheet leads down to the deck at a more acute angle from the clew, the leech is stretched too tight and the foot is too loose. The remedy in that case is to move the fairleader farther aft. If, however, the sheet leads to the deck in a flatter, more obtuse angle from the clew, it means that the foot of the sail will be stretched too tight while the leech will not be stretched tight enough. The remedy in that case is to move the fairleaders forward.

These principles determine the angle of the jib sheet lead in a vertical plane. In addition, you must determine the proper angle in a horizontal plane. This is more difficult because it varies somewhat with the flatness to which the jib is trimmed. When you are on the wind, the best location for the fairleader is near the inboard edge of the deck, close to the cabin-house or the cockpit coaming. If you are sailing free and your jib sheet is started, the best location may be out near the rail. I have seen successful Star boats with no less than a dozen fairleaders located at different points of the deck to care for the varying angles of jib sheet lead. There are, however, various devices that are capable of quick adjustment. I do not know whether or not any of them are patented, but I mention this possibility to avoid a danger of patent violation. One such device is in the form of a circular track or plate with a radial arm mounted in the center and the fairleaders affixed to the arm. Thus, by moving the arm to various points of the circle, and moving the fairleaders in or out on the arm, the jib sheet may be trimmed down to any point in the circle. Another device consists of a pair of parallel tracks affixed in a fore and aft direction on the deck and a cross member arranged to slide fore and aft upon these tracks. The fairleader is affixed to the cross member in such a manner that it may be moved out or in. Thus, by moving the fairleader on the cross member and moving the cross member forward or aft on the tracks, the jib sheet may be trimmed down to any point between the two tracks.

On any jib a hollow leech must be carefully avoided. By a hollow leech I mean a leech that is curved back toward the wind. The after edge of a jib should stand perfectly flat for at least a third of the distance to the luff. On a loose-footed jib the only means of controlling this curvature is the jib sheet, and this control can be effected only by being able to trim it down to various parts of the deck.

On a jib provided with a club, this problem is less acute but another problem arises to take its place. That problem is the determination of the correct position of the block on the club through which the jib sheet is rove. If that block is too far forward, the jib will stand too flat. If the block is too far aft, the jib will never stand flat enough. There is also one critical point at which the jib will wave and flap, swinging back and forth around the block as a center. I owned one sloop on which this critical point was located less than two inches from the position at which I got the best possible results. The only way to determine the best position of the jib sheet block on the club is to move it forward and aft and try numerous experiments. In making these trials, observe the curvature of the jib at a point directly above the forward end of the club. If there is a sudden and pronounced belly at this point, it is a pretty good indication that the block is too far aft. If the whole forward part of the jib stands extra flat, it is an indication that the block is too far forward. The belly at the luff should be smooth, symmetrical, and continuous. There should be no point at which it is more pronounced than the other points.

After you have determined the correct lead of the jib sheet, it is most important to study the best possible trim. With the main sheet trimmed to the proper point, sail as close to the wind as you can without luffing. Then start the jib sheet until the jib begins to luff. Note the angle of the jib and the length of the jib sheet between the jib and the deck. That is the outer limit to which you may go. Now sail on exactly the same course, trim the jib sheet until the jib begins to back-wind the mainsail. Note the angle of the jib and the length of the jib sheet between the jib and the deck. That is the inner limit to which you may go. Somewhere between these two limits is the correct trim of the jib sheet when you are on the wind.

Now, within these limits find the place where the helm is lightest. If your helm is heavy, it may be corrected by trimming the jib sheet flatter, but this result may also be attained by moving your crew forward or aft. The correction of a weather helm by moving the crew may further be complicated by its effect on the boat in general. You may lighten the helm by burying the bow or by burying the stern and, in either case, killing the speed of the boat. In other words, you must attain a light helm; you may gain it by trimming the jib sheet or by trimming with your live weight, or by both. You must, therefore, use both the factors of jib sheet and live weight in such a way that you do not destroy the proper waterlines of the hull and do not impair the efficiency of the jib. This sounds complicated and it is. The problem differs with every boat. I have seen two boats sailing side by side in a one-design class with the same hulls, the same masts, the same rigging, the same sails, and each boat had to be trimmed differently.

The trim of the jib sheet should also be judged in the light of the following considerations. In general, when the jib sheet is started, the jib is more efficient. When the jib sheet is trimmed, the mainsail is more efficient. This is due to the fact that greater driving power is developed by the leeward side of a sail than by the windward side. When the jib is trimmed flat, it increases the pressure on the leeward side of the mainsail and accelerates the velocity of the wind. It is impossible to lay down a law to govern the trim of every jib sheet. In general, however, we may state that when the jib is relatively large, it is better to try to get all possible efficiency from the jib than to try to increase the efficiency of the mainsail by trimming the jib too flat. If, on the other hand, the jib is relatively small, it is better to sacrifice the efficiency of the jib by increasing the efficiency of the mainsail. On the wind, the trim of a Genoa jib should always be governed by the resulting efficiency of the mainsail because the very large part of the Genoa jib's area that overlaps the mainsail has very little driving power of itself, but is most important in its effect upon the efficiency of the mainsail. On my own boat I have two jibs of the same size but of slightly different cut. With one jib I get better results by trimming for jib efficiency; with the other I get better results by trimming for mainsail efficiency. The difference is about four inches in the length of the jib sheet between the jib and the fairleader.

When you have once determined the proper trim of the jib sheet when on the wind, note the angle which the jib makes with the lee shrouds and the length of the jib sheet between the jib and the fairleader. If you are using a single-ended sheet, mark it at the cleat with a seizing of sail twine. Your crew can then trim to the exact point of greatest efficiency every time you go about.

At all costs you must avoid back-winding the mainsail by the jib. You can tell when you are back-winding if the mainsail appears to luff when the jib is trimmed flat, but does not appear to luff when the jib sheet is started while sailing on the same course. Back-winding may be due to causes other than the trim of the jib sheet. It may well result from a hollow leech in the jib. The hollow leech must be done away with by means of the battens or by adjustments of the leech line.

Now, if both the jib and mainsail are trimmed correctly, and if your live weight is in the right place, the boat will be pointing close to the wind and sailing fast without any perceptible rudder drag. The tiller will be in the center of the boat and you will be able to manage it with a light hand, steering with thumb and forefinger. The next thing to determine is the correct windward and leeward trim. Up to this point you have moved your crew forward or aft to attain freedom from rudder drag and the proper balance of the waterlines of the hull. Now it becomes necessary to get the boat down to her sailing lines.

You can readily determine the angle of heel at which the boat travels best. A properly designed boat has a longer waterline when heeled over than when sailed upright. In general, this increase of waterline increases potential speed. But there is a point beyond which a boat loses power and efficiency. A boat with hard bilges slows down when she buries her bilges too deep. The boat with a flat floor or insufficient keel, or too shallow a centerboard, will also make increased leeway when she is heeled down. All of these factors must be studied closely. In general, a boat is at her best when her rail is five or six inches out of the water and she is heeled gently without too much of a wave at her lee bow. If she buries her bilges too far, you will notice a pronounced bow wave at the lee bow and disturbed water all along the lee side.

When it is blowing hard, stiffen your boat by placing the crew up to windward. If the air is very light, move the crew down to leeward to make the boat heel more. With a heavy crew and a small boat you can work wonders by moving them to the right position.

Now let us examine the rest of the boat. First let us see if anything interferes with the correct aerofoil curvature of the jib and the mainsail. The jib loses its curvature principally through a hollow leech, or through improper sheeting. The mainsail may lose its curvature by having the runner, the backstay, the topping-lift, or the lazyjacks cut into the lee side of the sail. Since lee backstays and the lee runner are usually slacked off whenever the boat goes about they are rarely offenders in this matter. But topping-lifts and lazyjacks must be watched constantly.

The mast too is a prime offender. If shrouds are set up too tight, the mast is almost certain to develop a dangerous S-curve due to the compression strain of the shrouds. This is aggravated in a gaff-rigged boat by the forward thrust of the gaff. An S-curve is remedied by slacking the shrouds and tightening the jack stay. These adjustments should be made carefully. Sometimes slackening or tightening a single thread on the turnbuckles will effect the remedy. If the mast curves forward, it may be due to the fact that the head stay is too tight. The forward curvature to the mast is almost certain to destroy the set of the mainsail. If the mast curves forward and the jib stay and head stay are slacked, it is a sign that the mast is very limber and that not sufficient power has been put into the trim of runners and backstays. In connection with the mast, always study the tension on the jib stay. The jib stay must be perfectly taut while sailing to windward. Any slackness or sagging of the jib stay greatly impairs the efficiency of the boat. Perhaps I should state that line in italics. It deserves strong emphasis.

With the boat then properly trimmed, and with nothing interfering with the effectiveness of the sails, let us try to work her to windward.

The cardinal sin of most helmsmen is that of pinching. They are so anxious to work up every inch into the wind that they luff too often, too much, and for too long duration. The helmsman must glue his eye to the luff of the sail high up on the mast. At the first sign of fluttering, he must pull his helm up slightly to windward and fill away. He must avoid luffing again until he suspects a slight shift in the wind, in which case he may then feel his way slightly closer to the wind and bear away at the first sign of a flutter. He must not do this suddenly or violently. He must bear in mind that any change in direction keeps the boat from going ahead. Your good helmsman will keep at the point where his sail just doesn't flutter. Perhaps the best warning against too much pinching may be stated in another way. Do not try to out-point your competitors. If you do it naturally, if your boat is more weatherly, well and good, but in general you will have a very good chance of winning the race if you point as high as your competitors and move a little bit faster. All good boats will point up to just about the same degree.

Bear in mind too that whereas some boats may point a trifle higher than others, it is not important unless they can make speed while pointing higher. The negative phase of pinching is just as bad. Some helmsmen are so afraid of pinching that they sail bare, that is to say, they point away from the wind farther than is necessary and might well make as much as a quarter of a point higher into the wind if they remained alert and dared to test their position every once in a while by luffing slightly. Pinching and sailing bare are the two great worries in helmsmanship while on the wind. A good helmsman never tires, never stops working, but is constantly holding his boat just as high as possible and never too high.

A word about tacking. The wrong way to put a boat about is to jam the helm down suddenly and hard and try to get about as quickly as possible. Yet this error is committed probably more frequently than any other. Skippers are so proud that their boats are "quick in stays" that they try to come about on a nickel and bear away and get sailing on the opposite tack as soon as they can. By doing so they kill their headway and, furthermore, they lose all the distance that they might otherwise eat up into the wind.

The correct way to come about is to put the helm down slowly and gradually, rounding up into the wind on a long slow gradual curve, bringing the helm back amidships so that the boat shoots a long way to windward, then putting the helm down once more to bear away on the other tack. By this maneuver the boat loses practically no headway. She does not fight herself. A good boat with heavy ballast or a good deep keel will shoot a long way into the wind. My own boat shoots seven times her length. It cannot be stressed too often that when you are sailing to windward, distance into the wind is of the utmost importance. You must not stay in the wind so long as to lose steerage way, but while you are still going ahead at a good rate of speed, bear away on the other tack. When you fill away, keep the helm up till you are just a little bit beyond the point where you should be sailing. This will enable you to gather way quickly on the new tack. But the instant you feel that you have gained way, bring the boat back as close to the wind as she will sail. Most helmsmen bear away too far when they go about, thus rapidly losing a large part of the distance they have gained by shooting up into the wind.

Proper tacking loses little, if any, ground. The distance gained by going into the wind more than makes up for the delay caused in going about. If you are sailing in close company with another boat which is endeavoring to cover you, and if your tacking is just slightly better than your opponent's, go about frequently, then tack back again. On every tack you will gain. And if your tacking is very well done, you will lose nothing to the other boats that are holding a course.

Of course, it is very important to have your crew handling the jib sheets efficiently. If your jib is so arranged that the sheets must be cast off and trimmed again every time you go about, you must watch the crew carefully to see that they do their trimming properly. The leeward sheet must be let go just as the boat is about to come up to the wind. If it is let go too soon there will be an unnecessary amount of flapping to the jib. This always interferes with headway. If it is let go too late, the jib will be trimmed to weather, will stop your headway and carry you to leeward too fast and too far. On the other hand, the man who trims the sheet after the boat goes about must start to trim just after the jib comes amidships and must have it down on the cleat as you fill away. If he trims too fast, the jib is aback before you are into the wind. This kills headway, makes you put your helm down unnecessarily far and may even prevent your getting about at all. If he trims too late, the efficiency of the jib on the new tack is materially decreased and the whole smoothness of the tack is spoiled.

In sailing on a puffy day, the helmsman must be on the alert to head up into every little puff of wind. He can always point higher in the puffs, and this he should do whenever possible. On a Northwest wind on the Atlantic seaboard, and generally on all land breezes anywhere, the wind shifts fairly constantly. In such a breeze, the wind while predominantly Northwest, will sometimes shift as far as West and sometimes as far as North. Let us assume that with the wind Northwest you are sailing on the starboard tack headed West. If the wind shifts toward the North, head up. If the wind shifts back to Northwest, bear away again. But if the wind shifts toward the West, go about at once. You will thus be sailing nearer to Northwest on the port tack than you could possibly sail on the starboard tack. That puff may be of short duration, the wind may swing back again toward the North. If it does, go about again even though you may have sailed only a hundred yards on the port tack. You may look foolish and feel foolish, but do not hesitate to go about every time the wind heads you. I have won more races through this policy than from any other single cause.

Two races come to mind. In one I tore my spinnaker from head to foot at the start of the first leg. When the boats ahead of me rounded the second mark and started to beat back to the finish, they were so far ahead that I could not distinguish the numbers or even the very large class symbols on their sails. I felt hopelessly beaten but settled down to the policy of tacking on every slight shift of wind. I think I must have tacked thirty times on that windward leg. By doing so I sailed through the entire fleet and finished second, a heart-beat behind the winner. It was solely due to the fact that I was always sailing closer to the base line, closer to the average wind, than any of my opponents. In another race two years ago I was hopelessly out-classed on the first leg by the only other boat in the race. The second leg was a beat. I tacked so often that the skipper of a boat in another class which I sailed through lost his temper. I had unwittingly interfered with him. He thought I was crazy and remarked that he was racing. When I replied that I was racing too, he clearly thought I was insane, but I rounded the next mark ahead and eventually won the race. On three occasions when close to the other boat, I tacked while the other boat held its course. The wind held for some time on each of those shifts and right there I won the race.

In sailing on the wind with too much sail there is one trick known to all experienced racing men but which most beginners do not seem to realize. When you have too much sail, trim the jib flat and start the main sheet. Thus the mainsail may be luffing for a full third of the distance from the mast, but the boat will foot very fast, will hold her course and keep going. Do not bear away too much in the lulls, do not try to head up too much in the puffs, just keep her footing. You cannot do this if the jib sheet is started. By keeping the jib sheet trimmed you steady the entire boat. This is universal practice among good racing skippers. It is illustrated in Fig. 25 in which two New York 30s, and a 6-Metre are shown with jib trimmed flat and mainsail started and luffing.

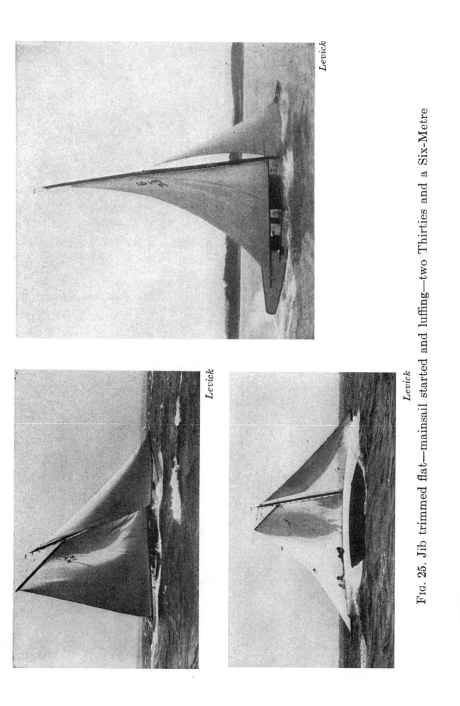

Fig. 25. Jib trimmed flat—mainsail started and luffing—two Thirties and a Six-Metre

Levick

Levick

Levick

FIG. 24. Nos. 24 and K28 are stamping badly. In such conditions a whippy mast will kill headway

FIG. 26. The tricing line on a Genoa jib

To many skippers this device is regarded as a substitute for reefing. They prefer to carry too much sail on the wind in order to have as much sail as possible while running. I cannot sympathize with this theory because I have won too many races by carrying reefs when other boats were struggling along under too much sail. The additional sail which you will carry by running before the wind on a very windy day does not materially increase your speed. If it is blowing hard your boat will attain its maximum speed even though reefed. Beyond that you can pile on sail until you carry the stick out of her without noticeably increasing the speed of the hull. But on the wind a boat will travel faster if she can "carry" her sail instead of "lugging" it. While, therefore, it is possible to make good speed by the device of trimming the jib flat and starting and luffing the mainsail, this is not to my mind an adequate substitute for reefing. The properly reefed boat will be more efficient than the boat with too much sail.

In sailing on the wind a boat makes more leeway than in sailing any other course. For that reason a centerboard boat should carry her board at the greatest efficient depth. Centerboards of the dagger type can generally be lowered as far as they will go. Most centerboards, however, are suspended by a pin at the lower forward corner of the trunk and the after end is hoisted or lowered by means of a rope pennant. As stated above, many sailors make the mistake of lowering the board too deep. It should be lowered just to the point where the top of the after end of the board is an inch or so above the bottom of the trunk. If the board is lowered beyond this point so that there is clear water between the top of the board and the bottom of the trunk, three retarding influences are set up: The first is the twist or warping which may occur in the board itself which thus becomes suspended at only one point and is not supported throughout the width by the sides of the trunk. The second is the eddy that is set up in the after end of the trunk itself and in the disturbance of the water below this part of the trunk. The part of the trunk in which there is no board acts somewhat in the manner of a hole made in the deadwood for the purpose of installing a propeller. The third retarding influence is the disturbance caused by the pennant which is thus dragged through the water. If the board is lowered to such a point that the pennant sets up a vibration, this retarding influence is increased. While in principle it is always necessary to carry the board as low as possible while sailing on the wind, in the case of a large board it is quite possible to lower it too far. The more it is lowered, the greater its wetted surface and consequent friction. The board, therefore, should be carried as low as is necessary to overcome leeway, but no lower. Experiment with your board while sailing, making careful note of your leeway by taking bearings of the angle of your wake. If raising the board a few inches does not perceptibly increase your leeway, it is probably better to carry it at that angle than to lower it all the way. Bear in mind too that the depth of the board will affect the center of resistance of the hull and therefore have a bearing on trim and rudder drag.

A chapter on sailing to windward would be incomplete without referring to the Genoa jib. This large, overlapping jib can be carried on the wind to impart greater power and drive. Undoubtedly, part of the success of a Genoa jib is due to the fact that under measurement rules the overlapping part of the sail does not count in sail area measurement. The fore triangle, determined by the jib stay, the mast, and the deck, is measured under the rules, but any part of the head sails that overlaps the mast and the mainsail is not counted. But beyond a doubt the Genoa jib does more than this. It increases the volume and accelerates the velocity of the wind passing the leeward side of the mainsail at its forward edge where it is most effective. The Genoa jib should always be trimmed as close as possible to the mainsail, but not so close as to involve back-winding. It is always trimmed outside the shrouds. A Genoa jib should always be equipped with tricing lines. Since these lines are of comparatively recent development, they deserve a word of explanation. A light cotton line is let into the miter of the sail somewhere about the middle. It is led forward to a small block on the jib luff, down to another block at the jib tack, and aft to the cockpit. When the boat goes about, the lee jib sheet is let go. One hand trims on the tricing line, pulling the whole sail forward. After the eye of the wind is passed, the tricing line is let go and the jib is again sheeted to leeward. The tricing line is clearly shown in Fig. 26. It is evident that the point at which it is let into the mainsail must be sufficiently far aft so that all the sail aft of this point can clear the mast and jack stay when the boat goes about. It is not wise, however, to place it any farther aft than necessary. A single line will do the work, but good practice calls for a double-ended line passing on both sides of the jib, both falls of which are trimmed at the same time. In this manner the tricing line acts as a lazyjack gathering forward the bunt of the sail. The similarity to a lazyjack must be stressed because the tricing line should be watched at all times to see that the leeward line does not cut into the belly of the sail. In general, Genoa jibs should not be carried on the wind on days when the wind is strong, puffy and shifting. Although it is still more efficient than the small jib even in a strong wind, it is so much harder to tack with a Genoa jib than with a small jib that it is usually wiser to use a small jib in such conditions.

Chapter XVI

REACHING

At the very outset it is necessary to distinguish between a close reach and a broad reach. Since the terms are somewhat elastic we will make a precise definition for the purposes of this chapter.

By a close reach is meant sailing with the wind abeam or forward of the beam. By a broad reach is meant sailing with the wind abaft the beam. When a reach is so broad that a spinnaker may be carried and guyed fairly well aft, it will be considered as a run and not as a reach.

It is necessary to make this distinction between the close reach and the broad reach because a boat is driven by different forces on the two courses. On the close reach the sails derive the greater part of their driving power from the leeward side and the lesser part from the windward side. On a broad reach the sails derive most of their driving power from the windward side and little, if any, from the leeward side. I do not wish to appear didactic in making this statement for it is one of those statements that authors sometimes live to regret. The scientific invasion of the art of sailing is still so recent that many of the findings of the scientists are subject to correction by new discoveries which may be made before this book is very old. Perhaps the safest statement to make would be this:

There is good, trustworthy scientific evidence that when a boat is on a close reach, the sails derive most of their propulsive force from the leeward side, and in the absence of scientific proof to the contrary, I am assuming what seems to be probable that on a broad reach the sails derive their propulsive force from the windward side. That re-statement should sound safe fifty years from now.

With this distinction in mind, there would appear to be two different principles for trimming the sheets on a close and a broad reach. On a close reach the trim should be of such a nature as to render most efficient the draft on the leeward side of the sails. On a broad reach the best way to trim is to get the utmost efficiency from the windward side of the sails.

That means that, with the wind abeam, or forward of the beam, the sheets should be started as far as possible and still avoid luffing. Let us begin with the main sheet. With the boat on her course, pay out the main sheet until it starts to luff. Then trim a few inches. Another way of attaining this result would be to sail the boat a half point, or three-quarters of a point higher into the wind than her proper course. Trim the sheet until the luff is reduced to a minimum, then bear away on the course. The trim of the jib sheet is somewhat more complex, for in the trim of the jib we must bear in mind the three factors that control speed: 1. The efficiency of the jib itself. 2. The efficiency of the mainsail by the increased flow of wind on the leeward side imparted by a closely trimmed jib. 3. Rudder drag. In general, however, it may be stated that the jib is slacked off more than when sailing close-hauled. If this were not so, the jib would lose its own efficiency and would back-wind the mainsail. Although the correct trim for the jib differs with different boats, in general it may be stated that on a close reach the jib is trimmed a trifle flatter than the mainsail, and it is not started sufficiently to make the helm heavy nor is it trimmed so flat as to lose the drive of its own lee side nor so flat as to back-wind the mainsail. Trial and error will quickly demonstrate the correct trim of the jib sheet. Many years ago when I was first learning to sail, the old fishermen and scallopers would warn me that there is no life in a flat jib and that power was derived only from a lifting jib. In those days, however, the jibs were bigger than they are to-day and boats were equipped with long nose poles. Furthermore, the jibs were farther away from the mainsails so that their effect on the mainsails' efficiency was impaired. I state this for the reason that many yachtsmen still believe in the time honored power of the lifting jib. On a close reach, and on most modern boats I believe this theory to be false.

On a broad reach, however, the theory is different. When the wind is abaft the beam, both jib and mainsail should be trimmed at right angles to the direction of the wind. In considering the trim of the main sheet, bear in mind that the sail must be at right angles to the wind, but this does not necessarily mean that the boom must be at right angles to the wind. As a rule mainsails sag. If the boom is trimmed at right angles, the gaff of a gaff-headed sail, and the upper third of a Marconi or jib-headed sail, will sag off beyond this angle. The skipper must average the part of the sail that sags and the part of the sail that is fast to the boom so that the average position of the sail is at right angles to the wind.

When sailing on a broad reach, the theory of

the lifting jib is absolutely sound. The jib sheet is generally trimmed a trifle flatter than the main sheet, but as a rule it is wise to start the jib sheet just as far as you can and still keep the jib approximately at right angles to the direction of the wind. This is almost certain to increase rudder drag somewhat, but in most boats it does not decrease the speed. The relationship between a started jib sheet and a heavy helm is well illustrated in Fig. 27. The leading boat is carrying her jib broad off with the consequence that her tiller must be held well across the boat. The second boat has her jib sheet trimmed flatter and the tiller is held amidships.

If the jib is small, rudder drag may be more of a factor in the speed of the boat than the efficiency of the jib. If the jib is large, however, it is generally wise to play for jib efficiency and forget rudder drag. It will be evident from this frequent re-statement of the problem that every skipper must make constant compromises, that he must barter advantages against disadvantages, and that it is only by close study of his own boat that he can ever be sure of attaining maximum speed. All that a printed book can do is to lay down the principles that govern speed, point where the advantages and disadvantages lie, and let the skipper manage his own sailing.

Only very rarely do equally matched boats pass one another in the short reach that is to be found on an ordinary triangular course. On port to port runs, cruising races, and night races which are of long duration and in which factors like tide, varying wind conditions, navigation, and general strategy enter to a large degree, the reverse is true. But even in a short reaching leg, the skipper usually has an opportunity of passing

Levick

Fig. 27. Showing the effect of a started jib sheet on rudder drag

Levick

Fig. 28. Stars "wung-out" with whisker poles

Levick

Fig. 29

Levick

Fig. 30A

Levick

Fig. 30B

Fig. 29. A ballooner that is more a hindrance than a help

Fig. 30A. A spinnaker working hard—but better if sheeted forward

Fig. 30B. A parachute spinnaker

another boat of approximately equal speed. If he does not do it often, it is because he pays insufficient attention to the varying factors and does not work hard enough to save the seconds that are so obviously savable on a boat. I remember sailing through the lee of another boat in the last short reach of a race on the Sound to win second place by a considerable margin. The following Monday a veteran skipper in the class called me on the telephone to learn how I had done it and stated that I had achieved the impossible, that boats in that class simply never passed one another on a reach, but I had done it and I have so often been passed on a reach that I do know it can be done despite its unusualness. The apathy of most skippers while sailing a reach is therefore inexcusable. The usual procession can be broken up by proper sailing and good strategy.

In sailing a reach one should always bear in mind the old geometric axiom that a straight line is the shortest distance between two points. To arrive at a straight line, however, does not necessarily mean that a boat should be steered directly toward the next mark. Tidal current must be taken into consideration. If the tide is running so as to set you to leeward of your course, you must steer to windward of the mark. If the tide is setting you to windward of the mark, you must steer to leeward. In general, the skipper does not have time to calculate his speed accurately, figure the exact strength of the tide, and make scientific calculations.

In sailing on a cruising run where the reach may be for a distance of twenty or thirty miles, he can afford to and should apply the well-known formula for correcting a course for current. The formula and its application are completely explained in the chapter on Coastwise Navigation in "Learning to Sail." The skipper soon learns how much allowance to make after he has sailed over a course a few times and even on a strange course he can ordinarily make the allowances if he can estimate the strength of the current and the speed of his boat. The length of the course has nothing to do with it. If one point is enough allowance in a leg a mile in length, the same allowance will be true for the same speed of the boat and the same strength of the current in a leg ten miles in length. For it is obvious that the current will be working all the way along the course setting the boat back from the course steered to the base line between the two marks.

It is most important to make this allowance when starting on the reaching leg and at all times to steer a compass course. Do not select a land mark and sail by that even though it should prove much less fatiguing. The trouble with steering for a land mark is that as the tide sets you down toward your base line, you are constantly making a wider angle of correction. If you should be sailing without a compass, which is never to be recommended, you will then have to resort to the land mark and will have to pick successively new land marks nearer the mark of the course.

For instance, you know from experience that the next mark lies in line with that sand bank with the beach plum bushes in the middle. You know that the tide is setting you straight across your course to leeward. From experience, you know that you should head toward the windmill that lies to windward of the sandbank. Gradually you should head nearer to the sandbank as you are sailing along. When you have run down half your distance you should head at a point half way between the windmill and the sand-bank. When you have run three-quarters of your distance you should have chosen a land mark half way between the middle point and the sand-bank. By this time the turning mark is in sight. Bear just a little high of it and as you approach you will find that you are being set down upon it. Make allowance for this set and you will hit the mark on the nose.

In sailing on a reach, fore and aft balance, proper trim and freedom from rudder drag are just as important as in sailing to windward. These factors are corrected on a reach in the same manner as they are on a beat by moving live weight, by the trim of the jib, by the proper depth to which the centerboard is carried, and by the rake of the mast. In general, the centerboard should be carried no deeper than is necessary to prevent leeway. On a close reach the board is carried just about as deep as on a beat. On a broad reach it is usually raised about half way. On a broad reach the consideration of leeway assumes less importance, but it must still be borne in mind, and in addition, the effect of the centerboard to prevent yawing and rolling must come in for consideration. If by lowering the centerboard all the way, the boat is steadier on her keel and lighter on her helm, the board should by all means be lowered, otherwise it should be raised just as much as possible without permitting rolling, yawing, or making leeway.

On a close reach a Genoa jib can be carried with great efficiency. On a broad reach a balloon jib is usually more effective. This is not always the case, however, and it will pay to experiment widely with both the Genoa and the ballooner. The Genoa is usually a better cut sail and even though it lacks the area of the ballooner it may be more efficient even with the wind abaft the beam. Genoas and ballooners are hoisted in stops in the same manner as a spinnaker. Stopping the sails is not necessary, however, especially in light airs, but they can generally be handled better and quicker if sent up in stops. If the reaching leg follows a beat, it is wise to send up the light sail in stops before rounding the mark and break it out and sheet it home the minute you bear away on the new course. It is good practice to have a separate stay just forward of the jib stay to carry the Genoa. In some boats the ballooner will be carried on this stay. In others, the ballooner will be carried on the head stay. In light to moderate airs one is always tempted to carry a regular jib inside the ballooner. Sometimes this is effective but usually it interferes with the pull of the ballooner much more than the value derived from the added sail would warrant. The sheeting of a balloon jib is always a problem. The racing rules generally prohibit sheeting it to any outrigger other than the main boom, but permit attaching it to the main boom. This is done by a snatch block on the boom through which the balloon jib sheet is rove and led inboard. In general, it is a good idea to sheet the ballooner either to the main boom or as far aft on the hull as possible. This gives lift to the ballooner and added speed to the boat. With the ballooner thus sheeted aft, it is sometimes difficult to preserve efficiency down to the very foot of the sail. The reason for this is that the pull is too much aft and not sufficiently down, yet if you were to pull down on the clew of the sail, you would curve it too much in toward the mainsail. I have often resorted to the trick of tying a bucket to the balloon jib sheet and filling it partially with water, pouring it out or adding to it until I got just the desired weight. It is very easy to find quickly just how much weight is necessary to hold the ballooner down at the same time that it is sheeted aft. Care should be taken to tie the bucket up close to the sheet so that there will be no danger of it getting into the water. And this trick should not be resorted to unless there is enough wind to keep a constant and strong strain on the sheet. While the ballooner can be used with the wind slightly forward of the beam, its greatest efficiency is with the wind abaft the beam. Care should be taken not to use a ballooner with the wind too far forward. The reason for this is not that you can't carry it, but that it doesn't do much good and frequently the smaller jib is much more effective than the big ballooner.

In the small boat classes, the boats are usually not equipped with either ballooners or Genoas, but most of them do carry spinnakers. If there are no rules to the contrary and no general rules about the sheeting of a spinnaker, the spinnaker is often effectively carried as a ballooner by letting the boom go forward until it is just clear of the head stay, then guying it to windward and strapping it down to the deck. The spinnaker is then sheeted outside the shrouds in the same manner as a balloon jib. It is not so effective as a ballooner of course, because the luff is free and will sag. The consideration of the straight luff, however, is most important when on the wind. If the spinnaker must be sheeted inside the head stay and inside the shrouds, as many racing rules require, it is usually better not to attempt to carry it unless the wind is a point or more abaft the beam. Even then, its efficiency will be greatly impaired by the fact that the head stay will cut deep into the belly of the sail. In reaching, as on every other course, it is possible to have too much sail. Especially is this true of the light sails that may take charge and cause the boat to yaw to such an extent that she will not be traveling nearly as fast as she seems. And carrying sail is not the purpose of racing. Making the boat go fast through the water and over the bottom is more important than seeming heroic.

CHAPTER XVII

RUNNING—LIGHT SAILS

STRICTLY SPEAKING, a boat is running when she is square before the wind. If the wind is over her quarter or farther forward, she is sailing a broad reach, but for the purposes of racing, a run and a broad reach should be considered together. As a matter of actual practice one rarely has a direct run in a race. It usually partakes of the nature of a broad reach, so that this chapter will be devoted to the business of getting speed out of the boat not merely on a course dead before the wind but on the ordinary course that would be covered by the running leg of a triangular course.

At the outset the skipper must decide whether he will sail a straight course or tack down hill. The straight course is the shortest distance between two points, but the shortest distance is not necessarily the quickest course. Strange though it may seem to the layman, a boat travels more slowly directly before the wind than on any other course. It is therefore frequently advisable to convert a run into a series of broad reaches, first on one tack and then on another tack, jibing successively to stay near the base line. The determination to sail the straight course, or to tack down hill, depends upon many considerations— strength of wind, strength and direction of current, stability of wind, and tactics and speed of opponents.

If the wind is strong, it generally does not pay to tack down hill. The reason for this is that your opponents, sailing directly before the wind, will be traveling fast and will probably cover the shorter course more quickly than you can sail the longer course. If the tide is foul and strong, it may pay to tack down hill so that you will be meeting the current at an angle instead of straight on the bow. If the tide is fair and strong, it may pay to sail the straight course because of the reverse application of this principle. If your opponents are faster than you are when sailing dead before the wind, it may pay to tack down hill even though the wind is strong. You will lose anyway if you sail the same course they do, whereas you may have a chance if you sail a different course. If the wind shows signs of being variable, it may pay to sail the straight course even though other considerations would lead you to tack down hill. In any event, if there is danger of a shift of wind, any deviation from the straight course should be made in a series of short legs, jibing frequently to keep close to the base line. Otherwise you may put yourself in such a position that you will have to sail dead before the wind while your opponents will have the advantage of a reach.

Nevertheless, when the wind is light and neither the mainsail nor the spinnaker seems to be doing its best work, it nearly always pays to avoid the straight course and approach the mark in a series of tacks or, more strictly, jibes. If you should decide to sail the straight course, you must, of course, make the same sort of correction for current as you do on a reach, but inasmuch as your speed will probably be less on the average run than on the average reach, you must make a greater allowance for a cross current.

When you are sailing dead before the wind, your mainsail should be at right angles to your keel. By mainsail I do not mean main boom. The upper half of the sail sags off more on a course directly before the wind than on any other course, and to keep the mainsail dead before the wind, it is necessary to trim the main sheet sufficiently so that the sail itself and not the boom is at right angles to the wind. The lower half of the sail will thus be a little nearer the wind than the upper half, and the average area of the sail will be at right angles to the wind. The jib sheet must be trimmed so that the jib will draw. That can be determined by the trial and error method. Usually the best angle for the trim of the jib is almost flat amidships. If the spinnaker is sheeted straight across the boat, it is sometimes advisable to take in the jib entirely, and it should be stated as a principle that any sail that cannot be made to draw should be taken in because, unless it is working all the time, that sail is more of a hindrance than a help. I remember watching the *Zaida* overtake in rapid succession all the boats in the cruising class in the New York Yacht Club Regatta of 1932. As she rounded the last leg to start her run to the finish she carried a great press of sail, including an enormous parachute spinnaker. Then, one by one, she took off all the sail she was carrying, with the exception of the parachute. Every time she took off a sail her speed increased perceptibly. Finally, she crossed the finish far in the lead under nothing but the parachute spinnaker, traveling like a steam engine in the light airs.

On small boats not equipped with a spinnaker, every effort should be made to make the jib draw. This may be accomplished by the use of either a whisker pole or a sprit. Whisker poles are standard equipment in the Star class and may be seen in Fig. 28. In its most usual form, the whisker pole is equipped with jaws on one end and a long bronze spike on the other. The spike is poked through the clew cringle of the jib and the jaws rested against the mast. The jib is then sheeted home on the weather side. The proper length for the whisker pole is the distance between the clew cringle and the mast when the jib is at right angles to the keel of the boat. You will notice in the illustration, Fig. 28, that the jibs are all whiskered out exactly at right angles to the boat, whereas the main booms are trimmed sufficiently close so that the mainsail, on the average, is at right angles to the keel of the boat.

In the small boat classes on Great South Bay, a large number of boats have their jibs equipped with a sprit in place of a club or a loose foot. The sprit extends from the clew of the jib to the jib stay, bisecting the angle of the clew and perpendicular to the stay. A spritted jib will behave pretty well when pushed out on the side opposite the mainsail and held there by the main sheet. It does not behave so well as a whiskered jib, but makes a fair compromise when a spinnaker is not available.

The correct way to stop a spinnaker has been described in Chapter XIII. Perhaps, however, a few words may well be added in explanation. It is very difficult to stop a spinnaker on any boat because of the size of the sail and the relatively cramped quarters. It pays to do this work ashore, spreading the spinnaker out on a dry clean lawn for the purpose. If the spinnaker must be stopped on board, it is well to develop a ritual and technique for handling it. On the *Old Timer* the work is always done down in the cabin. Near the companionway is a large hook and the swivel ring at the head of the spinnaker is hung on the hook. The first six or eight feet are then rolled up and stopped and all of the sail that is thus stopped is hung in a loop over the hook. This gives us plenty of room to tackle the next stretch of sail. As each successive length of sail is properly stopped, it is looped up on the hook and out of the way. Inasmuch as the sail hangs from the hook, it is very easy to get the luff and leech together and roll the bunt of the sail into a tight furl.

Even in the lightest of airs, it pays to hoist your spinnaker in stops. This is true even in the smallest classes where the spinnaker is no more than a pocket handkerchief. If the course is sailed in two or three laps, it may be too distracting to stop the spinnaker between runs. In that case it is set flying. To the beginner, a spinnaker is a fearful thing. It is so big, so cumbersome, so apparently difficult to use that the novice is terribly afraid of it. But, as a matter of fact, the spinnaker is a very easy sail to set, to take in, and to handle. It requires very little man power and very little skill when the principle of the thing is once understood.

If you are sailing before the wind, there is no power whatever in a spinnaker flying from a boom that is pointing forward. Therefore, the proper way at all times to handle the spinnaker is to push the boom out forward. If the spinnaker is in stops, it may then be guyed aft. A slight pull on the sheet will break the lowest stops; the wind will get into the part of the sail that is broken out and break the remaining stops. The sail may then be sheeted and is set and drawing. I wish to repeat that only the lightest grade of cotton thread, preferably basting thread, should ever be used when stopping a spinnaker. This is sufficiently strong to hold a stopped spinnaker in all but the most powerful winds, and a spinnaker that does not break out its stops loses its efficiency. Such a spinnaker is shown in Fig. 22. It can be seen that the whole top of the spinnaker is not working and that the balance of the sail is working inefficiently. It is hard to tell from the illustration whether the stops have failed to break or whether the head of the spinnaker is twisted. Either of these faults has the same effect—that of decreased efficiency.

The spinnaker is taken in in reverse order to that in which it is set. One hand goes forward, releases the sheet and holds it in his hand. Another hand pays out the guy. If the boat is large and the crew ample, a third hand should go forward, take the spinnaker boom off the mast and push it back along the deck. He should make it a point to look aft when he is doing this, otherwise he is apt to brain someone in the crew. As he does this, the other hand gathers together the clew and the tack, releases the snap hook which holds the tack to the boom and gathers the sail into his arms. The man who has just housed the boom then goes to the halliards and lowers away while the other man collects the sail as it comes down. If the boat is large enough to have a hatch forward, the man who is collecting the sail should stow it down the hatch as fast as it descends. The halliard is unsnapped from the head board and both ends of the halliard are then made fast to the proper pin or cleat.

If the boat is small, it should never be necessary to send more than one man forward and the remainder of the crew should crowd aft to counteract his weight. A man forward while running on a small boat will so throw the boat out of balance that she will steer badly and slow down perceptibly. In that case, the following procedure should be observed in hoisting the spinnaker. We will assume that it is set flying. One hand goes forward from the cockpit on the side opposite to that on which the main boom is carried. He takes with him one end of the spinnaker guy which is neatly coiled in the cockpit and passes it outside backstays, runners, and shrouds as he goes. He snaps the hook into the ring at the end of the spinnaker pole, then he casts off the halliard, snaps one end to the swivel at the head of the spinnaker and leads the other end aft. He snaps the tack into the ring in the spinnaker boom, finds the sheet and either holds it or makes it fast. At a signal from him the helmsman or another man in the cockpit hoists on the halliard and sends the spinnaker aloft. As the spinnaker nears the truck of the mast, the hand forward picks up the boom and pushes it straight forward on the windward side of the head stay and rests the jaws on the mast or the inboard end in the socket. He lifts the boom high so as to get a slightly downward thrust. With a gaff-headed rig, he places the jaws of the spinnaker boom above one of the lower hoops. In a Marconi rig, it is well to have a bight of line around the mast to hold the boom up. As soon as the boom is on the mast, the helmsman or another hand trims the guy aft and the hand forward belays the sheet. This takes a long time in the telling. With a well-trained crew it can be done almost in the twinkling of an eye. All this is achieved with just one hand forward. With the spinnaker halliard led aft, it can be taken in in the same way with the one man forward gathering the sail in his arms. This is easily accomplished when he does not have to attend to the halliard.

If the boat is pursuing the strategy of tacking down wind, the halliard must not be allowed to stay aft as it would interfere with the frequent jibing necessary. But there is no reason why it cannot be taken aft after the last jibe as the mark is approached so that the halliard can be handled from the cockpit.

In a small boat one guy and a sheet are the only lines necessary for the correct handling of a spinnaker. On a larger boat it is always advisable to have two guys; one forward and one aft. On a still larger boat where the spinnaker boom is very long and heavy, it becomes necessary to have a lift. This lift is made fast to the outboard end of the spinnaker boom and is handled in much the same manner as a topping-lift. On the very large boats, the spinnaker booms may be equipped with tracks and outhauls. In such a case the boom is swung outboard and supported by the lift, guyed to its correct position by the forward and aft guys. Then the tack of the spinnaker is hauled out on the track by means of the outhaul and the spinnaker is broken out by a pull on the sheet.

The correct handling of a forward guy deserves consideration. On all but the largest boats this guy should be long enough to lead from the outboard end of the spinnaker boom to a ring or fairleader in the bow and aft to the cockpit. When both forward and after guys are trimmed hard they will effectively prevent the spinnaker boom from swinging up against the mast and taking charge. In light airs, even on large boats, a forward guy is frequently unnecessary. I find that I make use of it about half the time, but I always have it ready for instant use. As soon as it is determined on which side of the boat the spinnaker will be set, I rig the forward guy by snapping it into its proper ring and leading it along the boom so that it will head straight inboard when the spinnaker is set. It is then stopped to the boom by a series of thread stops in the same manner as the spinnaker itself. At the inboard end of the boom the guy is coiled down on deck. In case it should become necessary to use the guy it is an easy matter to lead the end of it through the ring in the bow and break the stops. With both forward and after guys leading to the cockpit, it is an easy matter to change the trim of the spinnaker boom. The forward and after guys are worked as a pair, trimming one and slacking the other at the same time. The correct trim of a spinnaker calls for close study. It differs somewhat in different boats and differs widely with two different spinnakers on the same boat. In most cases, the spinnaker is sheeted hard right straight across the boat and is trimmed at right angles to the wind. The principle is easy to state. The spinnaker should be trimmed at right angles to the wind and should be guyed as far aft as it will go without breaking at the luff. The luff of a spinnaker is the line that runs from the head of the mast to the outboard end of the spinnaker boom. The luff may always be distinguished from the leech in that it has a wire or heavy rope luff line. The opposite side is finished like the leech of any sail. Sometimes the luff and the leech are of the same length, but the side that is the more heavily reënforced is the luff. Take it as a principle that the luff should not break. If it breaks it means one of two things—either the spinnaker is not sheeted flat enough or the boom is guyed too far aft.

A spinnaker is most powerful when the air can escape from it. With the spinnaker, as with all other sails, the drive must come from live air. The dead air must escape. With the wind directly aft it is usually possible to carry the spinnaker sheet forward to the bow so that the wind blows on to the spinnaker and off at the leech. In this way the spinnaker is most powerful and gives a wonderful lift and drive to the boat. With the spinnaker thus sheeted forward and the mainsail trimmed a trifle flatter than is customary in sailing before the wind, it is possible to spill the air off the mainsail into the spinnaker, and off the spinnaker into the jib, thus keeping the air moving and giving an extra drive to the boat. It is not often, however, that the sheet of the spinnaker can thus be carried forward. The wind must be dead aft to do it. Most spinnakers seem to be cut too long in the foot. Sometimes the spinnaker with the shorter foot can be sheeted forward when a spinnaker with a longer foot cannot be.

The customary use of the spinnaker is when the wind is dead astern. The spinnaker can be carried, however, until the wind is almost abeam. If the boat is provided with a balloon jib, it does not pay to carry a spinnaker with the wind too far forward. If the boat lacks a ballooner, the spinnaker can be guyed very far forward, particularly if attention is paid to the proper use of the forward guy. Without the forward guy, a spinnaker boom that is too far forward tends to lift. By trimming the forward guy hard, this tendency can be corrected. If the rules permit, a spinnaker that is guyed forward can be made most efficient by passing the sheet around the head stay and outside the lee shrouds. In that way the spinnaker practically becomes a balloon jib. It pulls like a mule. Most racing rules, however, require that the spinnaker shall not pass to leeward of the head stay and must be sheeted inside the lee shrouds. This means that the spinnaker rubs against the head stay which cuts deeply into its belly and destroys a large part of its effectiveness. It means, too, that it cannot be sheeted efficiently and is almost certain to back-wind the mainsail. Unless the spinnaker can truly be said to be working hard, it is a poor sail to carry. It should be taken off and the jib should be given a chance.

Jibing the spinnaker is an easy matter with an alert crew. This is the procedure: One hand is sent forward. He frees the forward guy from its fair leader and leads it aft, outside the lee shrouds and runners. Then he casts off the sheet and holds it in his hand. Another hand aft pays out the after guy until the boom strikes the head stay. The hand forward then unships the boom from the mast and passes it aft on the lee side of the boat underneath the main boom, gathering the spinnaker in his arms, close to the mast. The mainsail is then jibed, the hand forward picks up the boom and thrusts it forward on the side of the head stay opposite to the side on which it had been set. The hand aft then trims on the guy that had been the forward guy before the jibe. The hand forward makes the sheet fast and reeves what had been the after guy through the forward chock so that it may act as a forward guy. To jibe the spinnaker, it is necessary that the forward guy shall be led through a chock or sister hook so that it can be freed before the jibe. Thus the forward guy becomes the after guy and the after guy becomes the forward guy. On big boats it is always wise to have two spinnaker booms so that it is not necessary to "jackass" the boom from one side to another on every jibe.

There are many skippers who believe that there is peculiar merit to a lifting spinnaker; they like to see the spinnaker bellying forward in a light round curve. To my mind there is little doubt that a well-rounded bellying spinnaker is more effective than a flat one provided, first, that the spinnaker is cut that way and, second, that there is plenty of wind. In very light airs it is easily possible to lose a large part of the power of the spinnaker by letting it lift too far. The wind does all its work in lifting the spinnaker instead of imparting drive to the hull. In general, therefore, a spinnaker that is cut rather flat should not be allowed to belly too much and it is better in light airs to have a spinnaker trimmed too flat than too full. The foot of the spinnaker may well be studied. The spinnaker that is carried high and lifting well may be spilling the wind off the foot. This gives an extra drive to the boat and, further, has the tendency of lifting and lightening the bow.

Of recent years a great development has taken place in the use of the parachute spinnaker. These enormous sails that cost a king's ransom and are most difficult to handle, are now generally regarded as an unfavorable development in yachting. Their use has probably come about through the fact that recent developments in the Marconi rig have tended to a very small area in working sails, with the result that these working sails are not particularly effective off the wind. Undoubtedly, legislation limiting or prohibiting the use of parachute spinnakers would have taken place long before this if it were not impossible to define them or to measure their area. They are carried from a short boom and sheeted around the head stay and around the lee shrouds. They are immensely effective and it is said that they can be carried with the wind as far forward as the beam. Whether a parachute spinnaker really adds power to a boat that has sufficient working sails when carried in this manner, it is too early to state with any degree of authority. In general, however, the parachute spinnaker is handled on the same principles as the ordinary spinnaker.

If it is possible to have more than one spinnaker on a boat, it is well to have a large one and also a small one, and to experiment with both spinnakers for different conditions of the wind. A small spinnaker that will draw is much better than a large one that will not draw. For ocean sailing it is well to have a spinnaker that can be reefed. Some of our most notable cruisers have small spinnakers with bonnets which can be laced along the foot. Thus one spinnaker and a bonnet will serve the purpose of a large spinnaker and a small one. By unlacing the bonnet, the spinnaker can be set high so that it is not in danger of being filled and torn away by the waves.

A fairly recent development in spinnakers is that of putting a series of large holes down the middle. These holes should be at least six inches in diameter and carefully reënforced. Their purpose is to allow the air in the spinnaker to escape. This probably adds efficiency to the spinnaker. The most noticeable result that I have observed in spinnakers with holes is that they are apt to stand steadier than spinnakers without holes, and steadiness in a spinnaker is a characteristic devoutly to be wished. Of two spinnakers of equal driving power, the one that stands steadier is the better.

As soon as the spinnaker is set, the skipper should pay off a hand to the after guy, the forward guy, and the sheet. These three hands should be trimming constantly. The spinnaker is most sensitive to very slight variations in the wind. I recall a private race in a strong wind from Newport to New London some years ago. We were tired and lazy and not particularly alert to the slight variations in the wind, which resulted in the spinnaker breaking from time to time. Our opponent, who sailed like a fiend, trimmed his spinnaker forty times to our once and gave us an outrageous beating. He declared afterwards that the only reason for his beating us so badly was his constant trimming and retrimming of the spinnaker. Other things being nearly equal, alertness on the trimming of the spinnaker will win on a leg to leeward. This failure constantly to retrim the spinnaker is probably the most usual omission on the part of otherwise alert skippers.

In a quartering wind, the combination of spinnaker and ballooner usually works well. With the wind somewhat farther aft, the combination of spinnaker and Genoa works even better. But if the wind gets too far aft, all light sails except the spinnaker are usually blanketed by the mainsail, so that they become more of a hindrance than a help. In Fig. 29, the ballooner is obviously holding the boat back by flapping around more than it is pulling her ahead. In cases like this it is far better to use an ordinary jib, or to use no headsails at all. In Fig. 30, we see a spinnaker that is working at nearly its maximum efficiency and no headsails are carried. But when sailing thus dead before the wind, I have always found it better to sheet the spinnaker forward and spill the escaping air from it into the jib.

When running in a heavy sea, or sailing in very light airs, it is wise to rig a preventer to the main boom, particularly in light airs when motor boats are kicking up a swirl. The preventer is worth all the trouble it takes to rig it. The preventer will work wonders in keeping the sail from slatting about. It will keep the main sheet from dragging in the water. It will steady the whole boat and it will keep the wind from flapping out of the sail. If the main sheet is rigged on bridles on the boom, the blocks should slide forward on the bridles when sailing before the wind. In light airs it sometimes pays to pull the blocks forward with a boat-hook, or even to make fast a piece of string to the blocks so that they can be pulled toward the forward end of the bridles when the boom is out at right angles to the boat. This is very effective in keeping the main sheet out of the water. Lacking a preventer, it is often worth while to send a man forward to sit on the tack of the mainsail with his feet braced against the house or the coaming to push the main boom forward.

When sailing before the wind, a baggy mainsail is a great help. A mainsail that stands too flat does not develop nearly as much power. It is possible to make the mainsail bag by slacking somewhat on the halliards and the boom outhaul, by trimming the windward topping-lift and even by tightening the windward lazy-jacks. These adjustments should be made only in light airs and only when the run is the last leg of the race. If there is another leg to windward and if it is blowing hard, it is sometimes impossible to get the sail back to the proper trim when the course is changed. Furthermore, in the excitement of the race, one is very apt to forget these little adjustments and if they are forgotten for only a few minutes while sailing on the wind, it may be enough to cost you the race.

In a shoal draft boat the centerboard is always hoisted clear out of the water on a run. The only exceptions are when the boat rolls, yaws, or steers badly. In that case, just enough of the centerboard is lowered to overcome the difficulty.

In sailing before the wind when it is blowing hard, or in a heavy sea, care must be taken not to jibe accidentally. The matter of the accidental jibe is fully discussed in "Learning to Sail." Suffice it here to say that the accidental jibe occurs when the boat is sailing by the lee: that is to say, when the wind is blowing from the same side of the boat on which she carries her mainsail. It must be borne in mind that the jibe is governed by the relation of the direction of the wind to the hull, not by the relation of the direction of the wind to the sail. If the wind is only slightly to port of the center of the boat, the mainsail may be trimmed flat on the starboard side without danger of jibing, even though there may be a very narrow angle between the direction of the wind and the trim of the sail. If, however, the sail is broad off on the starboard side and the wind comes only slightly over the starboard quarter, the danger of an accidental jibe is very great. Let us discuss for a minute the technique of the jibe. I have always maintained that the safest jibe is also the fastest jibe. To jibe in a race, bring the wind distinctly over the quarter opposite to that on which the boom is carried, and trim the main sheet as fast as possible. When the main sheet is amidships then, and not until then, put the helm up gently. When the boom has crossed over to the other side, hang on to the sheet—do not let it run—then pay out slowly. In this way you keep the boat footing all the time. Most yachtsmen like to go into a flying jibe in the North River manner, letting the sails swing violently from one side to another and letting the sheet run. This is dramatic, exciting, and hard on the gear, but the sail, flying forward stops the boat more than it drives her ahead. Trimming in quickly does help drive the boat ahead but paying out slowly should always be the order of the day. On a big boat it is always wise to make the sheet fast just before the jibe is completed. Then the sheet can be cast off and payed out.

The trim of the hull should be watched carefully in sailing before the wind. As a rule the bow tends to bury itself. The weight of all the sails is carried forward. The pressure of the wind on the sails tends to bury the bow. This is usually counteracted by moving the crew aft and by getting as much lift as possible to the spinnaker. This should not, however, be taken as an unalterable rule. I know two ancient and honorable skippers in the 30-Foot class, both of whom have had long and successful records. One always carries his live weight forward when sailing before the wind; the other always carries his live weight aft. It will pay to study your boat in company with other boats and move your weight forward or aft to the best advantage. In very small boats I have always made it a rule to carry my weight aft.

Chapter XVIII

TURNING MARKS

The correct handling of a boat at the marks has been stressed by every writer and speaker on the subject of yacht racing. On any leg, beating, reaching, or running, the boats may sail a widely divergent course, but they must all round the marks and usually round as closely to the marks as possible. This means that boats that have been sailing clear of one another for several miles draw together in the narrow zone at each corner of the course. Furthermore, it is at the marks that precious seconds are won or lost. The business of rounding marks correctly is usually complicated by a highly competitive situation so that we must consider our turning not merely in the light of getting the utmost speed possible out of the boat, but also in the light of bringing her into the best tactical situation for both offensive and defensive purposes.

When sailing close-hauled on the wind, the first problem in turning is the correct approach to the mark. Care should be exercised to approach it on the starboard tack to obtain and maintain right-of-way over your opponent, and neither to fall short of the mark nor to overstand it. In general, boats go about in eight points, four points from the wind on the starboard tack and four points from the wind on the port tack. In other words, in going about, they are usually able to make good a course at right angles to the course on which they were sailing. Occasionally very close-winded boats can do a trifle better than this. Heavy cruising schooners, boats with baggy sails, and boats that are improperly tuned take from eight and one-half to nine points to go about. It is essential that you should know just what course you can lay and make good. If you can make it in eight points, you should go about exactly when the mark bears abeam. The skipper should arrange some means whereby he can sight directly abeam from his position at the tiller. On some of the small boats I have owned, it has been an easy matter to lean backward a little and sight along the after edge of the cockpit. Two brass nails driven flush into the cockpit coaming and the rail make an excellent sighting vane. On the *Old Timer* I place a hand in the companionway to sight along the after edge of the cabin-house. Any line that runs directly across the boat from side to side at right angles to the keel makes a good sighting vane to tell when the mark is abeam. In any close-winded boat that will go about in less than eight points, or in any boat that takes more than eight points in going about, you should have a specially constructed sighting vane laid to the new course.

If the boat is equipped with a binnacle and sighting hood or an azimuth ring, or other means of taking accurate compass bearings, it is possible to note the exact course which the boat makes good on both the starboard and port tacks. The one hand at the compass can sight along the correct compass bearing and report the time when the boat can lay the mark on the opposite tack. A boat is certain to lose valuable seconds at the mark without some means for determining accurately whether or not she can lay it.

There are many skippers who take great pride in sailing a windward leg in just two tacks, being able to stand right up to the mark on the second tack without overstanding. Such an achievement is proof of great skill, but is not the best of racing strategy. In the first place, a boat that is properly tacked loses little time, if any, in going about. In the second place, regardless of skill of the skipper, a boat may very easily overstand the mark if she approaches it on too long a tack. In such circumstances, a slight shift of wind may upset all calculations and compel the boat to sail much farther to windward than would otherwise have been necessary. In the third place, the tactical considerations around the mark are usually highly involved, and a boat should get into this zone of combat if possible before reaching the mark in order that she may legally interfere with her competitors. Of course, in doing so she runs the risk of being interfered with by her competitors, but unless the skipper faces that risk, he runs the chance of another boat getting by, which otherwise he could have stopped. The rule, then, is to take your long tacks early in the beat to windward, but approach the mark on several pairs of short tacks. If the windward mark is not set out directly to windward, it is usually the best strategy to sail on the course that lies nearest the mark for the greater part of the distance, to get on that tack as early as possible, hold it until near the mark, then tack successively so that you can lay it on the starboard tack.

In calculating whether or not you can lay the mark, it is always necessary to allow for leeway and for current. The better the boat, the less allowance need be made for leeway, but it should be remembered that it is the course made good that counts, and not the course

steered. If current is against you, you must, of course,
head higher than the mark; if current is with you, it
may be depended upon to set you ahead toward the
mark. The considerations of current, leeway, and the
varying conditions of going about, make this business
of laying the mark deliciously complicated without any
consideration of the tactics made necessary by the competitive situation. When they are added to it, it is very
seldom, indeed, that a yacht is handled with absolute
perfection at the important turning points.

When it comes to the business of turning the mark
itself, the preservation of speed becomes of paramount
importance. Speed must be preserved all the way
around from one course to the next. To preserve speed
it is first necessary to know the exact radius in which
your boat is capable of turning efficiently. A small boat
turns in a small radius, a large boat in a large one, a
boat that is short on the bottom, with long overhang-
ing ends will turn in a much shorter radius than a boat
with a long straight keel. A boat with long overhangs
will turn in a short radius in light to moderate airs, but
requires a much longer radius when it is blowing hard.
The only way to determine the turning radius of your
boat is to practice rounding marks from every conceivable angle under varying conditions of wind. You will
soon get the hang of getting around while keeping the
boat moving at all times. If somewhere in your turning, the boat definitely loses headway, it means one of
two things: Either the sails have not been trimmed
properly to the constantly changing relative angle of
the wind, or it means that you have turned in too short
a radius. As a rule, the fastest course around the mark
is steered as follows: You do not approach the mark
too closely; you start to turn quite some time before

you are up to it; and your turn is practically complete and you are sailing on your new course just as the mark draws abeam. Turning in that way you preserve the natural turning radius, maintain full speed throughout the entire turn, and hold the inside of the course all the way. If you run close to the mark and then turn,

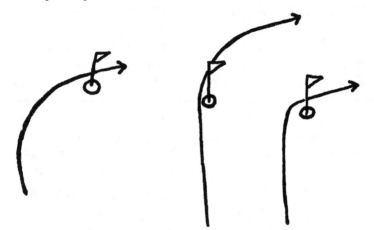

Fɪɢ. 31. Right and wrong courses around a mark. Left —correct. Center—incorrect. Too close to mark before the turn; too far away after the turn. Right—incorrect. Turning radius too short.

the turn is generally too short for the natural turning radius, and when you straighten out on the next course, you are far on the outside and not so far ahead. The diagram in Fig. 31 will make this clear. Such a course can be steered around a mark only when there are no other boats to interfere. If there are other boats attempting to squeeze between your boat and the mark, it is necessary that you should stay close into the mark to prevent them getting an overlap between you and the mark in rounding, or so that you, on your part, will have an overlap on any boat outside of you. This will be explained later.

You can lay it down as an axiom that in rounding the windward mark, you should always approach it on the starboard tack. If your race is so planned that you approach it on the port tack, you have committed an error in tactics that is excusable only when there is no other boat within striking distance. The starboard tack is at all times important, but never more important than at a mark. If two boats meet out in the course, one on the port and one on the starboard tack, the boat on the port tack gives way or goes about and no harm is done. If her skipper is wise, he will tack under the lee of the boat on the starboard tack, back-wind him, stop him, and climb out ahead. But if these two boats meet at the mark, the boat on the starboard tack forces the other boat about when she distinctly does not want to go about, carries her wherever he pleases, then goes about at his leisure, with full command of the right-of-way. This is inevitably disastrous to the boat that held the port tack. There is no possible way of turning it to his advantage. If, therefore, there is any remote possibility that you will meet a boat at the mark while you are on the port tack, go about before you get there and have your dog fight before you get near the mark. If you should hold the starboard tack at the mark and meet a competitor on the port tack, force him about, then carry him away from the mark. Look all around you to see that no other boat is using this opportunity to slip in ahead of you. If you have a fair lead over your other competitors, hold the starboard tack for some distance beyond the mark, carrying your competitor farther and farther away. This always has the effect of making him uneasy and usually upsets his temper to the point where he sails a poor race thereafter. He never realizes that in order to carry him away from the mark you are sailing away from it yourself. Just when the air is getting sufficiently blue around the competing boat, and the profanity begins to trickle across the water, then go about quickly but smoothly. Your competitor will be so upset that he will follow slowly and you will gain an immense advantage. This is absolutely allowed under the racing rules, and is fitting punishment for any boat that approaches the mark on the port tack.

If you are approaching on the port tack while your competitor is approaching on the starboard tack, be prepared to make a fake tack; notify your crew that the tack you plan is a fake, then if you see that your opponent is holding his course in order to force you about, push down the helm as if you meant it, cry "Hard alee" at the top of your voice; have your crew scurry around as if they were trimming for the other tack. Usually at this point your opponent will go about, especially if you are both pressed by another boat. You will have shot your boat up a little into the wind, and the minute you see your opponent's tiller go down, bear away again and you will follow him right around the mark without losing the distance you would have lost in tacking.

The question of room around the mark is not always clearly understood. If you are approaching the mark, let us say, on your starboard hand, and another boat overtakes you to starboard so that she has an overlap of her bow past your stern or any other part of your sail, spars, or rigging, she can call for room around the mark. If that is the case, you must give her room by bearing away if necessary, and must not interfere with her until she has rounded the mark. In other words, she has right-of-way from the time of the overlap until you are around and sailing on your next course. It must be understood that this right-of-way is contingent upon proximity to the mark. It does not apply except in the immediate vicinity of the mark and just as the boats are about to round, otherwise the rules governing overtaking apply and not the rules for turning marks. If, however, you are right up to the mark and have altered your helm for rounding, the other boat cannot establish an overlap between you and the mark but must go outside of you. The question of right to room around the mark is usually a disagreeable situation to fight out, not because the rules are not clear, but because questions of fact are so difficult to establish. It is always hard to determine whether or not the overlap was gained before or after the right to demand room around the mark had ceased. It is also usually a question of fact as to whether the rules for overtaking boats govern the situation or rules for turning marks. If you are the overtaking boat and want room around the mark, call out in loud, clear tones, demanding the right to room around the mark in those very words so that your intention and the basis of your rights may be clearly established. You may not claim room until after you have established an overlap. If, as sometimes happens in light airs, you lose that overlap before you round the mark, you lose the right to room.

It is a general rule of yacht racing to keep between your competitors and the mark. In later chapters it will be seen that this rule does not always apply; that there are times and conditions in shifting winds when the rules should be abandoned for other considerations, but at any approach to the mark that rule should predominate. Suppose, then, that your opponent tacks to approach the mark on the port tack. Should you cover him, or should you approach on the starboard tack? The answer is to cover him, then go about in time to take a short hitch to the mark on the starboard tack, making sure that you have allowed enough room to gather full headway after making the last tack to the mark. In a light, shifting wind you may be approaching the mark on the starboard tack with a competitor behind you and to weather. The wind shifts and you are about to start your sheet and travel a bit faster and lay the mark. The temptation to do it is almost irresistible, but if your opponent stands higher than the mark, you should stand just as high as he does, because if the wind should shift back again, you will find yourself to leeward of the mark while your opponent can sail to it with a rap full.

On any reaching or running course it is important to hold the inside position at the mark. Not only will an overlap guarantee you room, but for some reason or other the inside boat always seems to be out ahead after rounding. A study of Fig. 32 will bear out the wisdom of this procedure. Study first the positions of the boats in Fig. 32A. You will note that 37 and 42 are about abreast but that 37 is nearer the mark, has the inside position, and is sailing with sheets trimmed a little closer and is therefore probably traveling a little faster.

In Fig. 32B, both boats have jibed and 37 has worked out a commanding lead.

Now let us go back to Fig. 32A and compare the positions of the next group of boats. Behind the mainsail of 42 may be seen the leech of 12. She appears to be a length ahead of 235 which, in turn, is slightly ahead of 1 and 33. These two boats are about on an equal footing.

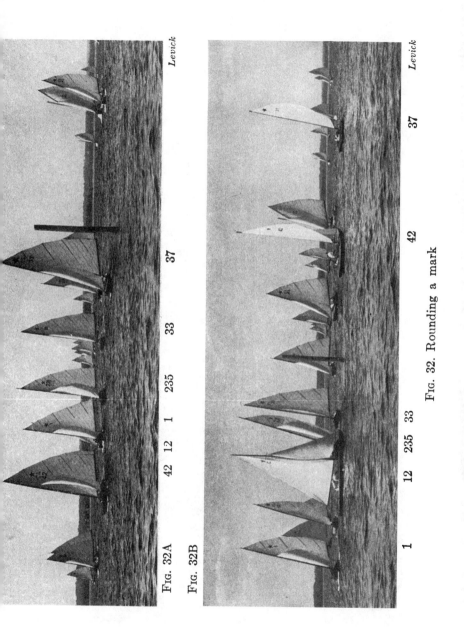

FIG. 32A

FIG. 32B

42   12   1   235   33   37   *Levick*

12   235   33   42   37   *Levick*

1

FIG. 32. Rounding a mark

FIG. 41. On the hair line between the leeward boat's backwind zone and the windward boat's wind shadow.

If we look at these boats in Fig. 32B, however, we will find that in each case the inside boat has improved her position somewhat. 12 is in the act of jibing, and 235 is altering her course to jibe. She will doubtless have an overlap, may blanket 12, and in general will be in a better position. Both 235 and 33 will beat 1 around the mark. If height of masts is compared, it will be evident that 33 is just as near the camera as 1 and the two boats are almost in the same relative positions as 37 and 32 in Fig. 32A.

If you are reaching or running to a mark, then turn it and lay a course to windward, it is always necessary to decide whether you will trim sheets and sail on the wind or tack at once. The decision is governed by the tactical situation. Let us suppose you are out ahead and are closely pressed by the second boat. If you trim sheets and sail on the same tack on which you approach the mark, the other boat will tack; if you tack, the other boat will trim sheets. Therefore, if you are closely pressed, the best situation is to trim sheets and tack when your opponent tacks. If you are not so closely pressed, the decision is more difficult. If you trim sheets and your opponent tacks, he will be so far behind you that you cannot cover him. If, on the other hand, you tack and he trims, the situation will be the same. In that case, the best tactics are to trim your sheets and sail for a short distance beyond the mark on the same tack on which you approached it, then tack before your opponent gets to the mark. You will then be in a position either by holding your course, or by tacking, to cover him whichever way he goes. You will lose nothing by this maneuver because it will place you to windward of your opponent and you can keep him covered regardless of his course.

Suppose you finish first in the run and the next course is a beat. No boat is pressing you sufficiently closely to worry you for the moment, but there are other boats behind you that you know are faster than you are on the wind. They are sailing down to the mark you have just rounded with sheets fully started and spinnakers guyed out. In such a situation it very often happens that if you tack at the mark you can sail right back into the fleet, holding right-of-way and compelling them all to go off their course, letting the spinnakers fly, trimming sheets, and otherwise disturbing the policy of their racing. Such tactics are legitimate and fair sportsmanship. But by all means make known your presence by loud hails, because the chances are always in favor of a boat that is running failing to realize that a boat that is beating may sail in directly the opposite direction and, with mainsail and spinnaker "wung out," it is frequently hard for the skipper to see ahead. You are justified in making a running boat alter her course; you are equally justified in protesting her if she fails to do so and forces you about, but you are not justified in colliding with her.

Jibing at a mark calls for the utmost skill of skipper and crew. It calls for nice judgment to know just when to take in the spinnaker. It is usually a fatal error to carry the spinnaker too long, but surely no boat is properly sailed on which the spinnaker is taken in too soon. The spinnaker should be carried until the last possible minute in which to take it in and get the men back to their stations for jibing. Since the course after jibing is always a reach, or a beat, the sheets are never paid out after the jibe beyond the point where they will be properly trimmed for the next course.

The principal faults in the jibing itself lie, first, in

jibing too soon. A boat should not be jibed until she can be trimmed on her new course. Second, in jibing too late. Many precious seconds are lost in boats sailing beyond the mark because of their inability to complete the jibe. Third, in letting the sheets run after the jibe has been completed. Fourth, in turning in too short a radius. Jibing too late is usually the result of insufficient man power to get the sheets in quickly, or the result of foozling the spinnaker. Jibing too soon is the result of a nervous skipper, underestimating the capacity of his crew to trim the sheets. When you jibe too soon, one of two things happens: Either the sheets are trimmed amidships many seconds before you reach the mark, the jibe is delayed until the mark is abeam, and these precious seconds are lost through destroying the driving power of the sails, or else the jibe is completed too soon and the boat is sailing by the lee up to the mark. Many a mark is fouled by this procedure.

It is not necessary to get the spinnaker completely housed, the halliard unbent and belayed, the guys and sheets trimmed and coiled, in taking in the spinnaker. Get it in below deck in any way you can, leaving halliards, sheets, and guys all in a mess if necessary. Jibe the boat, then tidy up your lines. If this is borne in mind, you will take much less time in stowing the spinnaker and can therefore carry it almost up to the mark. It must be borne in mind that the spinnaker is much more effective at the end of a run than at the beginning of a run. Occasionally, it is a distinct handicap to break the spinnaker out too soon. Even if the spinnaker is set, it may take several minutes to get it drawing properly. But at the end of a run you have been monkeying with it for several miles and it is at its greatest efficiency. Hence, the reason for carrying it just as long as possible. If, after turning the mark, the next course is to be a run, it sometimes pays to sail a little beyond the mark in order to get a course as far as possible to leeward before altering your course. The boat that is farthest to leeward can trim her sheets a trifle closer than her competitors and will, therefore, travel faster. If, after turning the mark, the next course is to be a reach, it will distinctly pay to place your boat on some course not directly astern of any competitor's. As a rule, the first boat to round the mark sails right on the proper course; the second boat to round the mark stands up to windward; the third boat around will stand up to windward of the second boat. In such a case, the fourth boat would do well to bear away to leeward. She would thus be nearer to the base line of the course, be out of the Zone of Interference of the other boats, and unless it is a very close reach, will probably sail a faster course. Naturally, considerations of tide and current will enter into such a determination, but as I write this I recall to mind one race in which we quickly climbed from fourth to first place by this little trick of bearing away after rounding the mark, despite the fact that the current was strong and all the other boats were heading "up tide." In light airs with strong currents, allow plenty of sea-room at the marks. Especially where government buoys are used as marks of the course it is well to beware of extra strong currents. Usually these buoys are placed where there is a sudden shoaling in the bottom around which the currents run with extra force.

Perhaps a word should be said about rudder action in general, although it is pretty elementary. A boat does not turn the way an automobile does. In the ordinary sloop the pivotal point is just about under the step of the mast. In other words, when you move your rudder, you turn the stern of the boat, not the bow. The place about which it pivots is forward of the center, not amidships. If, therefore, you find yourself being set down upon a buoy and have barely pushed your bow past it, turn the bow toward the buoy, not away from it. What you will really do is turn your stern away from the buoy. The bow already having passed it, is clear and may safely be turned toward the buoy since you are moving forward. Any attempt to steer the boat the other way will drive the stern into the buoy and disqualify you. It is well, in turning the mark, thus close aboard, to warn all hands not to touch the buoy. If you or your crew should be inspired to helpfulness and try to hold the buoy off, touching it with hand, or foot, or boat-hook, you are disqualified. Also, see to it that no articles of clothing, lines, dragging spinnaker guys or Irish pennants touch the buoy in rounding. I have known a boat to be disqualified because the collar of a sailor blouse blew out from the wearer's back just at the moment that the flag on the buoy dipped in a sea. Neither the wearer of the blouse nor anyone on board perceived this foul, but it was clearly noted by the entire crew of the following boat and the result was a protest and disqualification. Use extra care to prevent the spinnaker or the spinnaker boom from getting into the water in making a jibe around the mark. If it is blowing, you are likely to lose your spinnaker and boom, but even if it is not blowing, the spinnaker that is overboard takes charge so that it is impossible to do anything with the rudder. If by any chance this should happen, the only way the skipper can save the situation is by putting his helm down promptly, using the rudder to turn the boat in the same direction in which the spinnaker is already turning her, thus cutting inside the mark, then, after the spinnaker is recovered, he can sail back and around the mark, losing a couple of minutes in the process, but not being disqualified. If by any chance you should foul the mark in rounding, withdraw from the race at once. Such a foul should never be the subject of a protest, because the rule requires that the offending skipper shall disqualify his own boat.

CHAPTER XIX

OPPORTUNISM—TIDES AND CURRENTS

THE TERMS used in the conduct of a race are usually loosely applied. Two words have gotten into the vocabulary of the racing yachtsman and are usually regarded as synonyms. They are "strategy" and "tactics." I will distinguish between strategy and tactics and would also add one other term, a manufactured term, "opportunism." Let us try to distinguish between the three. Strategy is the general plan of a race, determined by the course, the natural conditions governing the course, the capabilities of the boat and crew, the capabilities of opposing boats, and the like. Tactics are those maneuvers which are determined by the course or position of an opponent. "Opportunism" are those maneuvers which are determined by natural causes over which none of the competitors have any control.

Let us elaborate these definitions. You are sailing on the starboard tack, an opponent is about to meet you on the port tack. Your strategy requires that you continue on the starboard tack to get a slant of wind and a favorable current which you know to be ahead, but you realize that by going about you can back-wind your opponent, stop him, climb ahead by using his wind as well as your own, and gain a great advantage over him. You go about. This is a tactical maneuver because it is determined by the course and position of your opponent. You have abandoned the strategy of the race to take advantage of this situation. You stop him, put him temporarily out of the race so far as you are concerned, then resort to your original strategy by standing over on the other tack to take advantage of a favorable wind and favorable current. This is "opportunism." It is determined by the wind and the current —factors over which neither you nor your opponents have any control. In the planning of this book I have placed opportunism before tactics, not because it is more important but because the business of racing can be more clearly understood if the beginner realizes how to get the greatest possible speed out of his boat without competition and then considers his competitive moves separately.

It must be understood that in any race, strategy, opportunism, and tactics overlap one another and crowd in upon the skipper's mind in no such clearly defined manner as this book might lead him to believe, but the only way to understand the problems is to dissect them on the operating table and consider them one at a time.

There are many factors which cover opportunism. The most important is the wind; the second most important group consists of tides and currents; the third group includes obstructions to sea-room and conditions of the water, the bottom, and other factors.

In this chapter we will consider tides and currents. Tides and currents are frequently used synonymously. This is an error. The term "tide" should be used only to refer to the height of water; the term "current" should be applied to the flow of water which results in a rising or falling tide. Tide has one dimension only—

height. Current has two—strength and direction. Most skippers depend for their tidal data on what is known as local knowledge, and local knowledge is generally a pretty undependable thing. This has been demonstrated to me so often by the erroneous local wisdom to which I have given credence that I have learned to distrust it entirely. The government publishes scientific data on tides and on currents. The tides and currents of the entire Atlantic coast are published in two little publications which can be purchased for twenty-five cents. Full instructions for the use of these publications are presented in the publications themselves.

A word about tides, however, will not be amiss. The tide is determined by two factors: The pull or attraction of the moon and the pull or attraction of the sun. Since the moon is so much nearer the earth than the sun, the moon exercises the greater attraction. When the moon and the sun are on the same side of the earth, they are pulling in the same direction. It is then we have what is known as the "springs" which result in a far higher tide and a far lower tide than the mean or average. When the sun and moon are pulling in opposite directions, however, the tide neither rises nor falls so greatly. These small tides are known as neaps. The exact height of rise and fall can be figured from the tide tables so that at any time you can apply the necessary correction for the tide to the height of the mean low tide on the chart. By means of these corrections, you can always tell pretty accurately without the use of a hand lead exactly how much water is beneath your keel, provided you know exactly where you are. The current tables give the time of the change of current due to the tidal changes.

The current tables are more important to the racing

man than the tide tables. They should be studied most
carefully. It is not the province of this book to go into
too lengthy a discussion on tides and currents, but certain things should be noted. Not every skipper knows
that the change in current direction does not coincide
with height of water. The current may not change
until an hour or two after the tide has turned so that
the time of high water as given in racing instructions
may really prove misleading if the skipper relies upon
it as an indication of the change of current. Another
thing that is not generally known is that the current
on the ebb does not always take the opposite direction
to the current on the flood. There are places where
both the flood and the ebb set toward the shore. There
are other places where the ebb runs almost at right
angles to the flood. Another consideration is that in
places just a mile or two apart there may be as much
as an hour's difference in the change and direction of
the current. Thus, there are noticeable differences in
time between the change of current direction on the
north shore of Long Island Sound and on the south
shore. There will be a difference in the current off
points and in the neighboring bights of the shore. At
the eastern end of Long Island Sound, where the whole
Sound empties and fills up through The Race, Plum
Gut, and Fisher's Island Sound, the tidal currents run
like a crazy quilt, apparently without rime or reason.
Thus at one and the same time a boat sailing East
through The Race could be stopped dead at one point
and a few hundred yards away be getting a tremendous
lift from the current. There is an hour's difference between slack water at The Race and slack water in
Plum Gut. These things will bear the closest possible
study. For nearly all navigable waters, tide and cur-

rent tables can be obtained that will give exact data for every hour of every day in the year, and no skipper should attempt to start a race without knowing in advance the strength and direction of the currents with which he must contend. There is a time between flood and ebb tide at which there is no perceptible current. This is known as slack water. It occurs three or four times a day, depending on the phases of the moon. As stated before, slack water is not necessarily coincident with high or with low tide, but slack water for every point along the coast may be figured from the current tables. Slack water is given in the current tables for a definite hour and minute, but it must be remembered that for an hour or so before slack water, and for an hour or so after slack water, current is a very unimportant factor and may practically be neglected.

What must be borne in mind, however, is that while you have slack water, your opponents a mile or so away may have a favorable or an unfavorable current to take into consideration. One would think that the current tables were all that are necessary in planning the strategy of a race, but height of tide enters into it too. Let us assume that you are sailing East on Long Island Sound in one of those calm breathless days in August. All the wind there is comes from the Southwest. Under these conditions there is usually no wind at all out in the middle of the Sound, but in under the shore a little breeze will be sucked by the difference in temperature between the land and the water. If you are sailing a boat of deep draft when the tides are at their springs, and it is dead low tide, you will probably not dare stand in sufficiently under the shore to get the advantage of this little suction wind. If, on the other hand, the tide is high, very much higher than the average, you can stand right in close under the shore without much fear of striking the bowlders with which that shore is dotted. You will know that you can carry a six-foot draft almost within a few feet of the shore. This, of course, is too dangerous to attempt but you can nevertheless sail well inside the string of black buoys. The knowledge of the height of tide may be the consideration that will win the race because it will enable you to venture much farther into the wind zone than your more timid opponents who may not have a tide table on board.

There is one other book which should make a general appeal to any racing man who sails on Long Island Sound. This is the publication of the United States Coast and Geodetic Survey No. 174, entitled "Tides And Currents In Long Island And Block Island Sounds." At the time this book is written, this is the only publication of its sort printed in the United States, but more publications will follow soon until eventually all the tidal data of all coastal waters will be presented in this form. What makes this book so valuable to the racing man is the series of charts, printed in the back of the book, which shows graphically, by means of arrows and figures, the exact direction and strength of the current for every part of Long Island and Block Island Sounds for every hour of the day.

If you will consult Fig. 33 which is a current chart, reproduced from the "Tides And Currents In Long Island And Block Island Sounds" you will note at the eastern end of the Sound in The Race, Fisher's Island Sound, and Plum Gut, the different directions at which the tide runs at the same time. It is obvious that what may be a head tide in one place will be a fair tide in

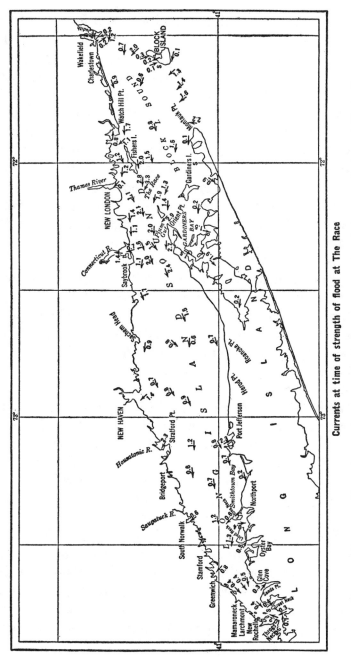

Currents at time of strength of flood at The Race

Fig. 33. Current Chart from government publication. Reprinted by permission of U. S. Coast and Geodetic Survey

another. There are times when you will get a foul tide
on one side of the passage, such as The Race, and a
fair tide on the other side. Currents rushing in one direction frequently set up eddies that go in the opposite
direction and are circular in motion. This is believed to
be caused by the friction of the shore and sometimes
by the friction of the bottom. It is well known that
water flowing through a pipe travels faster in the center of the pipe than around the edges. In the same way,
the current runs stronger in the center of a river or the
center of a creek. Where there is a bend in a river or a
creek, the current is strongest along the inside of the
bend and weakest along the outside. So true is this
that as a general rule the deepest water of the channel
follows the inside of the bend. Off the end of a point
the current is usually strong and follows the direction
of the main current, but along the sides of the point
and along the bights of shores between points, a reverse eddy is sometimes noticed. Playing these reverse
eddies in a foul tide is a very great help in winning a
race.

I remember one race to Block Island in which we
were a very bad last. We had drifted all night in a calm
and had been unable to get any noticeable steerage
way. When morning broke we were to the north of
Orient Point and through the dim mists we saw the
last of the fleet ahead of us already through Plum Gut.
The tide had been running flood for an hour through
The Race and for two hours through Plum Gut. With
this foul tide I concluded that it was better to go
through The Race, bucking a weaker, unfavorable tide
for a longer time, rather than to attempt the Gut
where I would have a stronger tide against me for a
shorter time. Furthermore, inasmuch as all the rest of

the fleet had gone through Plum Gut, my only chance of making a showing was to sail through The Race even if the circumstances had been such as to make The Race seem less desirable. I was beaten anyway so it seemed best to gamble on getting a break rather than on following the rest of the fleet blindly. Therefore, we sailed through The Race, hugging the shore of Plum Island and Great Gull and Little Gull Islands. Presently, we struck a current that stopped us as if we had hit a stone wall. The boat was thrown back on herself, and then I noticed that the water had a circular motion. I tried again, a little closer to the shore, and was given a forward lift that sent the boat tearing ahead. Thereafter, I kept my eyes on the water. I have never seen eddies so distinct and recognizable. Without any difficulty at all I could see from the motion of the water just where it was flowing in our direction. We altered course perhaps twenty times, but when we emerged beyond Little Gull Island, eight of our competitors were astern. It is not often that you can pick the eddies with the certainty with which I handled them on that misty morning, nor are they always as pronounced in their effect.

The business of catching the tide is a most disturbing element in the handicapping of boats in distance racing. At points where the current is strong, such as in The Race, or Plum Gut, or Fisher's Island Sound, a large fast boat may have worked out a lead, saved her time, and then be stopped by the tide. She may wait there two or three hours while the smaller, slower boats, coming up through a stretch in which the current is weaker, will catch the bigger boats just as the tide turns. The favorable current will then whisk the small boats on almost as fast as the big ones, particularly if the air is light. In such a case a large boat has not the slightest chance of overcoming the handicap given to the smaller boats. On the other hand, a large boat may get out ahead and get through a place like Plum Gut or The Race on a favorable tide. The smaller boats, struggling along an hour or two later, may still be well within their time allowance, but when they strike the unfavorable tide they stand still, while the big boats, having passed the neck of the bottle, romp on to victory. I have known races from Execution Light to Stratford Shoal and back in which the big boats, working out ahead, had a favorable tide all the way to the Light, turned the Light at slack water, and had a favorable tide all the way home; the smaller boats, lagging behind, would have a fair tide half way to the Light, a foul tide the rest of the way to the Light, a fair tide perhaps a third of the way home, and a foul tide two-thirds of the way home. Such a tide would prevent the smaller boats from winning even though their handicaps were two or three times that of the time allowance tables.

Occasionally, this turn of the tide is very dramatic and very sudden. I recall one race from Newport to New London with a strong East wind behind us and spinnaker flying all the way. Before we reached Point Judith my opponent had worked out a comfortable lead and was wallowing along in the big seas safely ahead. We tried hard to catch him, but succeeded only in preventing his gaining further. By the time we reached Watch Hill at the entrance to Fisher's Island Sound, he had a lead of perhaps five minutes. It is hard to estimate time in such circumstances, but I recall that I could still distinguish his racing number. When he passed the entrance to Fisher's Island Sound,

I still had hopes of catching him. In those waters, with their tricky currents, it was still anybody's race. Possibly five minutes later, we reached the same point and seemed to stand still. The water was boiling around us. The helm was bucking and kicking in my hands. The boat was wallowing uncomfortably in the huge and now broken seas, but the boat ahead seemed to be traveling faster than ever. All through Fisher's Island Sound I was fighting and struggling with the tide while my opponent dwindled to a speck, altered his course for New London Light and sailed up the Thames River. When I finally got my hook down beside him, he had been anchored for over twenty minutes, had stowed sail in a snug harbor furl and was inviting us to come aboard his power tender for afternoon tea which there had been time to prepare. His complete and decisive victory was due to the fact that he entered Fisher's Island Sound on the very last of the flood and carried the fair tide on his way through. Just a few minutes later I had struck the first of the ebb which was increasingly against me on the way through the Sound. Just those few minutes made all the difference in catching a favorable tide, and the tide made the wide difference in our finishing times.

The lighter the airs, the more important does current become. In the summer of 1933 the entire fleet of the New York Yacht Club battled the tide for two hours off Race Rock. I remember seeing the *Vanitie* and the *Weetamoe* with their huge hulls and lofty rigs a mile or two ahead, bearing down on the Rock while I was still fanning along in a very bad position. The boat took all my attention for the next few minutes and then I was amazed to see *Vanitie* and *Weetamoe* both about half a mile behind me. I had struck an eddy that was not unfavorable while the two America's Cup defender candidates, caught in the strength of the tide, had been whirled back like chips in a mill race. By the greatest of good fortune I caught another eddy and a puff of wind at the same time and our nose was up to the Rock. It seemed that of the entire fleet we had been one of the two or three boats to win through. We were tremendously excited. If we got by, the cup for sloops for the entire fleet would undoubtedly be ours, for with our enormous time allowance, we would almost certainly make up for anything that might happen later in the day. The next instant we had lost the eddy, and lost the puff, and were traveling backward like an express train. About two hours later we escaped at Little Gull Island into Gardiners Bay and, leaving The Race, began to make progress toward Newport. *Weetamoe* and *Vanitie* broke through about ten minutes before we were able to. I relate this experience because it shows the tremendous importance of working a strong tide correctly. It was very foolish of us to have attempted to pass Race Rock when the big Cup defender candidates had been unable to do it. Had we at the outset played the other side of The Race, as eventually we were forced to, the outcome might have been different. On this occasion one of the smaller boats worked her way to the Rock just as we had done, but when she felt herself going backward, she had anchored promptly. Thus, for a long time she was one of the leading boats in the fleet, and, as I recall it, she finished well up in that day's run.

This business of anchoring in a foul tide is of the essence of racing strategy. I recall one other race in which I anchored and "passed" three boats. I can recall numerous other occasions on which I have lost an otherwise good position through failure to anchor. In any current at all, the current becomes more important than the wind if there is no wind, and if the current is foul, the anchor should be prepared and ready for use immediately upon the loss of steerage way. There is no rule against anchoring, but a boat that anchors may not buoy her anchor but must weigh it again.

In all these calculations with the tide, there is an omnipresent danger of being too clever. One should not trust to experience unless the experience has been tempered with absolute knowledge. For instance, you know that in a foul current off a certain point you have worked through the entire fleet by hugging the shore. The next time you are in a similar situation you decide to adopt the same strategy. But there may be an hour's difference in the set of the tide and that hour's difference may cause a complete reversal of your first experience. This time the position that proved so favorable may be the worst possible place for you to stand.

Then too, in the consideration of tide and current we must not forget the relative importance of the wind. I recall another race in which my principal competitor was the boat that beat me on that run from Newport to New London. On this occasion we were sailing from Newport to Vineyard Haven and by the time the Vineyard Lightship appeared my opponent was out of sight ahead. The day was a little thick, but he was so far ahead that I doubt if I could have seen him if the weather had been perfectly clear. The wind was from the Southwest and as we entered Vineyard Sound I determined to stand as far to the Southward as the course restrictions would permit. There on our port hand rose the high bluffs of Cuttyhunk. It was evident to me that any wind blowing across Vineyard Sound would have to go over the top of Cuttyhunk, and that if I stood too near that shore, the wind would be passing over the top of my sails leaving me becalmed. As we left Cuttyhunk behind, I saw close in under Nashawena Island the flapping sails of my opponent. She was absolutely standing still, flapping idly without a trace of breeze. Two miles to windward of him we were carrying a strong quartering breeze that was driving us at a great rate through the foul tide. At the finish line off West Chop we beat him by over eleven minutes. In the post mortem that inevitably followed, my opponent maintained that he had played the course the right way. He had sailed through Vineyard Sound for so many years that he knew just where to find the best possible tides. He had stood in under the shore to avoid the foul tide and get the benefit of the eddy and of the peculiar circular motion of all tides in the entrance to Vineyard Sound. So far as the tides had been concerned, his reasoning was absolutely correct, but he had failed to take into consideration the fact that by standing in close under the shore he ran the risk of losing the wind, and that had been his downfall.

Let us assume, then, that by means of the tide tables, the current tables, and the new tables that give strength and direction of the current, you can determine where the current is strongest, where it is relatively weaker, where there is slack water. Suppose you can determine where the current will turn in your favor, and when. It is comparatively easy in the course of a long race, or even in a short race, to place your boat to take the greatest advantage of a favorable current and to be hindered the least by an unfavorable current. In this connection you should give close attention to the problem of lee-bowing the current, or as it is usually inaccurately stated, lee-bowing the tide.

If you are sailing to windward and have the current pressing on your lee bow, you are sailing under the most favorable conditions. It must be borne in mind that when you are sailing to windward your objective is to get up to windward and not merely to get ahead on your course. Thus, current on your lee bow is more favorable than current in your own direction, pushing you ahead. Let us assume that the mark you wish to reach is to the Northeast, and that the wind is also blowing from the Northeast. Let us assume further that the direction of the current is North. In connection with this it should be stated that the direction of the wind is always the direction *from* which the wind blows: the direction of the current is always the direction *toward* which it flows. Thus, current North means that the current is flowing *to* the North, whereas North wind would be a wind that is blowing *from* the North. With these conditions in mind, then, we know that we must sail one leg to the North and one leg to the East in order to progress to the Northeast. On which leg will the current be more favorable?

When we are sailing North, the current will be going with us and helping us to make faster time but it will be helping us to make faster time to the North, whereas our destination is to the Northeast. On the other hand, if we are sailing East, the current will be setting us to the North so that at the end of our leg we will be much nearer to our destination in that the current is progressively setting us to the North while we are sailing East. If the current is relatively strong and our speed is relatively low, we may be sailing a course

to the East and making good a course to the Northeast, which is exactly what we want to do. This explanation, then, should make clear the advantage of
lee-bowing the current whenever possible.

An incident of lee-bowing the current may serve to
make this more clear. In a long distance race sailed
in the summer of 1933 our course was almost due East
and the wind came somewhat from that quarter. From
the start off Scotch Caps at Rye, we sailed to a finish
line off Port Jefferson. My guess was that the wind
would hold East. Most of my competitors guessed that
the wind would haul to Southwest. In accordance with
all Long Island Sound yachtsmen, they determined to
play the part of Long Island clam diggers and hug the
Long Island shore in short tacks. The tide was against
us at the start but was not very strong, and my con-
sultation of the tables showed that there was no ap-
preciable difference between standing boldly out into
the Sound or hugging the Long Island shore. It was
apparent, however, that as we neared Port Jefferson
the tide would turn and would be favorable and strong.
That determined my strategy for the race. After one
tack to the Long Island shore, I stood boldly across the
Sound, fetching up near Stamford, then I short-tacked
along the Northern shore of the Sound until beyond
Darien. By that time the tide had turned. Then I
sailed in a lightening breeze across the Sound and all
the time the tide was setting me down toward Port
Jefferson. My boat was in very bad condition for that
race; we were short handed and did not take it very
seriously. But we finished well up among the big boats
and beat very badly a number of boats that had often
proved their superior speed. Lee-bowing the tide across
the Sound where it was widest at a time when the tide

was running strong gave us a tremendous advantage over the boats that had short-tacked along the shore. It might be contended that the boats in-shore sailed approximately the same number of miles on the starboard tack as they did on the port tack and therefore there could be no difference. But the difference is this. When the tide was unfavorable to all of us, I suffered no disadvantage by standing over to the Connecticut shore of the Sound. Then, when the tide turned and was favorable, I sailed a long tack with the tide on my lee bow. The other boats which had stood in toward the Long Island shore could not do this.

While the tide was favorable to them they sailed half the time with the tide on the lee bow and the other half with the tide astern. Thus, for half the time after the turn of the tide, I had a distinct advantage over them. The strategy of lee-bowing the tide must always be worked out with this thought in mind.

If, of course, the race is a short one and the tide does not turn in the middle of it and you must sail a certain distance on one tack and a certain distance on the other, with the tide of equal strength on both tacks, it is hard to figure out how to take advantage of lee-bowing.

Perhaps the situation in which lee-bowing the tide becomes most important is when the skipper has the opportunity of taking the current on either bow. Let us suppose you can lay the next mark on a close reach with the current on your weather bow. Sailing thus, you will find yourself set to leeward by both wind and current, and the going will be tough. But by pointing high of your mark, and pinching, perhaps, you can get the current to bear on your lee bow. You may not sail so fast through the water, but you will make better progress over the bottom. Then, as you near the mark, you can start sheets and leg for it. If your opponents continue to take the current on their weather bows, they will be forced to trim sheets steadily as they go along. The current will be stopping them instead of helping them. And by the time you have started your sheets and are tearing down on the mark, they will be slogging along close-hauled far to leeward.

But let me relate another incident in which I was not so smart as in the race just recorded. It was long ago in one of my early races and I had had very little experience with tidal currents. I was sailing the last leg of a strange sort of course, a triangle with a pigtail on it. I had rounded the triangle and hauled on the wind to sail the pigtail. I noticed that the boats ahead had done no tacking, yet I was amazed at the way they could lay the mark. All of them seemed to be headed right for the finish whereas I noticed that I could not lay within two points of the line. Sensing possible difficulties at the finish and realizing that if I had to go about near the finish line I would be approaching a mess of boats while on the port tack, I went about immediately, took a short hitch to windward, then went about to lay the mark. To my amazement the finish line drifted off to leeward. In a few minutes I found that I was pointing much higher than the mark. I had to bear away to fetch it. I thought the wind had changed. It was only then I realized that there was a strong cross current on my lee bow, setting me progressively up to windward. I started the sheets some more and bore down on the finish line, sailing very free indeed. As I approached the finish, the current was so strong that it almost swept me into the buoy at the end of the line and I was nearly disqualified as a result.

I won that race more by good luck than by good management. The other boats, more familiar with the currents, had realized that lee-bowing the tide would set them up to windward and they sailed their course aiming far to leeward of the finish line and trusting to the current to help them cross the line.

Chapter XX

OPPORTUNISM—WIND

Wind is caused by a difference in pressure. It flows from regions where the pressure is high to regions where the pressure is low. Wind is not horizontal; it blows upward at an angle of about four degrees. Apparently, strong winds formulate their direction in the upper air and then come down to earth. If you watch the movements of the clouds and note that they are traveling in a different direction from the wind that you are getting, you may expect sooner or later that the wind which is blowing the clouds will come down to earth and blow in the same direction as it is now blowing the clouds. Watching the movements of the upper clouds is one of the best means of forecasting a change in the direction of the wind. I do not know whether the following statement is scientific or not, but I am making it with the hope that it will clear up a situation that is often puzzling. I distinguish between pressure winds and suction winds. Perhaps no difference exists in fact, but if we will assume that there is a difference between pressure wind and suction wind it may help us in our sailing. I remember noting the candles on the dining-room table one evening last summer. The door to the pantry opened outward from the dining room and the flames of the candles on the side of the table nearer the door inclined toward it.

A second later the flames of the candles farther away from the door followed suit. In other words, when the door was opened the air in the dining room rushed out of that door. The first particles of air to move out were those near the doorway. This left a partial vacuum into which other particles of air rushed. The air around the near candles then started to move. Then the air around the far candles started to move.

Now, if those candles were boats somewhat separated on the water, we would have noted a phenomenon that often occurs. A portion of the atmosphere rises. The air near that portion of the atmosphere rushes in to take its place; the air farther away follows suit so that the boats to leeward in such a situation would get the wind before the boats to windward. The candles nearer the door were like the leeward boats. They got the wind before the candles farther away. Such would be a typical suction wind. I do not know how to tell the reader to watch for suction winds or to know when to expect them, but if he realizes that some winds start from the leeward and work to windward, whereas others start from the windward and work to leeward, he will be able to judge his local conditions more intelligently.

Often the wind on light days is particularly freakish. Sometimes in the flattest calm a wind will be found in a definite spot and nowhere else. I recall a race in a vicious thunder storm in which we had worked into first place by driving hard through the heaviest squalls. Suddenly there came a flat calm. We were well out ahead with one boat on our starboard quarter and one boat on our port quarter. The mark was scarcely a quarter of a mile away. We stayed in that position with our sails flapping. Suddenly, the boat on our port was struck by a vicious squall on her port side and she plowed along with her rail buried to her cabin-house, her mast inclined toward us. The next instant another squall hit the other boat on her starboard side. She, too, buried her rail and inclined her mast toward us. The two boats passed us less than a hundred yards away, both with more wind than they could carry, and not a breath of it reached us. We were third around the mark.

When freaks of the wind are mentioned, old time yachtsmen all recall a run in a New York Yacht Club cruise of many years ago. The famous New York Thirty, *Oriole,* had worked out a wonderful lead not only on her own class but also on most of the bigger boats. A hundred yards from the finish line she ran into a bald spot and remained there for over an hour while every boat in her class and nearly every other boat in the fleet sailed past her on either side, carrying a good breeze to the finish. *Oriole* was absolutely helpless, for the wind went everywhere except where she was.

On a hot muggy afternoon there is always danger of a thunder squall. This should be prepared for not merely because of the danger it entails but also because the boat that is properly handled in a thunder squall will win the race and such a squall is almost certain to upset the best laid plans of the racing skipper. In "Learning to Sail" I advised my readers to listen for radio static before starting out on any sail. This advice may well be taken by any racing man. Static is one of the best indications of the approach of a thunder storm and is used for that purpose by the large electric companies who are so often called upon to deliver extra power during the period of darkness which accompanies a storm. It is a far better indication than the barely perceptible changes in the aneroid barometer. One of the 12-Metres which has been very successful on Long Island Sound carries a radio set in her cabin and on any suspicion of a thunder squall listens for static before determining her course. In the vicinity of New York, thunder squalls nearly always come up from the Northwest, usually on a Southwest wind. This means that the skipper who correctly anticipates a squall can place his boat where he will get the advantage of the first wind and also where he can plan his course so as to run free to the next mark. Thunder squalls always produce pressure winds, never suction winds.

Even without means to detect static, no sailor should ever be surprised by a thunder storm. The fastest working storm gives warning hours ahead. The low-lying dark clouds in the Northwest with their hard edge of white cumulus are a certain forerunner of trouble. The direction of the storm can be determined by the direction in which the clouds move and it should always be borne in mind that thunder storms follow tides.

One of the hardest winds to guess on the Atlantic seaboard is the Northwester. It does, however, follow certain rules. First, it is always puffy; second, it shifts rapidly back and forth across the whole quadrant from North around to West. There seem to be two types of Northwesters: One in which the puffs are few and far between with relatively long periods of calm intervening, the other in which the puffs come thick and fast with relatively short periods of calm intervening. It is easy to study the character of the wind for it does not change much throughout the day provided it is blowing hard. The character of the breeze will have an effect upon your reefing, and correct reefing is an important element in winning in small centerboard boats.

If the intervals of calm are relatively long, reef for these intervals; if they are relatively short, reef for the puffs. The Northwest wind on the Atlantic seaboard is a land breeze. It is brought about by the relative temperature of the land and the water during the night. If a Northwest breeze is light in the morning, it will peter out about noon and blow from the Southwest some time between noon and two o'clock. At the Western end of Long Island Sound it usually strikes later in the afternoon because the Southwest wind must blow across the heated area of New York City where the rising column of hot air from the city streets and tall buildings diverts the breeze upward. If a Northwest wind is strong in the morning, it will probably blow from the Northwest or from that quadrant until sundown. It generally blows pretty hard all day.

A dry Easter—an East wind not accompanied by rain—will usually blow from the East all day long, and possibly for several days in succession. The dry Easter seldom moves around to Southwest in the daytime in the manner in which a Northwest wind moves. When an East wind storm with rain starts to clear, the wind goes around with the sun. It generally moves in definite four-point shifts from Northeast to East to Southeast to South and finally to Southwest. A Southwest wind often goes down with the sun and particularly so late in summer and in September. In July it is less likely to do so. When a Southwest wind goes down with the sun, the wind is generally Northwest at night.

If you will bear in mind the distinction between what I have called pressure winds and suction winds, you will be able to see two strongly contrasting effects in the lee of the land. On days when the air is light, the wind is sucked off the land by the rising airs over the water. Therefore, in light airs there is generally a streak of wind close under the lee of the land that is stronger than out in the open water. When the wind, however, is a strong pressure wind, it is usually lighter under the lee of the land than it is out on the open water. A headland, however, sticking out into the water is quite apt to cut off the breeze.

I remember winning a race in 1933 through the recognition of this principle. Sailing toward a mark under the lee of a point of land, I found as I expected that my wind was cut off. I rounded the mark third in my class. Then, instead of sailing toward the finish line, I stood boldly out into the Sound until I found the wind exactly where I had left it, then I sailed to the finish, winning by over thirteen minutes. Only one other boat in an enormous fleet followed these tactics to the intense amusement of the newspaper reporters. The others all hugged the land, waiting for a suction wind which did not come. They did not realize that the Easter which was blowing that day rarely changes its direction nor did they realize that the lift which comes under the lee of the land occurs only in suction winds. The land will often turn the direction of the wind. There is one stretch of shore to the east of Hempstead Harbor where a Southwest wind is distinctly more Westerly than at any other place on the Sound. Nearly every racing man at the Western end of the Sound knows this and stands in close to shore to get the Westerly slant. There is danger in it, however, for if he stands in too close he loses all the wind.

Land to leeward has a curious effect. As the wind approaches it, it gets up off the water to blow over the high bluffs. Thus, the wind may be blowing strong at the top of a hill and there may be no wind at all for a half-mile out on the water. Go out another half-mile, however, and you will have a strong breeze. The wall of land to leeward deflects the air upward, often so high upward, that you will lose all wind if you stand in too close.

On calm days racing men often go wind-hunting. This policy is not to be recommended without keen knowledge of local conditions. It is not enough to guess where the wind is because by the time you get there the wind may be somewhere else. The only sensible way to hunt wind is to guess where the wind is moving to and go there if possible. In hunting wind, do not neglect the distant signs. If two steamers are approaching miles apart and the smoke plume of one is ascending straight up in the air while the smoke plume of the other is being blown down by the wind, you will have a very good indication of what the wind is doing in those two spots. If a flag on shore is whipping out from its staff, or a windmill is turning, it may indicate the presence of wind close under the shore. If boats at a distance are heeled down and moving, they indicate the presence of wind, but this indication is usually dangerous because the boats that seem to be sailing fast may have no more wind than you have but may be driven along by auxiliary motors.

Chapter XXI

OPPORTUNISM—WHAT HAPPENS WHEN
THE WIND SHIFTS

LIKE EVERY other yachtsman in the world, I have lost many races because the other fellow got the breaks. But when the race is over, and the crew has held the last post mortem, and you're sitting with your bedtime cigarette, you get to wondering why it is that the other fellow is always in a position to get the benefit from a shift of wind, and whether there isn't something that he did, and you did not do, that turned the tide and brought him across the line first.

In such a mood, I sat one evening with drawing board, dividers, and pencil, and sketched out some race situations that were fresh in my mind. Before I got through, I had gone completely geometrical. I sat up half the night shifting cardboard models, measuring dotted lines, writing down impressive-looking gibberish like "AB — CD = O." Along toward morning, I staggered off to bed, dizzy with some amazing conclusions. I had learned that if one boat on the wind is directly behind another and the wind shifts four points aft, the trailing boat instantly finds herself on even terms with the leading boat, no matter if she were five lengths or five miles astern before the shift. (There is one exception to this rule. It does not apply if, after the shift, the trailing boat can lay the mark.) I learned that the one position which nearly every racing man avoids—a berth dead to leeward of a leading boat—is the only position in which a yacht gains on any shift of wind. There were other things as well—enough to make me worry when I considered my years of racing in which I had never exactly realized what had been happening in those abrupt changes of fortune we call "breaks."

For months thereafter I became the yacht club bore. I drew diagrams on the backs of hundreds of envelopes, and when they were used up, shamelessly resorted to the tablecloths. I had to test the ideas on the acknowledged experts. And I learned some astounding things about the knowledge of racing men. The real top-notchers, the men who had names to conjure with, knew what I was talking about. The alacrity with which they agreed showed that I was on the right track. But there were dozens of first-class racing men to whom my dope was either news or nonsense. That made me feel better. One old-timer who has made yachting history answered me, in part, as follows: "Yes, I know that. I learned it in Larchmont Race Week in 1912. I thought there were only five men on the Sound who knew it, but now I see there are six."

So at the risk of being pedantic and mathematical, I am going to reproduce my diagrams and cases and draw some conclusions therefrom. I have confined my cases to situations in which the competing yachts are on the wind.

If we were to take a line four times the height of a yacht's mast and describe a circle with the line as a radius and the heel of the mast as a center, we would have the "Zone of Interference" of that yacht. Any other yacht, sailing into that Zone of Interference, either interferes with her or is interfered with by her. Within that Zone of Interference, the principal consideration must be given to blanketing, back-winding, broken water, and the relative positions of the two yachts concerned.

Outside that Zone of Interference, the power of boats to interfere with one another is almost negligible, and the skipper's attention may be turned to wind, current, and other matters beyond the control of any of the competing yachts. For the most part, yachts sail in the Zone of Interference of other yachts for a relatively small part of any race. For the rest of the time, they may seek their opportunities without consideration of interference. Thus, in beating to windward, within the Zone of Interference, the worst possible place to be is directly to leeward of another yacht. But, outside that zone, it can be proved that a yacht directly to leeward of another yacht gains on any shift of wind. Therefore, in the cases to be cited, let us assume that the yachts are outside of all Zones of Interference—too far away from one another to be involved in what are commonly known as "racing tactics."

Most racing yachts will go about in eight points—in other words, can head up four points from the wind. I realize that this matter is controversial, and that every proud racing skipper will maintain that his particular ship will do better than that. But I am talking not about courses sailed, but about courses made good—and made good without pinching or killing headway. There is a difference in pointing ability; but the difference lies not so much in being able to look high as in being able to maintain speed while looking high. The *Enterprise* was famous for her ability to out-point the finest aggregation of fast yachts ever built; yet in his book, "Enterprise," Commodore Vanderbilt describes going about in a full seven and one-half points and having to pinch to lay the mark.

We "kid" ourselves a great deal in the matter of pointing. Yet nearly every racing man waits until the mark comes abeam before tacking for it—pretty good evidence that in his heart of hearts he knows he can make good only four points from the wind.

But let us avoid controversy by excepting the high-pointers and direct our attention to the average boat. It will simplify the mathematics. Eight points, then, to go about. Each new course at right angles to the old course and at 45° from the wind. For the sake of clearness—even at the danger of seeming too elementary—let me say that by points I mean points of the compass. There are thirty-two points on the compass card and each point is a thirty-second of a circle. Between the cardinals, such as from North to East, there are eight points. Between a cardinal and the intercardinal, such as from South to Southwest, there are four points.

Some skippers are a bit hazy as to the distance between two boats on the wind on the same course. It may be expressed thus: If two boats are on the wind on the same course, the distance between the two boats is the sum or difference of two factors. Draw a line through the mast of the trailing boat at right angles to her course until it intersects the wake of the leading boat. The length of that line is one factor. The distance from the mast of the leading boat to that point of intersection is the other factor. The line at right angles to the course counts for the windward boat. The other line counts for the leading boat on the course. The boat that has the longer line is ahead by the difference. If one boat is to windward and ahead on the course, she is ahead by the sum.

Now, if it is clear how to measure the distance between boats on the wind, let us place some boats in different relative positions, all outside the Zone of Interference, and let us see what happens to them if the wind shifts four points, or 45°. To avoid confusion, I have limited the examples to four-point shifts. The changes in position due to greater or lesser shifts may be easily determined by interpolation.

Now, it is important to know what happens on a four-point shift, because a shift of that amount occurs so often and so definitely. Think how often you have sailed in a light South wind, have felt the breeze failing, and then suddenly had it strike in strong and true from the Southwest. Four points! How often you have sailed in a fluky Northwester and had the wind strike in suddenly from the North. The next shift is Northwest again. And the next may be either North or West. Four points each time. When a rip-snorting Northeaster is blowing and the sky starts to clear, the wind seems to step around by fairly definite four-point strides—to East, to Southeast, where it hesitates a long time, to South, and finally to Southwest.

Here, then, are six cases for study:

CASE I. Fig. 34.

Assume wind to be from S.W. Then both boats would be headed S. Boat 2 is directly to leeward of Boat 1.

The distance between the two boats is AB (the distance of Boat 2 astern) + BC (the distance of Boat 2 to leeward).

The wind shifts aft four points to W. Then boats would head S.W. Boat 2 would then be directly astern.

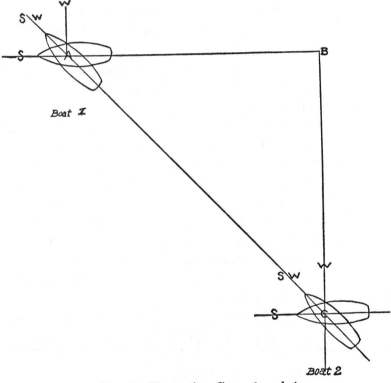

FIG. 34. Illustrating Cases 1 and 4

The distance between the boats is now AC, for Boat 2 is nothing to leeward.

Before the shift, the distance is the sum of the sides of a right angle triangle. After the shift, the distance is the hypothenuse of the right angle triangle.

In the illustration, before the shift, Boat 2 is 5 lengths to leeward and therefore nearly 7 *lengths be-*

hind. After the shift, she is 5 lengths astern—5 *lengths behind.*

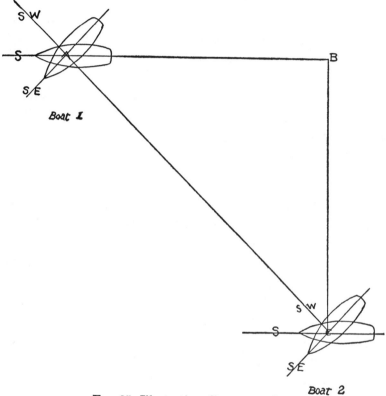

Fɪɢ. 35. Illustrating Cases 2 and 5

Cᴀsᴇ 2. Fig. 35.

Assume wind still to be from S.W. and boats headed S., as in Case 1. Boat 2 is directly to leeward of Boat 1, as in Case 1. The distance between the boats is the same: AB + BC.

But, in this case, assume that the wind shifts four points forward to S. Now both boats head S.E. Boat 2 is now directly abeam. Boat 1 is to windward.

If both boats should go about, they would be exactly in the position of the boats in Case 1 after the shift. Therefore, distance abeam is equal to distance astern. And the distance between the boats is now AC (the hypothenuse); not AB + BC (the sum of the sides). In the illustration, on a four-point shift of wind forward, Boat 2 gains nearly two lengths.

Conclusion: A boat directly to leeward of another boat and outside the Zone of Interference gains on any shift of wind, forward or aft.

CASE 3. Fig. 36.

Assume the wind to be from W. Both boats are headed S.W. Boat 2 is now 5 lengths directly astern of Boat 1. The distance between them is AC.

The wind shifts aft four points to N.W. Then both boats head W. Boat 2 is now the distance BC astern of Boat 1 and the distance AB to windward of Boat 1. But since AB and BC are equal, there is no distance between them and the boats are tied. If Boat 1 should go about and head N., the two boats would meet at B. Boat 2 has gained all of the distance AB to windward and cut down the difference between AC and BC (or CD) in distance astern.

If the wind shifts less than four points, Boat 2 would still gain, but not so much. Her distance behind would equal BC — AB, but BC would have a greater value, and AB would have a lesser value, than in the case of a four-point shift.

If the wind shifts more than four points, Boat 2 would be ahead of Boat 1 and her distance ahead would equal AB — BC, but AB would have a greater value and BC would have a lesser value than in the case of a four-point shift.

Conclusion: Any shift of wind aft favors the fol-

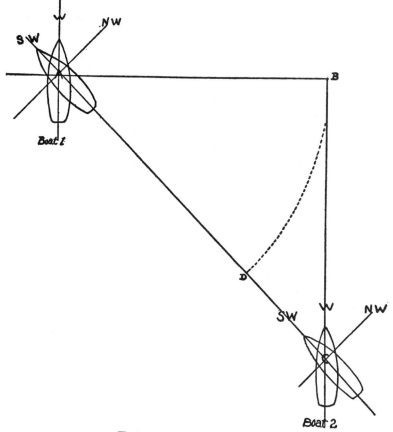

FIG. 36. Illustrating Case 3

lowing boat. If the following boat is directly astern of the leading boat a shift of four points aft places the following boat on equal terms with the leading boat, *regardless of her distance astern before the shift.* A shift of more than four points aft places her ahead, regardless of her distance astern before the shift.

The only exceptions to this rule are when Boat 2 can overstand the mark because of the shift, or when Boat 1 can outpoint Boat 2. (It is obvious that Boat 1 cannot lay the mark unless Boat 2 can do so, as Boat 2 is the weather boat.)

In the event of Boat 2 being in such a position as to overstand the mark, Boat 1 will still be the leading boat. The reason for this is that the only conditions under which Boat 2 can catch Boat 1 are when the shift places Boat 2 to windward as far as Boat 1 is ahead, so that she can cut down the lead of Boat 1 at the same rate as Boat 1 cuts down the distance of Boat 2 to windward. If Boat 2 can overstand, she gains to windward more than she needs, and Boat 1 will not have to sail so far to windward as Boat 2 will have to sail ahead. Of course, Boat 2 should be able to sail faster with started sheets and that may even things up. So Boat 2 may be able to catch Boat 1 *after the shift* by virtue of sailing faster with started sheets. But if the shift enables Boat 2 to overstand the mark, she is not at that moment on equal terms with Boat 1. I have seen much rejoicing on boats that have thus been enabled to overstand the mark. But it is a matter not for rejoicing but for regret.

Case 4. Fig. 34.

Assume the same initial conditions as in Case 3— wind from W.; both boats headed S.W.; Boat 2, five lengths directly astern of Boat 1. As in Case 3, the distance between them is AC.

Now assume that the wind shifts four points forward

to S.W. Both boats now head S. Boat 2, instead of being five lengths directly astern is now five lengths directly to leeward and nearly seven lengths behind. Before the shift, her distance behind was AC (the hypothenuse). Now it is AB + BC (the sum of the sides). This is the reverse of Case 1.

Conclusion: Any shift of wind forward favors the leading boat. If the following boat is directly astern of the leading boat, a shift of four points forward places her directly to leeward of the leading boat regardless of the distance between the two boats. A four-point shift forward causes the maximum loss to a boat following another directly astern. A smaller shift will not place her so far to leeward. A larger shift will place her farther ahead than the dead-to-leeward position, for Cases 1 and 2 prove that any shift favors the boat that is dead to leeward, and a shift of more than four points first puts her directly to leeward and then lifts her out of that position.

Case 5. Fig. 35.

The wind is from S. and both boats are headed S.E. Boat 2 is abeam of Boat 1. She is to leeward, but not directly to leeward. The distance between them is AC. (If both boats should go about and both boats should head S.W., Boat 2 would be the distance AC astern.)

Assume that the wind shifts aft four points to S.W. Now both boats would head S. Boat 2 is now directly to leeward of Boat 1. She is behind by the distance AB + BC (the sum of the sides instead of the hypothenuse).

This is the reverse of Case 2.

Conclusion: When two boats on the wind are abeam,

any shift aft favors the windward boat. A shift of four points places the leeward boat directly to leeward regardless of the distance between the two boats. A four-

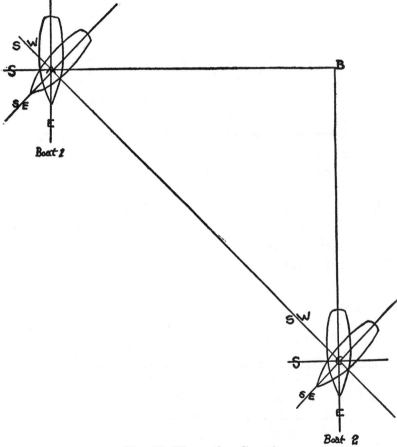

Fig. 37. Illustrating Case 6

point shift aft causes the maximum loss to the leeward boat, directly abeam of the windward boat.

CASE 6. Fig. 37.

Assume the initial conditions of Case 5. The wind is

from S. Boats 1 and 2 are both headed S.E. Boat 2 is to leeward and directly abeam of Boat 1. The distance between them, as in Case 5, is the distance AC.

Now the wind shifts four points forward to S.E. Both boats now head E. Boat 2 is now even with Boat 1, for the distance between them is AB — BC = O. If Boat 2 should go about and sail S., she would meet Boat 1 when Boat 2 had sailed a distance equal to AB and Boat 1 had sailed a distance equal to BC.

If the wind shifts less than four points forward, Boat 2 would gain but would not catch Boat 1. The distance between them would be AB — BC, but AB would have a greater value and BC a lesser value than on a four-point shift.

If the wind shifts more than four points forward, Boat 2 would be ahead of Boat 1. The distance between them would be BC — AB, but BC would have a greater value and AB a lesser value than on a four-point shift.

Conclusion: When two boats are on the wind and one is directly abeam of the other, any shift of wind forward favors the leeward boat. A shift of wind four points forward places the leeward boat on an equal basis with the leading boat *regardless of her distance to leeward* before the shift. A shift of more than four points forward places her ahead, regardless of the distance between the boats before the shift.

The only exceptions are when Boat 1 can overstand the mark by tacking, or when Boat 1 can out-point Boat 2. (It is obvious that if Boat 1 can overstand the mark by tacking, Boat 2 can do so as well, for she is ahead, and would be the weather boat if both boats went about. The same conditions would then govern as in Case 3.)

Chapter XXII

OPPORTUNISM—TAKING ADVANTAGE OF
A SHIFT OF WIND

In the preceding chapter, we saw just what happens on a four-point shift of wind. What are we going to do about it? Let us assume that the boats are in the positions described. Never mind just yet whether or not they should have permitted themselves to get into that position. Let us consider the best strategy for each boat to employ in each case.

Case 1. Fig. 34.

If a further shift in the same direction is expected, Boat 1 should go about. Another shift of equal range would put Boat 2 on equal terms. Boat 2 should also go about to hold her gain. If both boats tack, the conditions brought about by the shift are unchanged for Boat 2 is the same distance abeam as she was astern before they tacked. If one boat tacks but the other doesn't, the tacking boat will benefit.

But a change in direction of more than four points does not occur very often except when the morning land breeze turns into an afternoon sea breeze or when an East wind storm clears and the wind walks around with the sun. In most instances, it can be expected that the wind will hold or will shift back to its original position. If it is expected that the new wind will hold, the boats can tack or not. It will not affect their distance apart. If it is expected that the wind will shift back again to S.W.—in general, the most plausible guess—neither boat should tack. If Boat 2 tacks, Boat 1 should *not* tack to cover. There will be time enough for that after the wind shifts back. If Boat 1 should make a mistake and tack, Boat 2 should not follow. Every foot gained toward S.W. is a foot directly to windward on the shift back.

CASE 2. Fig. 35.

If a further shift in the same direction is anticipated, both boats should hold their course. If no further change is anticipated, they may tack or not. If a change back is anticipated, both boats should tack. Boat 1 is usually tempted to hold her course to cover in this instance, and on the whole, that is playing safe, as a shift back will place Boat 2 directly to leeward again and her gain from the first shift will be wiped out. But Boat 1 could make a huge gain in the direction of the anticipated wind by going about. In any case, Boat 2 should tack at once. If Boat 1 does not follow suit, Boat 2 should split tacks until she is at least two lengths to windward of the wake of Boat 1. Then tack again, far behind but to windward. If the wind shifts back as anticipated, Boat 2 will be ahead.

CASE 3. Figs. 36, 38 and 39.

This case is complicated by the possibility of Boat 2 being able to overstand the mark. In Cases 1 and 2, this situation does not arise, for if Boat 2 could overstand the mark, Boat 1 could also do it with equal facility (on her course in Case 1 and by going about in Case 2) and the only strategy would be for both boats to start sheets and scoot for it with all the money bet on Boat 1. Of course the skipper who starts his sheets banks pretty heavily on the wind not shifting back again before he reaches the mark.

But Case 3 is different. Let us assume that Boat 2 cannot overstand the mark. If a further change in the same direction is anticipated, Boat 1 should go about at once and engage in a good, old-fashioned, dog fight. Boat 2 will welcome the fight. It is a great stiffener of morale for a boat that has been trailing. And if, as in the case shown, she has the starboard tack, she will undoubtedly go to it. But if she is really counting strongly on a further shift of wind, she should avoid the dog fight and use all her effort in going about and taking advantage of her position. If the anticipated further change comes, she can then tack with a commanding position.

If no further shift is anticipated, both boats should hold their courses for a time at least. But Boat 1 should go about before it becomes necessary. On no account should Boat 1 hold a starboard tack until by going about she can lay the mark. Such a delay would mean that she would meet Boat 2 at the mark on the port tack, and this would be fatal. Boat 1 must force a dog fight before reaching the mark and long enough before it to go about in the lee of Boat 2, work out a lead, and reach the mark on the starboard tack without an overlap.

If a reverse shift to the original wind direction is anticipated, neither boat should tack. Such a reverse shift will rob Boat 2 of all the gain, but there is nothing she can do about it. If she should tack, her position would be still worse. If she should tack, Boat 1 may tack to cover without losing the advantage she would have if both boats held their courses. But Boat 1 would gain infinitely more by holding her course.

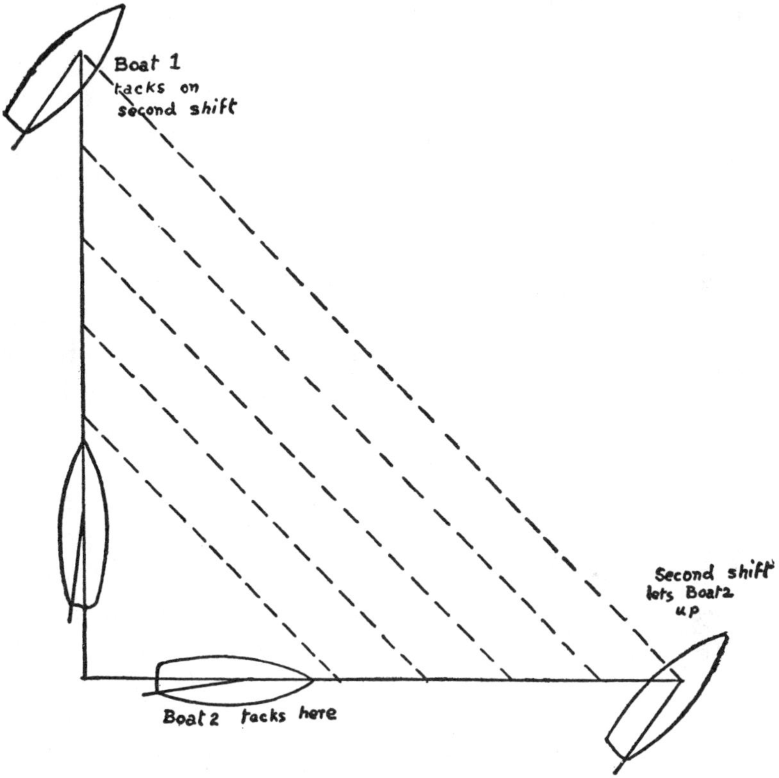

Boat 1
tacks on
second shift

Second shift
lets Boat2
up

Boat 2 tacks here

Fig. 38. When to tack on an anticipated back shift

Her gain would increase directly as the hypothenuse of the right angle triangle of which the course and distance of each boat are the arms. In Fig. 38, the distance sailed for equal intervals of time, are laid off on the courses. If the wind shifts back to the original position at the end of any interval, the gain is repre-

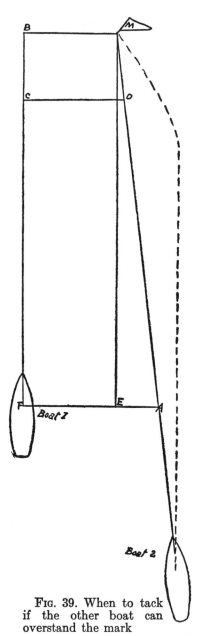

FIG. 39. When to tack if the other boat can overstand the mark

sented by the hypothenuse, which is the square root of the sum of the squares of the distances both the boats sail.

But now let us suppose Boat 2 can overstand the mark. Unless she anticipates the wind shifting back to the original position, she should start sheets and lay the mark. Otherwise, she should sail high until close to the mark and then reach for it. Assuming that Boat 1 cannot lay the mark when should she tack?

Refer to Fig. 39. If Boat 1 should go about at once, she would meet Boat 2 at A. But Boat 2 should be sailing faster with started sheets and would probably wade through Boat 1's wind and blanket her. Furthermore, Boat 1 would have to sail the distance FA + AM. If Boat 1 holds her course to B whence she can lay the mark, she will sail FB + BM, a much shorter distance. But this would offer the disadvantage of possibly meeting Boat 2 at the mark. This is the best strategy if Boat 1 holds the starboard tack at the mark; but if as in this diagram, Boat 1 would lay the mark on the port tack, she should go about at C, tacking again at D. It is not advisable for Boat 1 to tack at F and again at E, from which point she can lay the mark, for Boat 2 is quite likely to blanket her before reaching the mark because of her greater speed with started sheets.

If Boat 2 should elect to sail full and by, her course would be along the dotted line. In that case, the strategy for Boat 1 would be unchanged. She should delay tacking as long as possible and tack for a dog fight only in time to win clear at the mark. The longer she delays, the shorter distance she will have to sail.

CASE 4. Fig. 34.

If a further shift in the same direction is anticipated, both boats should hold their courses. Boat 2 will benefit from such a shift but there is nothing Boat 1 can do about it.

If no further shift is anticipated, both boats should hold their courses—Boat 1, because she has Boat 2 covered; Boat 2, because on any shift in any direction, she is bound to gain.

If a wind shift to the original direction is anticipated, Boat 2 should tack at once and sail until she is two lengths to windward of Boat 1's wake, then tack again. From this position she would become the leading boat when the wind shifts back again.

Boat 1 should tack at once to cover and to keep Boat 2 directly to leeward on the other tack. If Boat 2 fails to tack and there is likelihood of the wind shifting back again, Boat 1 should tack and abandon her covering tactics.

CASE 5. Fig. 35.

If a further shift in the same direction is anticipated, both boats should go about. If no shift is anticipated, both boats may tack or not. If a shift back is anticipated, both boats should hold their courses. While the boats are in the same position as in Case 2, they got there from different initial relative positions on an opposite change of wind.

While the strategy outlined is directly opposite to that of Case 2, the reasoning is precisely the same.

CASE 6. Figs. 37, 38 and 39.

It is evident that this situation is precisely like that of Case 3 except that the positions of the boats are reversed. In this case Boat 1 is to windward and behind —in other words in the position of Boat 2 in Case 5. Boat 2 is to leeward and ahead—or in the position of Boat 1 in Case 3.

If both boats go about, they will be in the same position as they were in Case 3, but on the other tack. In case of a dog fight, the advantage of starboard tack would rest with the other boat. In this case, Boat 2 might be able to overstand the mark by going about. With these differences in mind, it is easy to apply the strategy outlined in Case 3.

With these cases as a basis, it is easy to work out all the rules for procedure on a four-point shift of wind when ahead, behind, abeam to windward, abeam to leeward, directly to windward, or directly to leeward of a competitor. Every other position on the water can be worked out, as it were, by interpolation. Similarly, it is easy to work out the changes in position that are caused by a greater or lesser shift than four points.

In general, we can lay down certain rules of thumb for taking advantage of an anticipated shift of wind. The application of the rules must be tempered by general conditions of the race. They do not always apply. But far more frequently than most racing men imagine, these rules should be followed. It will be seen from the six cases cited that the old maxims of always covering the most dangerous competitor and always keeping between your most dangerous competitor and the mark do not invariably apply.

Here, then, are the rules of thumb, for an anticipated four-point shift:

1. If you expect a shift of wind forward, get out ahead. On a four-point shift it does not matter how much you are to leeward, if you are two lengths forward of your opponent's beam.

2. If you expect a shift of wind aft, get out to windward. On a four-point shift it does not matter how far you are behind if you are two lengths to windward of your opponent's wake.

3. Stay on the side from which you expect the new wind.

4. If the wind heads you, tack at once.

5. If the wind lets you up, don't tack—not even to cover.

6. If you are behind and cannot guess the wind, the only position from which you will gain on any shift of wind is directly to leeward.

This last is directed to those who lack the gambling spirit. From this position the gain is certain, but small. One does not win races from this spot, except on time allowance.

With good guesswork on the part of the skipper who follows these rules, a slow boat can beat a faster boat whose skipper guesses wrong or does not follow these rules. Of course, where wind is considered, the guess-work is frequently wrong, even among the most weatherwise. But it pays to know how to play the cards even if the dealer is sometimes unkind.

CHAPTER XXIII

OPPORTUNISM—OTHER FACTORS

GETTING THE breaks is the best possible way to win a race. We have discussed the best methods of getting the breaks on wind and current, but a change of wind or a fortunate finding of a favorable current always seem more like good planning—good racing strategy— than like breaks. The obvious breaks that yachtsmen discuss long after the race is over are the steamer which crosses one's bow, the tug boat with its mile-long string of barges that plows through a racing fleet, the entirely fortuitous things against which there seems to be no provision.

By far the greatest group are the obstructions to sea-room. Among these we may list anchored vessels. These are to be found most frequently near the finish line even on a well-policed course. An anchored vessel near the finish may prove to be an annoying obstruction to sea-room. You are drifting in with a fair wind with black clouds gathering in the Northwest. The finish line is distinctly marked ahead of you at right angles to your course and you are planning to cross it about the middle. The wind dies out, leaving you becalmed, the threatening thunder squall approaches and there come the first faint puffs of the new wind dead ahead. Your spinnaker is aback and is quickly taken in, sheets are trimmed and you find yourself tearing along close-hauled, planning to finish in two tacks. You are busy, your eyes are on your boat, your opponents behind you tack long before they can lay the finish line. It seems bad strategy because the clouds seem to be moving in your direction and if the wind changes again you will be able to sail free while your opponents will still have to beat. You hold on. You have planned it perfectly. You go about, head for the buoy end of the line, and just then you notice a large power yacht that had anchored near the finish and entirely out of the way has been swung around her anchor by the new wind and is directly across your path. That obstruction to sea-room costs you the race.

An alert skipper should at all times be able to avoid anchored vessels, but sometimes the unforeseen happens. The anchored vessel changes its position without weighing or shifting its anchor; or the anchored vessel, suddenly discovering it is in someone's path, will as suddenly weigh anchor and move out right in front of you; or an anchored vessel in a bad sea may drag anchor. I have known racing finishes completely upset by large power boats carrying mail under the command of a self-important skipper who would not waste two minutes to pass astern of the competing yachts.

Moving vessels present a somewhat different problem from anchored vessels. The problem is most annoying to the skipper who does not know the little trick of taking bearings. This is how you do it. When a vessel is approaching, take a bearing right over your own deck. You may find that her smokestack appears, let us say, just forward of your lee shrouds. Then hold your course very carefully and two minutes later take another bearing. If the distance between the boat and your shrouds has widened out so that her bearing is farther forward, she will pass ahead of you. If the second bearing places her stack aft of your shrouds, she will pass astern of you. If, however, that bearing has not changed, it is reasonably certain that the two boats will come together.

In the case of a long tow, you should take bearings on the bow of the tug and also on the stern of the last barge. If you find the bearing of the bow of the tug moving forward and also the bearing of the stern of the last barge moving forward, you will know that the entire tow will pass ahead of you. If, however, you find the bow of the tug working forward and the stern of the last barge working aft, you will come together somewhere along the line and you must alter your course accordingly. If you can locate the point of the tow line where the bearing does not change, it will indicate the point at which you will come together. If this point is up near the tug, you should alter your course to pass ahead of the tug; if it is way back near the barges you should alter your course to pass astern of the barges. A racing vessel has right-of-way, of course, over a tow, but towboat skippers do not always respect this right-of-way.

It is often necessary to change course several times when a long tow passes ahead, simply because the tug-boat captain respects the right-of-way of the racing boats and tries in all decency to clear them. In clearing one batch of boats, he may so alter his course as to interfere with another batch. The only thing to do in this case is to take bearings all over again every time the course is altered and it is essential that you re-check the situation frequently to make sure that the course has not been altered.

To my mind the most disturbing obstruction is the

sightseeing power boat. Whereas these boats do not often lie across the course, nor inject the danger of a collision, they are constantly churning up the water and interfering with the progress of the racing fleet. More profanity is caused by the sightseeing power boats than by anything else. If these boats distributed their interference with an equal hand, throwing up disturbing wakes on all racing boats alike, it would not be so bad, but they will plow through ahead of your boat and astern of another, interfering but little with the latter and stopping the former dead in her course. I recall one race in which I had sailed all night long and had second place cinched. There were three of us fighting it out for second, third, and fourth places. We had proved ourselves to be the fastest of these three boats and were a hundred yards or so ahead. The wind had left us but it was certain that we would soon be favored with a reviving breeze. Just as the fresh breeze struck in, a huge power boat, traveling at high speed, came out from nowhere and circled our boat twice. Her wake was mountainous. We lay there and flapped for five minutes before we could gather way. The two other boats were but little affected and tore off to the finish line. When we gradually overcame the effect of the wake and got steerage way, we rapidly overhauled and passed one of these boats and followed the other a heart-beat across the finish. That five minutes' delay cost us second place. That big power boat that dealt us the death blow was flying the Commodore's flag of one of the country's largest yacht clubs.

Shoal water is an obstruction to sea-room, and by shoal water I mean not only water so shallow as to carry a threat of running aground. There is a drag or friction caused by the bottom that distinctly slows down a moving boat. It is the opinion of experts that this friction of the bottom is exercised whenever the water is less than seven times the draft of the boat. In waters deeper than seven times the draft of the boat, bottom friction is practically non-existent, but where the depth of water is only slightly greater than the draft, the friction becomes a considerable problem. As evidence of this friction, consider the stern wave in a power boat while sailing in deep waters and also in shoal waters. In deep waters, the wave is small; in shoal waters it rolls up in two enormous waves to port and to starboard. When the water becomes very shallow, these waves break. The power boat sailors on Great South Bay are constantly looking back at their stern waves as the best possible indication of the depth of water under their boats. I have seen stern waves break even when in a sail boat. All of this means that, if there is any choice, the skipper should keep his boat in deep water in order to avoid friction of the bottom.

But a more serious obstruction to sea-room is the rock or shoal which makes it necessary for you to change your course. If you are in such a position that you cannot change your course without fouling another boat which has right-of-way, you must hail that other boat and ask for sea-room. It is necessary that you make your hail while sailing *toward* the obstruction, not after tacking away from it. If you are sailing into danger and call for sea-room, the other boat must immediately tack and you must tack at the same time, or an instant later. You may not change your mind about the obstruction and hold your course. If you tack first and hail for sea-room while tacking, or after tacking, the other boat may hold her course and you must get around her the best way you can because you are not then sailing into danger. This rule is one of the most frequently misunderstood of any of the rules in the book.

In the races in which you are permitted to disregard government buoys, you may frequently seize an opportunity by cutting inside of them. If you have a shoal draft boat and are racing against deep draft boats, this is a notable advantage. It is also very necessary to know at just what point you may safely cut across inside a channel buoy. Let us suppose an instance which occurs quite frequently. There is a high hill running out to a point and the point continues under water for a mile or so. Then there is a stretch with deep water, twelve or fifteen feet, then the rocks begin again, rising to a point where they are but two or three feet below the surface, then dropping away to deep water. Outside this last patch of rocks is placed a government channel buoy. Assuming that you are all desirous of cutting this corner as closely as possible, it is obvious that the best place to cut inside the buoy is where the water is twelve or fifteen feet deep. It is not only the safest place but also the place that will give you the shortest possible cut. If you have a sextant, you may cut across by means of the danger angle, the instructions for which are explained fully in Bowditch and also in the Coast Pilot. The skipper is strongly urged not to take a chance on cutting inside government buoys unless he has dependable local knowledge and some means, such as bearings or ranges, for fixing his exact position.

Among these entirely fortuitous obstructions to searoom may be rated the flotsam with which our coastal waters abound. It is very easy to run into a large floating log that may damage the hull so as to cause you to abandon the race. There is almost no experienced sailor who has not suffered hair-breadth escapes from this source. Perhaps the most annoying form of flotsam is the great patch of seaweed that is frequently found in points where seaweed covers the bottom. Sometimes these patches are a half-mile long, an eighth of a mile wide and three or four feet thick. A boat sailing into them is stopped dead in her tracks. On occasion I have also been stopped by sewage and once by the fragments of a recent wreck. These low lying objects are harder to discern than tows, steamers, motor boats and the like, and we are usually close upon them before we see them. It is always necessary to make a decision as to whether to sail around them or to try to plow through them. Usually it is better to try to sail around if you can do so without altering your course to too great an extent. After sailing through a floating mass of seaweed it is wise to make some sort of inspection to see whether any has stuck to the bottom of the boat. A mass of seaweed on a fin keel is a very effective brake. When sailing a centerboard boat, I always make it a rule to raise the board at intervals even when on the wind in order to free any particles of seaweed that may have caught at the forward end. Fin keels, centerboards, rudders, and scags will on occasion catch an enormous amount of weed. In an auxiliary, the propeller is constantly picking it up. I have known keels of boats to foul lobster pots, fish nets, moorings, and floating lines. It is not only necessary to get these things off the keel; it is wiser still to avoid them.

If a choice of course permits you to sail in smooth water rather than in rough water, with no accompanying loss of wind, it is always wise to choose the smooth water. Seas stop a boat more than we imagine. Close-hauled, every slap of a wave delays progress. With a beam wind I have sailed in such high seas that when in the hollows, my sails have been blanketed. In sailing before a high sea, and particularly with a quartering sea, the boat yaws and rolls so badly that progress is greatly impeded and you are further slowed down by the necessity for constant rudder action.

The avoidance of any of these obstructions—seas, seaweed, shoal water, floating wreckage, sightseeing power boats, moving or anchored vessels—plays an important part in the winning of any race. The skipper who avoids them is said to get the breaks, but the avoidance is part of racing and the skipper who is alert gets the breaks of this nature.

Chapter XXIV

TACTICS—HOW BOATS INTERFERE WITH ONE ANOTHER

In general, boats can interfere with one another by the use of the wind and by the use of the water. As a rule, it is not possible for a boat to bother an opponent at a greater distance than four times the height of her mast. If we take the foot of a boat's mast as a center and take four times the length of her mast as a radius, and with that center and that radius describe a circle around that boat, we will cover just about all the territory in which we can interfere with another boat. For lack of a better term, we will call this the Zone of Interference. When one boat sails into the Zone of Interference of another boat, all her sailing must be governed by her power to stop that boat or by the power of that boat to stop her. The maneuvers in which a skipper engages to take advantage of conditions outside the control of any of the contestants we have defined as opportunism. The maneuvers which he makes within the Zone of Interference where conditions can distinctly be affected by the maneuvering of one boat or another we will term tactics. By far, the most important consideration in tactics is the use of the wind. The wind may be shut off or it may be bent—turned in such a manner as to help one boat and hurt another.

The first of these tactics is known as blanketing. One

boat blankets another when it cuts off her wind. The second one of these tactics is known as back-winding. The wind is turned in such a way as to be unfavorable to the other boat. On some points of sailing blanketing and back-winding merge swiftly into one another so

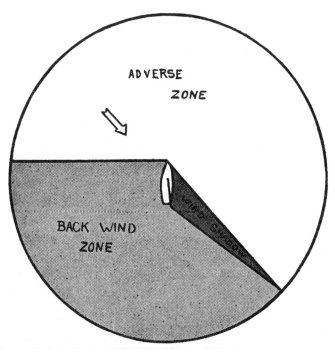

FIG. 40. The Zone of Interference on the wind

that perhaps the term "back-winding" is not all inclusive for the tactics of turning the wind. It will, however, suffice for a beginning and will be made more clear in the following chapters.

In Fig. 40 the Zone of Interference for boats close-hauled on the wind is shown schematically. It is roughly represented as a circle with four times the length of the mast taken as a radius. If another boat follows within the area labeled "wind-shadow," the boat shown in the diagram will blanket her; if she follows into the back-wind zone, the boat in the diagram will back-wind her. But, if she sails within the adverse zone, she will either blanket or back-wind the boat shown in the diagram. The essence, then, of racing tactics is to place yourself somewhere in the other boat's adverse zone and to avoid at all costs her wind-shadow or her back-wind zone by placing yourself in her adverse zone.

Your boat has a Zone of Interference exactly similar to that of every other boat, except that if your boat is larger the zone will be correspondingly larger, or if your boat is smaller than the other boat your Zone of Interference will be correspondingly smaller. It so happens that when you are in a position either to back-wind or blanket the other boat, she can neither back-wind nor blanket you and vice versa. Yet the line of demarcation is a narrow one. If you place yourself on the windward side of the boat shown in the diagram just forward of her back-wind zone, she will fall in your wind-shadow, and very frequently, in maneuvering for a blanketing position, you arrive just too late; your opponent is forward of your wind-shadow and you fall into her back-wind zone. In Fig. 41 we see two boats exactly on the hair line. If the windward boat were a foot ahead, she would certainly blanket the leeward boat. If she were a foot behind, she would certainly be back-winded by the leeward boat.

In Fig. 42 is shown the Zone of Interference of a boat before the wind. She casts her wind-shadow ahead of her and cannot use it in defense against a boat that is overtaking her. Her adverse zone is shown as a column of air stretched out behind her. There is no zone for her back wind. This does not mean that there is no back-wind effect from a boat that is running before the wind. It means merely that it is impossible for a boat that is running to use her back wind in any way that will be harmful to a competitor. Therefore,

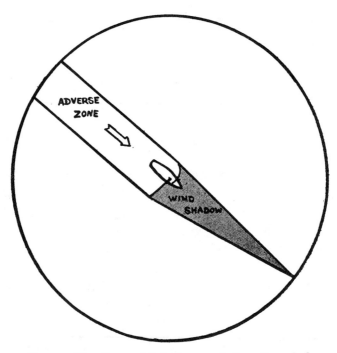

Fig. 42. The Zone of Interference before the wind

back-winding does not function as a means of offensive or defensive tactics between boats running before the wind. For the overtaking boat, blanketing is a most effective weapon against which there is no defense other than jibing out of the way.

Fig. 43 shows the Zone of Interference for a boat that is racing with a beam wind. It is somewhat similar to the Zone of Interference of a boat close-hauled except that the wind-shadow and the back-wind zone are different in area and direction. So much for interference by wind.

Boats can use water to interfere with other boats in

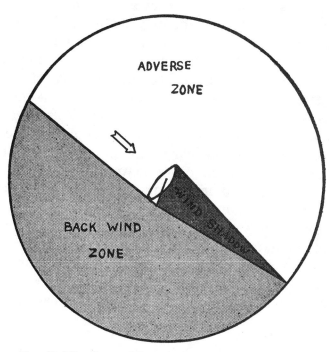

FIG. 43. The Zone of Interference with a beam wind

three ways: 1. By so turning or placing the boat that her bow wave interferes with the other boat. 2. By doing the same thing with her stern wave. 3. By interfering by means of her wake. Boats may also be forced into broken water, such as backwash from docks, shores and headlands, or forced into the bow wave, stern wave, or wake of another boat. Boats perform badly in broken water. If normal waves are turned up in a normal manner by the wind and proceed in a regular procession, a boat will swiftly adapt her rhythm to the rhythm of the waves and make rapid progress. If the rhythm of the waves is broken from any disturbance, the progress is interfered with seriously.

It is possible, too, to pocket a boat in such a manner that she cannot escape or get ahead. This pocketing is very difficult to achieve where one boat is racing against another. In team races, it is a very important tactical consideration. It has the same effect as the pocketing of the favorite in a horse race and somewhat the same effect as the stymie in golf. It is generally considered poor sportsmanship to employ tactics of this nature in an ordinary race in which each boat is pitted against all the other boats, but inasmuch as it is a legitimate and important factor in team racing, it deserves mention.

These, then, are the general considerations of racing tactics: blanketing, back-winding, using broken water, forcing a boat off her course, and pocketing. For every attack there is some means of defense and these means of defense will be considered in relation to each attack.

Chapter XXV

TACTICS—BLANKETING

The entire subject of blanketing will be made clear if one considers the wind as though it were light, and the blanketing area as though it were a shadow. In fact, the term "wind-shadow" is generally accepted and recognized by racing men. It is not easy to define the exact dimensions of a wind-shadow. It is generally assumed to be conical in form, with its base immediately in the lee of the sails of a blanketing boat, its apex four mast-lengths to leeward, and its sides sloping uniformly from the base to the apex. This description is probably inaccurate. I have long suspected that there are holes and hollows in the wind-shadow and bumps along its surface. Probably the wind-shadow is different for different shapes of sails and may also vary with the velocity of the wind and the speed of the boats. But the conical shape is probably near enough to the truth to guide us in our tactics. The most important points to bear in mind are the length of the shadow—four times the height of the mast, and its direction—directly to leeward of the blanketing boat.

It will be evident from this description of the wind-shadow that the power to blanket decreases very rapidly in proportion to the distance between the two boats. It will also be evident that near the apex of the wind-shadow cone there is an increased need for ac-

curacy, because the area of the cone is so small near
its apex.

By far, the most frequent error in blanketing is to
misjudge the direction of the wind-shadow. An opportunity, for instance, is presented when two boats
converge on opposite tacks, one somewhat ahead of
the other. The boat that is ahead must go about precisely on the wind of the following boat in order to lay
her wind-shadow across the other boat's sails and thus
cut off her wind and stop her. It is very easy to make
the mistake of tacking too late so that the leeward
boat finds herself not in the wind-shadow but ahead of
it and thus in the best possible position to escape.
When sailing close-hauled on the wind, the blanketing
boat must have the other boat four points abaft the
beam or, in other words, must look back at her at an
angle of 45°.

It is important, in tacking on another boat's wind,
and thus blanketing her, that the two boats be very
close together. If the leading boat is at a considerable
distance ahead, the blanketing will not cause much
damage. In Fig. 45 we see two well-defined instances
of blanketing on the wind. In each case the windward
boat is heeled noticeably more than the leeward boat
and is evidently therefore getting more wind. In Fig.
45B, the boats are farther apart but it is evident that
the topsail of the leeward boat has had its wind cut
off.

In the start among the 10-Metres shown in Fig. 46,
it is evident that No. 5 has been blanketed by the leading boat and that No. 6 has been blanketed by No. 2.

As a rule, however, the leading boat instead of
blanketing resorts to another device. She crosses the
second boat's wind and goes about directly ahead of

Levick

Fɪɢ. 45. Blanketing on the wind

Levick

Fɪɢ. 46. Blanketing in a start

FIG. 47. An ill-advised luffing-match. The second and third boats are letting the first boat escape. The fourth boat will presently bear away

FIG. 48. A case of blanketing while running

the following boat, thereby attacking her with two
weapons. First, she bends the wind; second, she breaks
the water. If you will refer to Fig. 40, you will observe
that if the leading boat goes about directly ahead of
another boat, the trailing boat will be in her back-wind
zone instead of in her wind-shadow. But she will be
stopped no less effectively. The following boat, sailing
directly in the wake of the leading boat, suddenly dis-
covers that she cannot point so high into the wind.
Actually, her ability to point has not been changed.
What happens is that the wind's direction has been
changed so that the following boat now gets the wind
more nearly ahead and therefore points farther to leeward. The following boat also finds her water broken
up by the wake of the leading boat. Struggling thus in
broken water, with her wind somewhat impaired and
seriously bent, she slows down and falls off to leeward
and is in what Dr. Curry calls the "hopeless position."
In this position her performance becomes progressively
worse until the leading boat draws so far ahead that
she is outside the Zone of Interference. From this position, it is impossible for the following boat to overtake
and pass the leading boat even though the following
boat may ordinarily be very much faster.

A small boat, employing these tactics, will seriously
interfere with a large boat, but a large boat, because
she is hard to blanket and because the puny waves of
the smaller boat do not interfere with her more powerful hull, may still beat the small boat from this position.

From the forward edge of the wind-shadow of the
leading boat, aft and clear around to a position directly
abeam of her to windward, the following boat is in a
hopeless position from which she cannot hope to escape

except by tacking. Even if she tacks, she is most likely to be pounced upon by the leading boat which, going about at the same time, is able to place her in the same relative position on the other tack. The only way in which the following boat can escape is to tack immediately when the other boat tacks on her wind or ahead of her. In that way she may put herself forward of the wind-shadow when the leading boat comes about to cover her again. If, however, it seems as if the leading boat would catch her once more, she should split tacks with the leading boat, tack for tack, without any let-up until one or the other draws free. Similarly, the leading boat should tack every time the following boat seeks to escape, always sailing on the same tack with her and always striving to be either directly ahead or on her wind.

The objective of the following boat is always to get free at the first possible instant. If she cannot escape by tacking, she should bear away immediately, thus sacrificing some of her gain to windward but maintaining her steerage way and getting out of the wake and out of the wind-shadow. Of course, if the leading boat tacks directly ahead of the following boat, it is hard to escape by bearing away, for she will bear away directly into the wind-shadow of the leading boat. She will, however, travel faster when she bears away and, if she is not too close, her added speed may carry her through the apex of the wind-shadow to a point where it is no longer annoying. It takes courage to throw away hard won yards by sailing to leeward when one is bound to windward, but the minute it is recognized as the only remedy, the bitter pill should be swallowed and the action taken promptly. If it is not taken, the following boat will find herself in a worse position with a much reduced hope of getting out ahead.

I have often suspected that when the leading boat either blankets the following boat or tacks directly ahead of her, that not only is the following boat hurt, but the leading boat is helped. Therefore, there is a double reason for the promptest possible escape from this position.

On a reach, the same considerations hold true as on the wind, except that the direction of the cone of the wind-shadow points farther forward. With a beam wind, the wind-shadow points directly abeam. See Fig. 43. On a broad reach the wind-shadow points about midway between the point abeam and the point ahead. On a close reach the wind-shadow points between four points abaft the beam and abeam. The opportunities for blanketing on a reach are somewhat limited, for most of the opportunities for blanketing on the wind come when two boats are converging on opposite tacks. On a reach, boats are always sailing on the same tack and therefore the only means of blanketing is when one boat overtakes another.

Let it be said here that with two boats of approximately equal speed, it is almost impossible for one boat to overtake another on the windward side close enough to the leeward boat to effect blanketing. So true is this that I make it a rule never to attempt to blanket another boat on the wind except when converging upon her on the opposite tack.

There are two reasons for this: The first is that the overtaken boat has right-of-way. She is permitted to luff as she pleases to hinder you from overtaking her to windward until she has reached the point where her bowsprit end, or stem-head if she has no bowsprit, would strike your boat aft of the shrouds. Thereafter her right to luff farther from her course ceases. In some interpretations of the racing rules, it is held that, if she holds this course and you continue sailing and she strikes you aft of the shrouds, you are disqualified. (I am not in sympathy with this interpretation of the rules, but feel that they should be interpreted to mean that if the two boats come together and the point of contact is forward of the shrouds of the overtaking boat, the overtaking boat is thereby disqualified, but if they come together and the point of contact is abaft the shrouds, the overtaken boat is disqualified.) At no time must the overtaken boat bear away on a boat to leeward. When an overtaking boat starts to sail through the wind of the overtaken boat, the overtaken boat usually indulges in what is known as a luffing match, or a dog fight. She puts her helm down, luffing sharply and compelling the overtaking boat to luff as well. Then, when they start to lose way, both boats bear away again and then commence the luffing match all over. There is always danger in a luffing match that one or other of the boats will be disqualified, but a more imminent danger is that some of the other boats in the race that are not involved in the luffing match will escape and win the race. In Fig. 47 we see Boat 4 luffing out the overtaking Boat 13. Boat 15 is also involved, whereas the boat in the foreground is romping on to win the race.

(Since writing this, I am not so certain that Fig. 47 really illustrates the point I am trying to make. The trim of the sheets of the leading boat convinces me that this picture was taken at a starting line and that the boats are heading for the line but that the leading boat is too early and is bearing away without starting her sheets. The impossibility of finding a better illustration, however, has induced me to print this with the explanation that although this is really not a luffing match it pictures a luffing match exactly as it would occur, except that the sheets of the leading boat would be started on the course she is sailing.)

But the danger of a luffing match is not the only reason why an overtaking boat should not attempt to blanket the overtaken boat. If the overtaken boat simply holds her course without attempting to luff, she is almost certain to draw ahead and to stop the overtaking boat dead in her tracks. This will be explained in the following chapter.

When the wind is abeam or forward of the beam, blanketing is a weapon that may be used by the leading boat only.

When the wind is abaft the beam, however, the use of blanketing is restricted to the overtaking boat. On a run a boat is blanketed by another boat which sails up directly behind her, or, in other words, directly on her wind. In Fig. 48, the leading boat is about to be blanketed by No. 62. The leading boat protects herself by luffing. It is essential, however, that this luff shall be started early enough. In other words, the leading boat must always keep herself to windward of the course of the following boat even though she is thereby driven òff her course. If she waits until too late to start her luff, the following boat will luff at the same time and will be able to hang on to her wind for three-quarters of a circle. Somewhere in that circuitous course the overtaking boat will blanket the overtaken boat and she can then bear away and pull out ahead. It is probably best for the overtaken boat to protect herself by luffing, but after the blanketing has commenced I have never seen it done. If the overtaken boat starts her luffing before the overtaking boat comes into the Zone of Interference, she will be all right. After that, it is too late. The only thing for the overtaken boat to do is to pretend to luff by trimming her sheets and actually altering her course nearer to the wind so that the overtaking boat does likewise. Then the overtaken boat should jibe quickly, steer wide of the overtaking boat, and either bear away or jibe again, depending on the location of the next mark. The luff, when executed in this manner, is a splendid ruse that draws the overtaking boat off her guard and, if the overtaken boat can complete her jibes just a few seconds before the overtaking boat, she will win clear and be able to resume the race without immediate interference.

It will be evident from this chapter that blanketing is an extremely valuable field of tactics, but that it has its distinct limitations. When it works, it stops the blanketed boat so decisively that all of us are tempted to use blanketing much more frequently than we are justified. On the wind it should be attempted only when converging on opposite tacks, and even then it is not usually more effective than tacking on her bow. To attempt to overtake a boat on the wind and to blanket in the course of that action is nearly always disastrous.

CHAPTER XXVI

TACTICS—BACK-WINDING

BY BACK-WINDING is meant the turning or diverting of a current of air by the sails of one boat so as to affect adversely a competing boat. When the wind blows on a curved sail, it is turned in much the same manner as steam is turned by the baffle plates of a boiler or the stationary vanes of a turbine. (See Fig. 44.)

FIG. 44. Showing how the boat ahead bends the wind of the following boat

A boat can back-wind another at any point in her back-wind zone. (See Fig. 40.) On the wind, this zone extends from the after edge of her wind-shadow aft and clear around to a point abeam to windward.

Back-winding to my mind is by far the most potent form of interference with another boat—the best tactical weapon in the hands of the yachtsman. Back-winding is most noticeable in two situations: 1. Where one boat is directly ahead of another. This situation has been explained in the chapter on blanketing. 2. Where one boat is to leeward of another and slightly ahead of her wind-shadow. In Figs. 49A, B, C and D, you will notice that in each case the boat to leeward is heeling more sharply than the boat to windward. This means that the boat to leeward is getting more wind and that she is throwing the back wind from her sails on the leeward side of the sails of the windward boat. When two boats of approximately equal speed are in this position, the leeward boat always draws ahead. In Fig. 50A, you will note that No. 3 is heeling more than her opponent to windward and throwing the wind from her sails back against the lee side of the windward boat's sails. In Fig. 50B, we see the same boats a moment later. No. 3 has drawn ahead.

The same situation is shown in Figs. 51A and B. In Fig. 51A, the middle boat is heeling more than the windward boat and the leeward boat more than the middle boat. In Fig. 51B a moment later taken from the same angle, it is evident that the leeward boat is clear ahead and the windward boat is behind the middle boat whose top-mast is just showing.

When both boats are on the wind, the leeward boat not only sails faster, but can also point higher. If the windward boat does not tack or make a successful effort to draw far to windward, she is certain to slip back, then to fall into the wake of the leeward boat, then to slide down to leeward into the so-called hope-less position. It is very difficult for the weather boat to escape from this unfavorable position unless she tacks. To my mind, therefore, it is important for the weather

FIG. 49A *Levick*

FIG. 49B *Levick*

FIG. 49C *Levick*   FIG. 49D *Levick*

FIG. 49. Back-winding

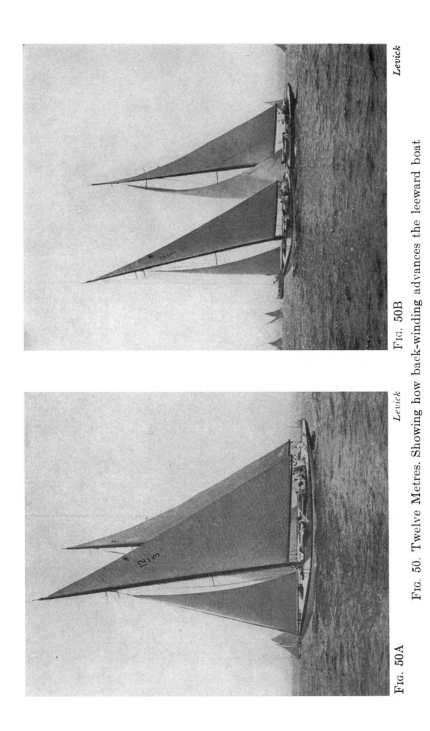

Fig. 50A

Fig. 50B

Fig. 50. Twelve Metres. Showing how back-winding advances the leeward boat

boat always to make a short tack to windward even though she can already lay the mark. Dr. Curry calls this position of the leeward boat the "safe leeward berth." I feel that this nomenclature is unfortunate because it gives the impression that this leeward berth is a defensive position and that the objective of getting into this position is to secure safety. The position from which one boat may back-wind another is distinctly an offensive position—a position from which she can interfere seriously with the progress of the windward boat. It is a position well worth maneuvering for and can be used to advantage not merely by a boat converging on another on the opposite tack, but also by an overtaking boat.

Assume, for instance, that two boats are converging on opposite tacks on equal terms. The boat on the starboard tack has right-of-way. It is always a temptation when you have right-of-way to force the other boat to go about, and there is sound reasoning behind this temptation, for by so doing you may disturb the well-laid plans of your opponent. It is far better, however, before your opponent goes about, to tack in his lee at such a time, and in such a position, that when you are on the port tack your boat will be forward of your opponent's wind-shadow. The wind is now striking your sails across the bow of your opponent. You are getting its full benefit, but the wind, striking your sails, is bent back against your opponent in such a way that he is not receiving the full force of it. You will begin very rapidly to draw ahead. Presently, your opponent's bow will be behind your stern. With dramatic swiftness he is forced to point farther from the apparent wind. He drops back into your wake. Presently, he is far behind and to leeward and soon you will be several minutes ahead. The decisiveness with which you stop him, push him back, and thrust him down to leeward is one of the most vivid phases of yachting. To my mind, this is more important than blanketing your opponent or going about directly ahead of him, because, from an equal or possibly inferior position, you achieve successively all the advantages—first, of back-winding, second, of thrusting your opponent into your wake, and, third, of dropping him into the hopeless position where he is blanketed by you. You must observe extreme caution in going about ahead of your opponent's wind-shadow. This means that you must go about in such a way that you will gain full headway before the wind-shadow creeps up and blankets you. If you are a heart-beat too late, the ominous wind-shadow will creep across your sails, you will be blanketed and thrust back into the hopeless position. If an opponent converges upon you and gains this back-winding position, the only thing for you to do is to tack at once. It is wise, of course, to wait long enough to see whether your headway will enable you to overtake his sails with your wind-shadow; but if your opponent goes about in your lee and it is evident that he is getting his wind across your bow, and he gains way fast enough so that presently he is going just as fast as you are, then do not wait. Go about at once.

Levick

Fig. 51B

Levick

Fig. 51. N. Y. Forties. Showing how back-winding advances the leeward boat

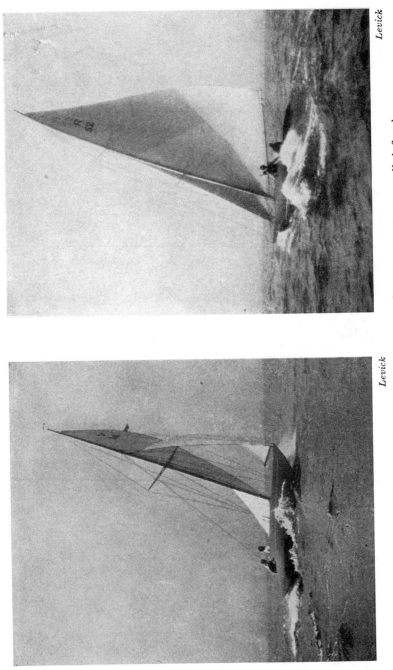

Levick

Levick

Fig. 52. Broken water—the bow waves and stern waves are well-defined

Chapter XXVII

TACTICS—BROKEN WATER

In an ordinary wave, the water moves but little. The undulation of the wave travels without disturbing the particles of water very greatly. Of course the very top layer moves somewhat, and also when the waves break to form whitecaps, there is considerable motion to the water particles. But they all move in fairly regular progression in a manner that is not greatly disturbing to the progress of a boat.

But when a boat has passed through the water, it is a different story. The particles of water are disturbed and pushed out of the way to make room for the boat. It is churned up for a depth equal to the draft of the boat and curled up in waves at the surface. After the boat has passed, the particles of water rush back into the position from which they have been displaced and whirl around in eddies. This displacement and replacement of the water particles interfere with the regular progression of the normal waves. The total effect on a boat that tries to sail through water thus broken is a destruction of the rhythm of its progress. Thus, if two boats are racing in close proximity to one another, and one boat is ahead, its broken water seriously handicaps the following boat.

Broken water is most clearly evidenced by three phenomena—the bow wave, the stern wave, and the wake. The bow wave, as its name implies, is thrown off by the bow of the boat. It starts to curl away from the boat slightly aft of the bow and is usually at a fairly sharp angle to it. This angle differs with different boats and in different conditions of speed and seas. It is also affected by the depth of the water. But, in general, it forms a fairly sharp angle, lying usually nearer to the boat than to a right angle from the boat.

The stern wave forms under the counter. It differs from the bow wave in that it rolls off more nearly at a right angle to the course of the boat. I do not believe that there can be any rule for the exact direction of the stern wave any more than for the bow wave, except that the stern wave always makes a broader angle with the course of the boat than the bow wave, no matter what angle the bow wave may take.

From the study of hundreds of photographs of bow and stern waves, I am forced to the conclusion that they are seldom equal in magnitude. Sometimes the bow wave is well defined and sometimes the stern wave. There is great similarity in the waves caused by all boats of the same design; and there are perceptible differences in the waves caused by boats of different design. Although the Victories and the Interclubs are very close to one another in point of size, there is a marked difference in their bow and stern waves. These differences will repay close study, but they are beyond the scope of this book.

Now it is apparent that if these two pairs of waves are not parallel, they must intersect. This point of intersection is most significant to the racing man, for at that point, the waves fight one another and seem to disappear. If the skipper of an overtaking boat can detect the point where these waves intersect, he can break through them at or just behind the point of intersection. The detection of this point, however, is not always easy. The bow and stern waves are not exactly continuous. It is necessary to trace their general direction from their points of origin and protract them to an imaginary and moving point where they will intersect.

One would think on the face of it that if a wave cannot be detected by the eye, it will offer no resistance to the passage of a boat. But the trouble is that these waves follow a definite direction but are not apparent at all times at all parts of the wave. If you aim at some part of the wave line other than the intersection, there may be no visible wave at one moment, but the next moment it may heave up and break at that very point. The intersection, then, is the only spot at which an overtaking boat should attempt to break through, whether the overtaking is to windward or to leeward.

In Fig. 52, the bow wave and the stern wave are pretty well defined. These two pictures are reproduced here to show exactly where the waves originate, because it is at these points that the overtaking skipper must seek the origin of these waves and try to trace out their direction. In Fig. 53, the white lines show the direction of the waves and the point of their intersection. It is evident that at this spot, neither wave will offer much resistance.

It very often happens that in overtaking a boat to leeward, the point of intersection of the two waves will very nearly coincide with the apex of her wind-shadow. When sailing close-hauled, it is always a good idea to aim at the point of intersection first. If then, no further progress is possible, bear away to get farther from the wind-shadow of the overtaken boat. There have been occasions when I have had to do this—to seek one spot where it was possible to break through my opponent's broken water, and another spot where it was possible to break through her wind. But more often than not, I have been able to get through the narrow and feeble wind-shadow right at the point where the waves of broken water crossed one another.

The overtaken boat can move this point of intersection around by suddenly yawing wildly and thus interfering with the plans of the overtaking boat. It is not easy to do, and it takes practice to get the timing right, but when the full value of broken water as a defense is realized, it will pay to learn just how to do this with your own boat.

The water streaming directly astern of a boat is her wake. The water in a wake is swirling around rapidly, not only on the surface, but to a considerable depth. It is very hard to sail fast through another boat's wake. It is this fact as well as the fact of back-winding that makes the position directly astern of another boat the worst of all positions on any course to windward.

In the conduct of any race, it is well to consider the effect of broken water turned up by your own boat and by other boats as well. By converging on a boat that is abeam, it is sometimes possible to erect a wall of broken water by utilizing the waves of both boats. If your most dangerous competitor is behind you at that moment, it is possible to keep him there for a very long time. In Fig. 54 we see a similar impenetrable wall of broken water between the boats that are strung out in a line. Behind them No. 19 is pocketed in such a way that her only avenue of escape is in sailing around rather than between the leading boats.

Fɪɢ. 52. The point of intersection of bow and stern waves

Levick

Fig. 54. An impenetrable wall of broken water

Chapter XXVIII

TACTICS—BREAKING THROUGH

WHEN TWO boats are close-hauled on the wind, the overtaking boat is faced with the difficult problem of breaking through. She may overtake to windward, or she may sail through the other boat's lee. Either course is fraught with danger. The danger in overtaking to windward is in sailing into the other boat's backwind zone, thereby giving her a lift ahead, having your own wind turned so that you cannot point so high, and being definitely stopped by the flow of back wind from her sails. On the windward side, too, you find the leading boat's broken water, her bow wave, and her stern wave. If you are aided by a sudden puff of wind and find yourself more ready to take advantage of it than your opponent may be at the moment, it is possible to break through. The only point where this is possible is where her bow wave and stern wave intersect. If you can sail through the intersection and keep going fast, staying to windward just as far as possible, you may be able to break through her back-wind defense, eventually blanketing her, and sail on to victory. If you are any closer to her than the intersection of her bow and stern waves, this is practically impossible. If the leading boat is alert, however, luffs when you luff, and keeps you from getting into a berth well to windward, she can effectively stop you.

275

Because of this fact, I never attempt to overtake a boat of equal size to windward. Unless it is unavoidable, I never overtake a small boat to windward because I deem it bad sportsmanship. A big boat, because of her superior speed, and because she is less affected by the back-wind of the small boat, can overtake to windward when a boat in the same class as the overtaking boat cannot do so. Of course, if you are sailing in a handicap race and the smaller boat has all the benefit of time allowance, it is perfectly good sportsmanship to sail through her wind and stop her all that you can.

To pretend to try to break through to windward, however, is very valuable as a feint, and I recall several races that I have won just by this device. To sail through another boat's lee is easier than it seems. There we have no back-wind area to contend with, but we do have a wind-shadow and we have the same bow and stern waves to break through. The best way to sail through another boat's lee is to pretend to overtake to windward; get up on her weather quarter just as though you were trying to break through to windward and stay there just long enough to reassure the other skipper as to your intentions. As soon as he has seen you in that position, he will conclude that you are not dangerous and will probably devote his attention more to sailing his own boat than to watching you. Inform your crew of your intentions beforehand so that they will be alert and ready to handle the main sheet and jib sheet. Then, when your opponent's attention is distracted, bear away suddenly across her stern, starting your sheets to their most efficient angle on the new course. The course should be two or three points freer than the course you have been sailing. By this means you will suddenly increase the speed of your boat and will be aiming at the intersection of the bow wave and stern wave of your opponent. Slightly beyond the intersection of these waves lies the apex of the cone of his wind-shadow. You will not quite clear the wind-shadow, but you will sail through it at a point where it is very narrow and not particularly effective. The extra jump which you will give your boat by sailing thus on a freer course will give you sufficient momentum to carry you through the point of the wind-shadow so that presently you will be receiving your wind across the other boat's bow. Hold on until your bow is on a line with his bow. Then trim your sheets just as close as possible and sail a parallel course, or, if he is not entirely close-hauled, trim closer so as to converge upon him. You are an overtaking boat and must keep clear, but there is no reason why you cannot sail just as close to your opponent as you can possibly lie. You are now forward of his wind-shadow and he is lying directly in your back-wind zone so that you will get a lift ahead from his sails. Your back wind will slow him up and presently you will draw up ahead to a commanding position. From the minute your bow becomes level with your opponent's you have won the skirmish. As soon as your bow is clear ahead and you are laying a course closer than your opponent's, he will start to go back like an express train. Soon you will be clear ahead and your opponent will be sailing in your wake. The distance between the two boats will widen and your opponent will also drop back to leeward. Then you can forget him.

The advantages of starting this maneuver from a windward berth are the following: 1. You mislead your opponent as to your intentions. 2. You will be able to sail a freer course through his wind-shadow and thereby gain the necessary momentum to break through. 3. You are affected less by his back wind than if you were directly astern. 4. You are affected less by the eddies and broken water in his wake than if you were astern or to leeward. There is no greater fun in yachting than breaking through in this manner.

On a reach, the business of breaking through is much more difficult than on the wind. The reason for that is that it is very difficult momentarily to increase your speed by altering your course. Furthermore, on a reach most boats sail more nearly at the same speed than on the wind. Helmsmanship seems to count for less. Furthermore, the wind-shadow of your opponent points so much farther forward than when sailing on the wind that it is very difficult to break through it and get your wind free across your opponent's bow. When sailing on the wind, you get your wind free as soon as your bow is level with your opponent's. In reaching with a beam wind your boat must be clear of your opponent's wind-shadow. Your back wind affects him less adversely because your sheets are started farther and your back wind does not flow so much to windward. We can conclude from this, therefore, that the better side to break through when reaching is the windward side. On the windward side your opponent's back wind is less effective, your windshadow, pointing farther forward than when closehauled, blankets your opponent's sails more quickly and you do not have to draw clear ahead to dominate the situation.

In overtaking before the wind you should endeavor to sail right in your opponent's wake if the wind is

dead astern. If your run is merely a broad reach, you
must get to windward of your opponent, then from
that position steer directly down on him. Sail up to
him just as if you were going to run him down and do
not bear up to clear him until the last possible moment.
In attempting this maneuver at sea you must use
special care. If your opponent drops down into the
hollow between two waves while you are riding on a
crest, you may gain a sudden momentum, rush up on
him, blanket him suddenly, and run your bow up on
his taffrail before you can bear up and escape him. In
calm waters this danger is not so great, but in sailing
before the wind you will seem to blanket your opponent not at all, then all of a sudden you will blanket
him completely and he will stop dead in his tracks.
This is a moment which tests the alertness of the
helmsman. The tiller must be moved rapidly in two
directions: First, down to clear him with your bow and
then up to swing back toward him with your bow in
order to clear him with your stern. Do not bear away
more than is necessary, however, and keep your mainsail across his boat to blanket part of his mainsail and
also his spinnaker, then before you strike his backstay with your boom, you must bear up some more in
order to go clear. In all of this maneuvering you must
be careful of a sudden luff on your opponent's part.
You are an overtaking boat, sailing the same course or
nearly so and any sudden luff on his part may cause
a foul which will put you out of the race. At this point,
too, watch for a jibe on the part of your opponent. If
he waits until you have blanketed him before jibing,
it is usually too late for you to do anything about it
except to avoid collision with his stern. If he starts to
jibe just before he is blanketed it is wise for you to jibe

too. If he luffs as you approach, you should be prepared to luff also. Have enough man power on the main sheet to enable you to trim quickly, and have a hand at the spinnaker guy ready to let it run. Nine times out of ten you can cut corners, get closer to him, blanket him completely, stop him, run around him, and draw clear ahead.

Chapter XXIX

TACTICS—GENERAL STRATEGY

EXCEPT WHEN a boat is so far ahead that she can sail her own race, her skipper must always bear in mind that every move he makes will have some effect upon his relationship to the other boats in the race. Let us take a situation which occurred frequently upon the home course of the club in which I sailed many years ago. The prevailing wind was Southwest and the starting line lay between the mark and the crow's nest of the yacht club perched upon the end of a large high dock. The buoy end of the line was always best. The line inclined somewhat across the course so that the buoy end was a little nearer the first mark than the crow's nest end in which sat the august Race Committee. Furthermore, on the prevailing wind you could jockey freely up to the buoy, whereas the size of the dock prevented you from maneuvering freely at the opposite end. The dock, with its load of spectators, its automobiles, and the clubhouse, combined to blanket boats that sailed too close to it. Therefore, the best skippers always chose the buoy end. But the prevailing Southwest wind was always a little stronger close in under the shore. Therefore, the boats that started at the buoy end on the starboard tack invariably made the best starts, but the boats that chose the dock end were soon able to tack inshore and work along in smoother waters and a better breeze. It was, therefore, always a problem for boats that started at the buoy end to sail through their opponents into the zone of better going along the shore.

This is how we would do it. For four or five minutes after the start we would hold along on the starboard tack, standing out away from the shore and almost parallel to it, then taking careful bearings on the boats that were behind and to windward, we would judge when the time was ripe to go about. If there was another boat bearing slightly more than four points abaft our beam, we would go about and endeavor to meet that other boat even though she held the starboard tack and we were on the port tack. Just before we came together, we would throw the boat about so that our bow would be just a little ahead of our opponent's and we would get our wind free over her bow. In a few minutes she would drop back into our wake and, if she were a dangerous boat, we would hang on and punish her. If we were not particularly afraid of her, but saw a more dangerous opponent to windward and four points abaft the beam, we would go about again, get a lift from that boat and thus continue, repeating the situation with each boat in succession until we found ourselves in the desired position under the shore where we could sail fast with the long string of our opponents behind us and to leeward.

It is to be noted that this excellent strategy almost always worked despite the fact that at no time did we have right-of-way. Each boat proved a stepping stone from which we made a distinct gain even on the boats ahead, and each boat we thus back-winded was placed definitely behind us. Whenever you see an opponent whom you can treat in this way, you should attempt to sail close to her and back-wind her not only because you stop her but because you will travel faster in the process and gain considerably on the boats ahead. There are two dangers in this process which must not be overlooked. The first is that your opponent is armed with a powerful weapon—the right-of-way. If you sail too close to him while he is on the starboard tack, he may suddenly go about on the port tack and, hoisting his protest flag, claim that you have put him in danger of a foul; and danger of a foul is considered nowadays as a foul. If you suspect from tenseness aboard the other boat that this is her intention, do not hesitate to hail her, telling her to hold her course and that you intend to go about. If, after that, she goes about and protests, you have established a clear defense, provided that you have not run so close as to make the danger of a foul really imminent.

The other danger, inherent in these tactics, is this: You are certain to lose some headway when you go about. You may misjudge the way which your opponent is carrying and if you go about just one second too late, instead of being in a position to back-wind him, he will be in a position to blanket you, for his superior way will carry him through your back-wind area and his wind-shadow will begin to creep across your sails. This places you in a particularly bad position because you will not be able to go about and you will be properly spanked and put to bed far down to leeward and far behind your opponent.

This danger is particularly great on puffy days. If just at the moment when you are going about, a strong squall sets in, it will kill your momentum instantly. At the same time your opponent, who is still sailing, will get increased speed from the squall so that he can sail right through you and blanket you while your sails are still shaking and you are lying helpless.

There are two general rules of yachting which should be borne always in mind. As has been pointed out, they do not always apply, for frequently opportunism is more important than tactics and it is better to take advantage of a shift of wind than to try to retard an opponent. But, in general, these two rules should be followed. They are: 1. Always keep between your opponent and the mark. 2. Always keep your most dangerous opponent covered. Another rule to bear in mind is to have all your dog fights in the open. Do not attempt them near a mark unless you have the advantage of right-of-way.

Occasionally, one is so fortunate as to be able to compound his offensive and defensive tactics. It is conceivable that a boat, by back-winding one opponent, may be in a position to drop him back so that he will seriously interfere with another and at the same time get such a forward lift from her that he will be able to sail through the wind-shadow of a third. This is usually achieved more by good luck than good management. But if a skipper thoroughly understands all that goes on in the Zone of Interference, it is easy to work out the combinations of possibilities in a closely bunched fleet.

The opportunities for the application of racing tactics apply most often at the starting line or near the marks. At the starting line one must consider the possibilities of both back-winding and blanketing. It is here that one must decide promptly whether to tack or to hold on. A boat that is hopelessly blanketed or back-winded should tack at once to free her wind, but once having her wind free, it is not always wise to hold the course. Usually, it is the part of good sense to go about and sail the same course as your opponents. The only justification for splitting tacks is when you know that you can gain an advantage from it or when you know that you are so hopelessly beaten that you split tacks to get a break which the other boats may not get.

This consideration should not enter into your racing strategy as long as there is any chance of out-sailing your opponents on the course which seems best to the majority. Very seldom does the boat that splits tacks gain any decided advantage from unforeseen breaks, but if you are losing anyway, it does not matter whether you are beaten by five minutes or by twenty minutes, and there is always just a chance that you may sail into more favorable conditions. An observing opponent of mine said recently that my boat was both the fastest and the slowest that he had ever seen; that there were days when it was impossible to catch me and days when I was beaten so badly that it did not seem as if I were in the same race. I think probably a large part of this is due to my favorite strategy of splitting tacks when I know I am beaten. Once in a while it makes me win, but far more often I am beaten by much wider margins than if I had sailed the logical and obvious course. To my mind this does not matter. If I am beaten anyway I may just as well be beaten badly, but I dread reading the Sunday papers the next day.

The proximity of an opponent is often the very best reason for not sailing a straight course to the next mark. If you have an opponent overlapping your stern on your weather quarter, and you sail a straight course for the next mark or for the finish line, your opponent will sail the same distance that you do and may catch you in the process. If, however, you sail to the next mark or to the finish line on a wide circle, you will compel him to sail a still wider circle until he either overtakes you or drops behind and heads for the mark. The minute he drops behind, you can head for the mark, too, thus cutting off a corner, but he must either deliberately slow down his boat, thus reëstablishing your lead, or else must sail a longer distance if you travel on the circumference of a wide circle.

In general then, the best ways to stop an opponent are: 1. Sailing close-hauled to tack directly in front of him. 2. Sailing close-hauled to tack directly to windward of him so as to blanket him. 3. Sailing close-hauled to come about in his lee, forward of his wind-shadow. 4. Sailing close-hauled to overtake him by sailing through his lee and stop him with your back wind. 5. Running before the wind, to sail directly down wind until very close and blanket him. 6. When reaching, to stop him with your back wind if you are ahead, or to try to get abeam and stop him by blanketing him if you are behind. 7. In general, to place yourself in his adverse zone. Always to avoid his back-wind zone. Always to avoid his wind-shadow.

Chapter XXX

RACING RULES AND THEIR APPLICATION

Second only to a boat and water to sail her on, a racing skipper must have a rule book. Since the racing rules are so necessary a part of his equipment, I deem it unnecessary to reproduce them here. Such a printing of the rules would pad this book unnecessarily, and it is already too lengthy. Furthermore, rules change from time to time, and the printing of any rules in this book might subject it to quick obsolescence at the hands of a rules committee.

The rules must be not only on the printed page but also in the skipper's head. Every skipper should study the rules very carefully, should review them every season, should make a thorough effort to understand them, and should keep alert to the changes which are enacted from time to time. In the course of my racing, the rules have undergone constant amendment and no less than four complete re-codifications. The rules as they stand at the time this book is written have been immensely simplified, but in the simplification they have lost somewhat of their former clarity. To understand the present racing rules, it is wise to go back to the older codifications; get hold of a rule book that is twenty years old and see how they ran races in those days. The changes are primarily verbal, yet little subtleties of meaning have crept in, and a comparison of the old rules with the new ones will go a long way toward making the present rules clear.

This study has a further benefit. As a rule, members of a Race Committee are old timers who are not sufficiently active physically to engage in the participation of a race. These older men formulated their ideas of the racing rules at a time when the rules were somewhat different from what they are to-day. I recall a freezing, water soaked session, arguing with the Race Committee in one of the two protests which I have made in my entire racing history and was amazed to find that only one man on the Committee was familiar with the rule under which the protest was lodged. If it had not been that I had studied an old rule book, and therefore knew the obsolete rules that were causing the misunderstanding, I would never have been able to clear away the confusion that reigned in the minds of these men. It is well to understand not merely the rules, but the changes, in order to be a good sea lawyer and, in addition, to realize the confusion that may possibly exist in the minds of your competitors if they are old timers at the game.

It is a very easy matter to sit down with the situation carefully drawn on paper and figure out the exact application of the rules to a definite situation. Clear, logical thinking and exact interpretation of the meaning of the wording of the rules will clear up nearly every situation that arises; but when you are in the middle of a race, watching your boat, watching the mark, watching the wind, watching your competitors, with the sail down to the water-edge on one side and the weather rail of your boat high in the air on the other side, green water breaking over the bow, and four or five boats involved in a close tangle all at once, it is pretty hard to define the exact situation or to recall the exact rule which governs it.

The only solution for conditions like this is to keep alert to the situation at all times. The relationship between two boats changes so rapidly that one should have three things in mind in order to clarify his thinking. First, the point at which one yacht enters the zone of collision with another yacht and the circumstances of that entry. Second, the moment of the foul. Third, the set of rules which governs the situation.

Let me explain. Boats A and B round a mark and sail off before the wind. Boat A is in the lead with clear water all about her. Boat B, coming up from astern attempts to blanket Boat A. Boat B is sailing the same course as Boat A or nearly so. Sailing very close to Boat A, Boat B's bow overlaps Boat A's stern. Boat B has now entered the zone of collision as an overtaking boat. She continues to close in on Boat A until her bow is about amidships of Boat A. She then draws farther off to the side but is still within the zone of collision and it is impossible for either boat to put her helm hard over in either direction without a collision resulting. In that situation the boats sail for two miles. Much time has elapsed; there has been kidding and conversation between the two boats and then Boat A starts drawing away. She is traveling very much faster than Boat B. Boat B, falling astern, tries to duck under Boat A's lee and in doing so her bobstay scrapes Boat A's stern. The alert skipper watches the first moment in which Boat B makes an overlap. He decides that Boat B has entered the zone of collision as an overtaking boat; therefore Boat A has right-of-way. Half an hour later when the actual foul occurs, Boat B is still an overtaking boat under the rules, despite the fact that Boat A is traveling faster. It is in a situation like this that the beginner becomes confused. In the excitement of being overtaken he may fail to note that Boat A has right-of-way. In the excitement of the foul occurring much later, he may conclude that Boat A is the overtaking boat inasmuch as Boat A is traveling faster than Boat B. But Boat B rates as the overtaking boat from the time she enters the zone of collision until she again draws clear. The time of entering the zone of collision and the moment of the foul are long separated in time and in distance but the question of right-of-way remains the same. The alert skipper is noting such situations constantly throughout the race. Every moment he decides, "I have right-of-way over No. 7; No. 13 has right-of-way over me; in a few minutes I may have to yield right-of-way to Boat 4; it depends on what she does; I'll watch and see."

A study of the racing rules reveals that a certain batch of rules governs the conditions of ordinary sailing, that another batch of rules takes precedence when in the immediate proximity of a mark, that still a third batch governs at the starting line. For instance, a boat overtaking to windward does not have the right-of-way in ordinary sailing and the overtaken boat may luff as she pleases to prevent the overtaking boat from passing her on the windward side, but if they overlap at the mark the overtaken boat must leave room for the overtaking boat to pass between her and the mark. Thus one rule takes precedence over another and the alert skipper must be careful at all times to note just what rule governs in the circumstances.

Any foul in yacht racing sooner or later winds up in a debate before the Race Committee and the most disagreeable situations arise when the competitors disagree on the facts of the case. No protest is ever disagreeable that is determined on a question of law; but when facts are in dispute, the protest can become genuinely nasty. It is my belief that no one should ever draw up a contract without the conviction that the contract will end up in a law court and the full meaning of the parties will have to be explained before a judge and jury. In the same way any ticklish situation should be handled in a yacht race precisely as though you were going into court. For example, two boats are approaching one another and are about to enter into the zone of collision. The skipper of one boat summons his crew to attention. "Look," he says, "we are approaching dangerously close to No. 11. Note that we are a converging boat, holding a better course. Everybody take a squint along the center line of the boat and note the difference in the courses each boat is sailing. I want you to be able to witness this." The crew looks and makes mental notes. They may see that on the boat on which they are converging the upper block of the runner tackle is in range with her mast. Five men note this. On the other boat no one pays attention to the converging boat until she is close aboard and forced to bear away to avoid a collision. There is a protest and at the trial a difference of opinion as to facts. The crew of one boat gives testimony. They all observed the situation accurately and clearly and can explain it to the Race Committee. The crew of the other boat are of the opinion that the boat which committed the alleged foul was an overtaking boat and not a converging boat. But none of these men took bearings or ranges, or closely observed how that boat entered into the zone of collision. The boat whose crew was properly prepared as witnesses will win the decision.

At various points throughout this book the duties of a lookout have been outlined. If the man designated as a lookout is a capable racing man, he should be able to inform the skipper not merely when there is danger of collision, but should also be able to report as to which boat has right-of-way. I have never been sufficiently fortunate to have a lookout so skilled; but if I had, I would unhesitatingly proclaim the interpretation of the situation as one of his duties.

It is my opinion that beginners are more confused over the apparent conflict of two sets of rules than from any other cause. Let us assume that Boat A is close-hauled on the port tack and Boat B is sailing on the starboard tack with her sheets started just a little bit and not trying to sail as close to the wind as she can. In that case Boat A has the right-of-way. Yet because Boat B is on the starboard tack, confusion results. Any boat that is close-hauled has right-of-way over any boat that is free regardless of the tack that she may be on. When two boats meet on opposite tacks and both boats are close-hauled, or both boats are free, the boat on the starboard tack, that is to say the boat receiving her wind on the starboard side with her main boom over the port side, has right-of-way. When two boats are on the same tack and are sailing free, the boat that is closer to the wind has right-of-way. When two boats are sailing the same course, or nearly so, the overtaking boat must keep clear. In general, that is all there is to the racing rules for ordinary sailing. Close-hauled has right-of-way over free; starboard tack has right-of-way over port tack when both boats are free, and when both boats are close-hauled, but not when one is close-hauled and the other is free. In converging boats, the boat holding the better course has right-of-way and, in general, the overtaken boat has right-of-way.

I cannot refrain at this point from preaching on behalf of an interpretation of a rule which has been variously interpreted in different clubs. When one boat overtakes another on the lee side and the overtaken boat bears away but does not strike the overtaking boat, a situation arises which may be interpreted in two ways. In the old established practice in this country the overtaken boat would be disqualified. The publication of certain books by foreign writers, however, has given rise to the opinion that the overtaken boat may bear away just so long as she does not strike the overtaking boat. This I firmly believe to be wrong and an interpretation inimical to the good of yacht racing. An overtaking boat has a hard enough time to get by the boat ahead. If she passes on the windward side she blankets the overtaken boat, and the overtaken boat has every right to luff as she pleases up to a certain point to protect herself. If the overtaking boat is decent, however, and elects to pass on the lee side, she should have a free and uninterrupted passage. That is the designated path for her to take and any interference with that on the part of the overtaken boat, to my mind, is a violation of the intent and the actual wording of the rule.

Chapter XXXI

DISTANCE RACING

IN THE past few years there has been a very great increase in the number of races held at night. Night races were started as a stunt—as a test of seamanship, or something of the sort. They have continued because of their wonderful fascination and their great value and charm. To my mind there is no race like a night race; nothing that calls forth so many qualities of seamanship; nothing that gives greater beauty, thrill, excitement, or fun. I know of no night race that is not a distance run. It would be a mistake to sail such a race around a short triangular course. A night race should be planned for such a distance as to last all night and finish, if possible, in daylight. The best night races are those which start while it is still dusk. The races which start in pitch blackness are not nearly so much fun because you cannot see your opponents and are racing alone or at most, in the company of red and green lights. If, however, you have an hour or two of daylight before darkness descends, you can size up your opponents, the courses they are taking, their relative speed, and your chances of beating them.

Starting in the dark is usually controlled by an audible signal in the form of a gun, and a visual signal in the form of a hoist of distinctive lights. The races I have sailed that were started with rockets seem to me to be much better than the gun and light system. A search-light from the Committee Boat playing on the buoy that marks the opposite end of the starting line is a very great aid in getting a good start.

Night races deserve special mention because of their present popularity. Essentially, however, they do not differ from ordinary cruising runs, most of which are started in daylight and many of which are not finished until long after dark. The usual run of the New York Yacht Club from Vineyard Haven, around the outside of Cape Cod, to Provincetown, combines all the fun of a day race and a night race. The New York Athletic Club's annual race to Block Island, starting at noon and finishing some time the next day, is also a daytime and nighttime run that has in it every worthwhile element of the distance race. The off-shore ocean races to Bermuda, to Gibson Island, the Fastnet race in England, and transatlantic racing do not fall within the scope of this book. Ocean racing is an art of itself and deserves, and has received, full treatment in several excellent books.

The organization and training of crews for distance racing is much more important than for the afternoon trek around a small triangle. In a long race the crew must be working watch and watch, and each watch must have in it men who would be perfectly capable of handling the boat if left to their own devices. Thus, in each watch there should be at least one good helmsman, and preferably two. There should be at least one good navigator who knows how to get a fix, and lay a course, and who has a keenly developed sense of responsibility. There should be at least one deck hand who is tireless in trimming and hauling on the sheets.

One hand should always be responsible for an alert

and adequate lookout. He should be placed forward where he can see beneath a bulging spinnaker if necessary, and his weight must be balanced by that part of the crew which remains aft. It is not a function of this book to set out at length the necessary equipment for this sort of race, for such a race partakes of the nature of a cruise and is sailed in cruising trim with much more weight than would be carried in the ordinary afternoon sail. But certain phases should be mentioned.

Supremely important are good lights. I use a storage battery and electric lights for running lights, for they are the only lights bright enough to give me any feeling of safety. If electric lights are used, it is most necessary to have oil lamps as stand-by equipment. Electric light in the cabin for navigation, cooking, and finding necessary equipment is a godsend, but again kerosene and candles are all important. I use an immense number of candles during a season. Open flares, of course, are dangerous in an auxiliary, but with care they can be handled on a sail boat without serious danger of fire. A candle can be lighted even after it has been dropped in the bilge water and may be depended upon to give light whenever it is sheltered from the wind.

The degree of light on the compass card is of great importance to the comfort of the helmsman. The light should be neither too bright nor too dim, but better too dim than too bright. A flashlight bulb operated by two large dry cells, gives a sufficient and comfortable light for steering. In a regular binnacle there is no difficulty in arranging such a light. If the compass is placed beneath a deadlight in the floor of the cockpit, a good arrangement is to have two compass lights; one to starboard and one to port of the compass. By means of throwing a two-way switch, the windward light may be lit and the leeward light extinguished. Thus at any angle of heel, the light is above the compass card and sheltered from the helmsman's eyes. On any system of electric lighting for the compass, the wires, of course, must be twisted together, for otherwise their polarity will cause deviation.

Flashlights should be on board in abundance. Every member of the crew should have his own flashlight. At least one very powerful focusing light should be handy to the helmsman. With that, he can study the trim of his sails, the angle of the fly, the motion of the boat through the water. He can pick up telegraph poles or other dangerous flotsam and see how to avoid them. He can even focus his light on the sails of a competitor half a mile away, recognize her, and plan his race accordingly. A good, husky, portable search-light will prove very helpful for these purposes.

The principal danger in sailing at night is being run down by a steamer or a tow overtaking you from the rear. If they approach from forward of the beam, they will see your running lights and avoid you, but a boat that shows no lights abaft the beam is not readily distinguished from that quarter. Hence, it is wise to hold a flashlight handy to show to the overtaking steamer and then to play upon the sail. Your little point of light may not be noticed from the deck of the steamer, but if you will play it upon your sail, lighting up its big white area, you are sure to be seen. I have often sailed on the steamer from New York to Boston and spent long hours watching the lookout at work. The distance at which he can discern and report a sail boat at night is perfectly amazing.

Perhaps I am getting too old and cautious, but I feel the need of special safety measures in all night racing.

The first and most necessary of these is a water light attached to a ring buoy. One end of the water light is attached to the ring buoy by about ten feet of line, the other end of the light can is made fast to the boat. If a man falls overboard, the buoy is thrown in after him. It pulls the water light overboard, breaking out the stopper which remains attached to the boat. When the water gets into the can, a bright light flares up which may be seen for many miles. The man who falls overboard swims to the light and hangs on to the life buoy while the boat can be worked back to what might otherwise be an invisible point in the darkness. The New York Yacht Club disqualifies any boat sailing in any distance race in daylight or darkness that fails to carry such a water light.

I also make it a rule to rig life lines whenever sailing at night in rough waters. Even if there is no wind, if there is a heavy swell and the boat slats and bangs around, life lines are always rigged before darkness. It is very easy to rig a life line. Put a deck plate down aft and to that screw a pipe with a "T" coupling at the upper end. Then run a line from the deck up and through this stanchion, forward to the shrouds and down to the bow. The purpose of a life line is twofold: First, it does prevent accidents on a slippery wet deck where a man cannot see to avoid stepping on a rolling jib sheet. It saves many a tumble overboard. Second, it greatly increases the efficiency of the crew. A man who must go forward will creep cautiously along if there is no life line, but run swiftly forward if he can place his hand on that guiding string. The windage of a life line is small; its dividends in safety and efficiency are great.

Two articles of equipment I have never had to use

are flares and a fire extinguisher. The only time I needed flares I had none on board. The only time I needed a fire extinguisher, it was empty. In both instances I lived to tell the tale, but I never sail at night without them. Flares, fire extinguishers, life preservers, water light, life lines, and plenty of flashlights are very necessary equipment for safe sailing at night. The screens of your running lights can cause a great deal of bother unless you give them proper attention. For the most part, running light screens are simply lashed to the shrouds. The weight of the lamps on the after end of the screens generally causes that end to sag. On the lee side the shrouds are usually slack and the screens and light slat around like mad things. The only place they can be fastened with any degree of security is down to the deck where a single wave will not only extinguish the light, but is apt to carry light and screen overboard.

I have overcome this difficulty to my own satisfaction. I have fastened deck plates on each side of my shrouds. Into these deck plates I screw pipe stanchions and fasten my light boards to the stanchions. Then, to be doubly safe, I lash the boards to the shrouds so that if any accident should happen and the stanchions should carry away, I would still have my running lights. Although this scheme works better than any I have ever seen, I have, nevertheless, lost some stanchions, principally through fouling by a clumsily handled spinnaker boom.

Sailing at night is very different from sailing in the daytime because the principal sense upon which the helmsman depends is so handicapped by lack of light. When you see your sail only fitfully in the gleam of a flashlight, when you cannot see the water racing past the hull, when you do not know where your opponents are, you must depend entirely upon other senses to drive the boat. Your ears and general feeling of the boat's angle of heel, her rhythm and pace, then become all important. The man who develops these senses to the greatest degree of perception is the best skipper in a night race. When the *Atlantic* sailed in the race to Spain, she arranged three powerful arc lights on deck to throw clear beams of white light along the luffs of her sails. I have often been tempted to adopt such a device, operating an ordinary search-light or automobile spot-light from a storage battery. This can be done on a small boat if the source of light is shielded so as not to violate navigation laws by showing a white light to an approaching boat. The device has one serious disadvantage, however; that of revealing your position to your competitors. Most successful night racers use a flashlight no more than they absolutely need to, and depend largely on other senses than sight.

When sailing at night, the steering of an accurate compass course becomes all important. This perhaps is more necessary from a navigational point of view than from the viewpoint of making maximum speed, for it does hold a boat down enormously if the helmsman glues her too hard to his course without permitting the boat the freedom and life that is so necessary for good speed. The best helmsmen average their compass course. If they sail for a minute or two a half-point to windward of the course, they'll average it by sailing the next minute or two a half-point to leeward of the course. By doing this it is possible to keep the boat perpetually on her course and at the same time sail her at greatly increased speed. When the navigator is taking bearings, however, it is essential that the boat be held "steady on."

The problem of navigation in general is simplified rather than complicated by the presence of darkness when sailing along a well-marked coast. A distinctive light is always easier to recognize than a misty headland which may have no distinguishing characteristics. But navigation at night is always complicated by one factor. A light gives direction only, it does not give distance. It is very difficult to estimate the distance of a light by its size or brilliancy. This means that cross bearings are necessary at very frequent intervals. Even in daytime cross bearings are necessary to obtain a fix, but in the daytime, when sailing through reasonably familiar waters, we are far less accurate in determining fixes. We can glance at a distant shore and estimate the distance pretty accurately just by guesswork, and unless there is a sign of fog, rain, or other disturbance to visibility, most of us are too busy racing to pay much attention to determining just where we are. Furthermore, in the daytime, the presence of another boat sailing approximately the same course offers a very valuable check. At night these other boats disappear from view and, if we are not careful to get frequent and accurate fixes, we are apt to run into danger and most apt to sail a longer course than would otherwise be necessary.

I always make it a rule to appoint one man in each watch as the navigator for that watch. They take their work seriously. I check their work at sufficient intervals to make sure that they are not committing any serious errors, but otherwise make them responsible for the course and position of the boat while I make myself responsible for her speed.

As a general rule I do not like to trail a log in a night race but always have it handy for bow and beam bearings if they should be necessary to determine my distance off shore. As a general rule, bow and beam bearings are not very accurate in a small boat when the air is light and the current strong. Good guesswork is better. I feel strongly, however, that no one should take a boat into a night race without understanding thoroughly the elements of piloting. These have been fully covered in the chapter on Coastwise Navigation in "Learning to Sail." They are also carefully explained in the Coast Pilot. It is perhaps unnecessary to mention that good charts, drawn to a large scale, are most necessary for all navigation, and particularly for navigation in a night race. The charts should be up-to-date. By notifying the U. S. Coast and Geodetic Survey in Washington of your desire to receive the weekly Notices to Mariners, you will be placed on the mailing list to receive these notices every week. File them or bind them into a book and before you start on any distance race, go over the charts that cover the race and on them note the changes reported in the Notices to Mariners. In one of the night races of 1933, the Bartlett Lightship was removed and a lighted bell buoy substituted the day before the race. The proposed change had been published in the Notices to Mariners and the skippers who had read these notices were prepared to find a buoy where they had previously had a lightship. The others spent a large part of the night looking for that lightship which marked a corner of the course at which they turned to run into New London.

A light list, published annually, should also be an important part of your navigational equipment. The data for each light should be taken from the light list rather than from the chart. The chart will give the location accurately, but with the many changes in the characteristics of the lights, the light list is more dependable. The lookout should be instructed to report not merely floating objects and other vessels, but also each light as it is raised. The navigator should notify the lookout to be on the alert for the lights he expects to see and describe the characteristics. The stop-watch with which you start the race should be on deck to enable you to time the flashes and the occultations.

If a light is designated as turning point for a race, it is better to steer for the light than to sail out your compass course, unless the compass course is arranged to provide for a large difference in leeway or current set. Unless these corrections are in order, I make it a rule to turn out the binnacle light as soon as the loom of the lighthouse appears so that the helmsman will have nothing to sail by except the lighthouse. If a lighthouse is used as a turning point, due caution must be observed in rounding it. Lighthouses are usually built on shoals and obstructions and even if there is a good deal more water noted than your draft requires, the danger of pounding on a rock is considerable if there is a heavy sea running. If you are not first in rounding such a lighthouse, it is usually wise to get right in the wake of a deeper draft boat and follow her around. If she does not strike, you are not likely to.

An important factor in winning a distance race is the freshness of the crew. In the excitement of the race, most of the men are on deck most of the time. It is an easy matter to sit up all night, chatting comfortably and speculating on your chances, but when dawn breaks and you have thirty or forty miles left to go, the entire crew is generally so fagged that they are under a serious handicap. The proper procedure is to see that the watch on deck is alert, capable, and understands its duties. Then, send the other watch below. Insist upon that absolutely. Drive the men below and make them sleep whether they want to or not. Do not give a call of all hands if the watch on deck can handle the situation. Except in the case of jibing in a stiff wind, reefing, or breaking out a spinnaker in a bad sea, the watch on deck can usually handle the boat without help from the watch below.

Certain provisions must be made for the comfort of the crew. They should have cushions or similar devices to sit on. A deck or a cockpit gets soaking wet if there is any dew at all. The crew should be warmly dressed. My teeth have chattered through many a long watch in July and August nights that were sweltering hot ashore. I make it a rule to warn my crew to bring adequate clothing and at least one complete change, for if a man falls overboard, or gets struck unexpectedly by the top of a sea when he is working forward, he must change his clothes promptly. I also make it a rule absolutely to prohibit anyone lending or borrowing any clothing. Too often I have lent my only spare sweater to another man only to get soaked through a few minutes later. Then, with one sweater for the two of us, I found myself utterly unable to take the sweater off his back and let him shiver. When this occurs, I invariably find myself hating my shipmates and that is a bad thing for the conduct of a race.

I deem it important to know what the other fellow is doing and to know how well we are sailing ourselves. Of the numerous night races in which I have sailed, two stand out as completely joyful experiences. On one occasion on a night of flat calm we ran into a little streak of wind. We got great speed out of the boat for a period of about two hours. One by one we saw the running lights of the other boats fade out of sight astern. Then, for the rest of the night our keenest observation was unable to reveal the gleam of any flashlight on any sail. The conviction dawned on us that we were ahead. We worked like maniacs to keep ahead, trimming and re-trimming for every stray breath of wind. Just as the gleam of dawn began to be sensed we rounded Stratford Shoal light. The lighthouse keeper was on his walk and we hailed him. "You are the first this morning," he cried. Later we found he was mistaken, but we sailed back along the course we had come with redoubled energy. The speed with which you drive a boat when you feel you are ahead is a wonderful contributing factor to your success.

On the other occasion, we knew we were pretty well up but just as darkness descended we saw ahead of us a boat with a remarkable record for winning. She owed us a little time but we determined to beat her. For three hours our starboard light winked into her port light as we raced side by side down the Eastern end of Long Island Sound and through the Gut. Then the wind fell flat. The other boat got a slant and ran away to finish in the money, but I know that we did better work by sailing in her company than if we had sailed alone, and I am equally convinced that if we had not put up such a keen fight the other boat would have had no silver to show for her efforts. I stress this at length to point out the importance of keeping track of your opponents. It adds immeasurably to the pleasure of the race and certainly makes you go faster.

One thing is certain of all night racing: It is very hard to keep driving a boat at night. In the daytime the little imperfections in your speed are so apparent that driving comes naturally. At night, however, one becomes more complacent, more contented with just making the boat go. If it is blowing hard and you are on the wind, the waves seem larger, the spray seems wetter, the strains of the boat more apparent. Also, your speed seems greater so that even though you may be bobbing up and down and not going ahead, you are not apt to notice the difference. After nightfall one is tempted to shorten sail. Hard though it is to drive a boat in a blow at night, it is harder still to make her foot through a calm. It is then that the little differences count most. I do not know why it is, but sounds seem louder at night. I have been scared to death by the slapping of my lee shrouds against a light screen, convinced that this loud knocking noise meant that I was about to carry away something important. In the daytime it would be apparent that the slap of those shrouds and the sound of their striking the screens were coincident. At night, when you cannot see anything, sounds take on a new and often sinister significance. I recall one race in which we had to beat back to the finish. It was blowing very hard. I was afraid to drive the boat too hard because of a rubber mast and shrouds that were not too trustworthy. We got back in three long tacks, but some of the other boats did it in one. I know now that if that race had been sailed in daylight, I could have estimated the degree of strain in the shrouds and the mast and we could have laid the mark in one tack, for I had often out-pointed and out-footed the boat that won the race. This business of driving at night is highly important. In ocean racing it is usually the difference between finishing well up or in the ruck.

Chapter XXXII

PUTTING THE BOAT TO BED

I MAKE the assumption that any man who ventures into yacht racing already knows how to care for his boat, how to put her away at her mooring so that she will be safe, and that further instruction on this point is unnecessary. But a finely attuned racing machine requires more than ordinary care, and the way the boat is put to bed will have an important effect upon her performance in future races. I remember cruising not long ago with a very able sailor who owned a large and powerful ketch. His crew were up with the sun, chamoising off his bright work, his brass was polished like pure gold, his lines were coiled with exactitude, but his sails were handled brutally. Throughout those two days, I was monkeying with outhauls and battens and leech lines and grommets, trying to put some power into his sails. A week or so later he sailed with me. He was appalled at the condition of my brass and varnish, but amazed at the care I took of my sails. He had never realized that his sails were his power plant and that they deserve at all times the utmost care.

In any hard race the sails are always wet. They should be dried most carefully. Yet drying sails at the end of a race is usually difficult because there are few, if any, hours of sunlight left. The best way to dry sails is by sailing on them. Yet that is difficult unless you have a large stretch of sheltered water in which you can sail back and forth until the sails are thoroughly dry. To dry sails in this manner, slack the halliards an inch or two and make sure that the outhauls are not pulled out too tight. If it is impossible to dry the sails by sailing on them, they should be hoisted and allowed to flutter, but in this case the halliards distinctly should not be hoisted all the way and the outhauls should be very slack. It is a good idea to hoist on the halliards until the sail is about two-thirds hoisted, then pass a stop over a hoop or mast-slide and trice up the bottom of the luff in order to give free access of the wind and the sun to the foot of the sail, because sails are usually wetter along the foot than at any other point.

On a small boat, the sails are dried, then unbent from the spars, stowed in a bag and taken ashore. On a large boat the sails are furled. In all cases the outhaul on the boom is slacked off and the sail pulled forward a couple of feet. Do this job thoroughly. Do not be content merely with slacking off the outhaul but clasp the sail at several points along the foot and make sure that it is thoroughly slacked and not stretched by a sticking slide. If the sail is laced to the boom, overhaul the lace line so that it is slack at all points. If the sail is gaff-headed, slack off the outhaul at the peak and overhaul the lace line along the head. Incidentally, a gaff-headed sail should always be laced to the gaff. Track and slides should never be used on the head of the sail because this hangs the whole weight of the sail on the peak cringle and rapidly pulls the sail out of shape.

A sail that is not quite dry should be furled loosely and not covered with the sail covers. A Marconi mainsail should not be rolled but should be flaked down with a flap of the sail to starboard and a flap to port until the head is reached. In putting the sail covers on a dry sail great care should be exercised in frapping the cover closely around the mast so that rain flowing down the mast will not get in under the covers. This is more important with the Marconi mainsail than with the gaff-headed mainsail because the Marconi mainsail lies closer to the mast.

On all but the largest boats, the sails should be taken ashore and dried properly. The best place to dry a sail is in a warm dry attic which has first been thoroughly cleaned. The sail should be hung over clothes lines and never supported by its cringles. The weight of the sail hung from the cringle is certain to pull it out of shape. It is a very easy matter to remove a Marconi mainsail from mast and boom if they are equipped with slide magazines. Needless to say, the sails should always be carried in a clean sail bag and it pays to have a bag somewhat oversize.

The jib is usually abused more than the mainsail. If a jib has a club, the club should always be loosened at outhaul and lace line. Even in a large boat it is such an easy matter to unhank the jib from its stay that it seems a crime ever to leave it exposed. A jib in a sail cover is most apt to be mildewed even on a warm sunshiny day, because if there is any sea running, a certain amount of spray will splash up on the jib and be dried there in the sun. A sail that dries while it is folded is almost certain to be mildewed. The worst way to treat a jib in a small boat is to roll it up around its club and throw it in the bottom of the cockpit. This is ruination.

As a general rule the battens in the jib are relatively

so short that it is not often necessary to remove them. The mainsail battens, however, should always be removed preferably as the sail is being lowered. They should be stowed on a perfectly flat surface. Otherwise they are apt to become warped and warped battens will produce hard spots in the sail. Do not dry sails on a freshly mowed lawn. Grass stains inevitably result.

When sails are properly taken care of, the skipper should police his boat carefully, examine every block, cleat, turnbuckle, and cotter pin. So often little things happen in a race that are unnoticed until the boat gets back to her mooring. The spinnaker halliard perhaps has started to chafe aloft. This means a new halliard or reversing the old halliard before the next race. One of the shroud turnbuckles has lost a cotter pin and has become loose. The cleat on which the spinnaker guy has been pulling all afternoon has started to pull loose from the coaming. There is a little extra play in the tiller. The top of the centerboard looks warped. All of these things should be noted while you are putting the boat to bed. That is the time to take out your note-book and write down the things that must be done before the next race. Really these things should be done before you leave the boat, but you are tired and wet and hungry and you put them off. That is permissible if you are certain to note everything and to allow yourself time to correct these little faults before the next race. If your spinnaker is wet, take it ashore for drying, and note in the book that you have taken it ashore so that you will not start the next race with the spinnaker neatly stowed in its bag in your garage. If the spinnaker is thoroughly dry, stop it up before you go ashore. It will save a lot of time on your next racing day. Then, before climbing into the dinghy or tooting for the club launch, pump your boat out dry. I am convinced that a boat takes on more weight from water in the bilge than she does from water seeping into her planking from the outside. A boat that is dry inside will be lighter and faster on the following week.

Chapter XXXIII

SPORTSMANSHIP

THIS ISN'T a sermon. It is a code and its application. It is written for the good sportsman, not for the bad one. Fortunately, there are very few poor sports in yacht racing, which remains one of the cleanest of all competitions. The poor sport needs no guidance. He is not reformed by reading books.

But the good, clean sportsman, with the best motives in the world, makes a good many mistakes. His highly commendable generosity of spirit often causes injustice. In his concern for his own decency, he overlooks two larger considerations—the rights of competitors and the welfare of the game. He is in a peculiar situation for he is often protagonist, witness, judge, and jury. With lightning speed, he must define a complicated situation. He must fit that situation into an involved code of racing rules. He must understand swiftly and clearly the rights of every boat. If he deems himself in the wrong, the good sport yields at once. But if he is in the right, he must make a further decision based upon his code of sportsmanship.

A recent instance will make this clear. The situation —a closely bunched leeward start in the New York Yacht Club thirty-foot class. A tough spot, this leeward start in a large boat class. No killing headway before hitting the line. Little chance to maneuver. Crews all busy with the spinnakers. And the boats spread out in extended order from main clew to spinnaker clew, occupying many times as much space on the starting line as they would in a windward start. A minute or so after the gun while confusion still reigned, *Old Timer* and *Minx* were sailing side by side out of range of collision, *Minx* slightly ahead. *Old Timer,* sensing trouble, had sent up her spinnaker in stops but had refrained from breaking it out. *Minx* had broken out her spinnaker but was having trouble in making it draw. At that moment, *Nachtan,* going like an express train, pulled into the wake of *Old Timer* and started to blanket her. *Old Timer* promptly trimmed sheets to escape from *Nachtan* and converged into collision range with *Minx.* The crew of *Minx* were too involved with her spinnaker to pay any attention to *Old Timer.* *Old Timer* hailed *Minx* calling for room. *Minx's* helmsman replied in a way that showed he did not understand the situation. He probably classified *Old Timer* as an overtaking yacht instead of a converging yacht holding a better course.

By that time *Minx's* boom was inside of and overlapping *Old Timer's* jib stay. But three inches separated them and there had been no collision. *Nachtan,* with her spinnaker aback, seemed less dangerous now; so *Old Timer* bore away from *Minx,* broke out her spinnaker, and escaped. *Old Timer* might easily have collided with *Minx's* boom, hoisted her protest flag and thus disposed of one competitor; but good sportsmanship ruled otherwise. *Minx,* however, presently withdrew from the race. I don't know why; but I have heard that her crew analyzed the situation, decided that *Minx* was wrong, acted as their own judge and jury, and with a high but misguided sense of sports-

manship, withdrew. It was entirely unnecessary. There
had been no foul, for *Old Timer* had not exercised her
rights, and her failure to hoist her protest flag clearly
expressed her intention not to do so.

Let us analyze this case. It is a common enough
occurrence and typical of the situation where racing
codes stop and a sportsmanship code controls.

No one can criticize *Old Timer* for converging into
range of collision with *Minx*. She was driven to it by
Nachtan and was entirely within her rights under the
racing rules. She altered her course not to attack *Minx*
but to escape from *Nachtan*. From the viewpoint of
sportsmanship, motive becomes important. Should
Minx have yielded when *Old Timer* hailed her? Undoubtedly. But let us plead her case. Confusion reigned.
It shouldn't have, perhaps, but it did. They were excited on *Minx*, on *Old Timer*, on *Nachtan*. There was
that bunched leeward start, the trouble with the spinnaker, too many things clamoring for attention. One
minute *Old Timer* was safely tucked away sailing a
parallel course to port. The next minute, her sheets
were trimmed and she was banging into the end of the
boom and yelling for room. With *Minx's* crew all
monkeying with that spinnaker, with no hands at the
sheets, it is doubtful if *Minx* could have gotten out of
the way if she had tried. With no chance to study the
situation, her helmsman jumped to the conclusion that
he had right-of-way. Who can blame him?

If the race had been three minutes older, the confusion of the start subsided, *Minx's* spinnaker drawing,
her crew at their stations, her helmsman with a clear
picture of the situation in his mind, *Old Timer* might
have been justified in striking *Minx's* boom and protesting. If *Old Timer's* skipper had forced the foul

to get rid of a competitor, he would have been a skunk. If, however, he had forced it to compel a stubborn antagonist to yield from a position he had no right to maintain, his action would clearly have been for the good of the sport.

It is interesting to note how distinctly the motives and the sportsmanship of both skippers were defined. *Old Timer's* was under no compunction to hail *Minx*. The hail was evidence of her skipper's good faith, of his desire to keep all the boats in the race and not kill them off by technicalities. *Minx's* answer was equally good evidence of her skipper's confusion. It said plainly that if *Minx* thought she were in the wrong, she would have yielded instantly.

Now we come to another point. Suppose *Minx* had tried to get out of *Old Timer's* way, but owing to the fact that no hands were at the sheets, had failed. Should *Old Timer* have protested? Under the racing rules she had the right, but under the sportsman's code she had not.

It is my thesis that many such situations are unavoidable. And that when a yacht does her best to abide by the rules, a sportsman should never protest.

I am reminded of another case in which a hail kept a skipper's record clean. It was in a catboat race many years ago on Great South Bay. The race was a windward and leeward course. *Kittery* was leading; *Modesty* a poor second; the rest of the fleet strung out behind. I was crew on *Modesty*.

Near the weather mark our skipper said, "If we go about, we'll meet *Kittery* on the run back. We'll have right-of-way and we may be able to make her foul us." It isn't a nice thing to confess, but we all agreed to this strategy. We waited until *Kittery* was busy jib-

ing around the mark, then went about to meet her.
Kittery bore down on us. She had an enormous, full-
cut sail, and her boom just cleared the water. It hid
us from sight completely. We held our course. The *Kittery's* bearings didn't change a hair. It was evident
that if we both held on there would be a collision. I
think we all felt pretty slimy as the two boats drew
together. I know I did. And then our skipper let out a
loud yell of warning. *Kittery's* crew awoke to their
danger, but instead of altering their course, they
grabbed all five parts of the main sheet and lazily
pulled in the boom. They were nearly clear when a
puff of wind struck them and the sail got away. It
crashed from their hands and the boom barely cleared
Modesty's head stay by less than an inch. Had it struck,
a protest would have been in order.

For, though *Modesty's* original motive was questionable, her skipper's sportsmanlike hail justified it.
It is perfectly acceptable for a boat with right-of-way
to compel a competitor to sail out of her course. *Kittery* deserved punishment for her lazy nonchalance in
trimming her sheet instead of really getting out of the
way. To-day, perhaps she might be protested under
the "danger of a foul" rule, but that rule was not in the
book in those days.

Another case: I was sailing *Lone Wolf* in the Star
class when I saw *Grace* foul *Gadget*. It was a deliber-
ate and inexcusable infraction of the rules. *Grace* on
the port tack slammed right into *Gadget* on the starboard tack. There was considerable heated conversation between the two boats. I was too far ahead to
hear the words. Then *Grace* rammed *Gadget* again,
twisting her around until she had to jibe to get clear.
Then they split tacks.

"We'll cover *Gadget*," I said. "*Grace* is out of it." But *Grace* wasn't out of it. I let her escape. She beat me and hung up a higher score than several other boats that had sailed a clean race, for *Gadget* wouldn't protest. When we discovered this, it was too late for any of the other boats to protest. *Gadget's* skipper was under a duty to his other competitors and to the sport. He should have protested. It was not a case for generosity. Another point: The protest flag had fallen into disuse in these waters. Without it, we had no means of discovering the intentions of *Gadget's* skipper. Had we known of his intention not to protest, we could have covered *Grace* and might have beaten her.

How often we have seen a course laid out so that the only sensible start is on the port tack. Yet all too often a boat will barge down the line on the starboard tack solely with the intention of causing fouls with the other boats. Often she must go about to cross the line at all. But if she can spoil the start of the other boats and dispose of one or two competitors by protest, she rejoices in her cleverness whereas she should be ashamed of her sportsmanship.

The proper headway rule is a wonderful litmus paper for discovering the presence of sportsmanship. If a competitor tacks so close to one's boat as to violate the rule, any alert skipper can put his own boat about in time to back-wind and stop the competitor. "Shall I protest him or shall I beat him?" It is hard to conceive of any sportsman yielding to a temptation to protest a boat that places herself at his mercy. The sportsman gets his kick out of pulling ahead of another boat, not from debating the pros and cons of a rule violation.

From these few cases we may formulate the beginnings of a sportsman's code applied to yacht racing:

1. The sportsman races for the fun of the thing. He does nothing to spoil his own fun or his competitor's fun.

2. He is never motivated by a desire to gain by putting a competitor out of a race, except as punishment for an intentional crime.

3. He never takes advantage of a competitor's honest mistakes in interpreting rules or situations.

4. Armed with the right-of-way, he never strikes at an unarmed foe, who, owing to circumstances, cannot escape—except as a matter of self-preservation.

5. In any situation he has the right to harass, delay, impede, or embarrass his opponents under the provisions of the rules without being subject to criticism of his sportsmanship. But the death penalty of disqualification should not be evoked lightly.

6. In the event of a situation in which the facts are clearly established but the rules are obscure, duty to the sport demands a protest. (Any decision on such a protest should be appealed to the North American Yacht Racing Union without acrimony or bitterness but solely for the purpose of interpreting the racing rules authoritatively. Rules like laws acquire their meaning from interpretation in actual cases.)

7. In any case of flagrant, intentional, stubborn violation of the rules, a protest is an important social duty. The good of the sport and the rights of your other competitors demand that it be prosecuted vigorously and without generosity.

8. The sportsman conducts his protest like a gentleman. The trial of a protest should be as orderly as a case in court. There should be no speaking out of turn,

no heat or recriminations. Questions of fact should be clearly segregated from questions of law. If possible, the facts should be agreed upon or proved by disinterested witnesses.

9. The Race Committee has no right to exercise its spirit of sportsmanship by the abrogation of any rules without the unanimous consent of all parties concerned. Only where boats have no steerage way or are otherwise out of control may the Race Committee look the other way. Even in such circumstances, the Race Committee must rigidly enforce the rules in case of protest.

10. In the event of fouling a mark or some other indisputable violation of rules in which a competitor is not directly involved, the sportsman disqualifies himself by immediate withdrawal. In the case of a questionable violation of this nature, he reports the facts to the Race Committee and abides by its decision. The sportsman who encroaches too often upon the province of the Race Committee becomes a nuisance.

11. Needless to say, the sportsman never hides behind a lie, a bluff, or his own failure to reveal facts unknown to his competitors or his judges.

A CATALOG OF SELECTED
DOVER BOOKS
IN ALL FIELDS OF INTEREST

A CATALOG OF SELECTED DOVER
BOOKS IN ALL FIELDS OF INTEREST

CONCERNING THE SPIRITUAL IN ART, Wassily Kandinsky. Pioneering work by father of abstract art. Thoughts on color theory, nature of art. Analysis of earlier masters. 12 illustrations. 80pp. of text. 5⅜ x 8½.   23411-8 Pa. $4.95

ANIMALS: 1,419 Copyright-Free Illustrations of Mammals, Birds, Fish, Insects, etc., Jim Harter (ed.). Clear wood engravings present, in extremely lifelike poses, over 1,000 species of animals. One of the most extensive pictorial sourcebooks of its kind. Captions. Index. 284pp. 9 x 12.   23766-4 Pa. $14.95

CELTIC ART: The Methods of Construction, George Bain. Simple geometric techniques for making Celtic interlacements, spirals, Kells-type initials, animals, humans, etc. Over 500 illustrations. 160pp. 9 x 12. (USO)   22923-8 Pa. $9.95

AN ATLAS OF ANATOMY FOR ARTISTS, Fritz Schider. Most thorough reference work on art anatomy in the world. Hundreds of illustrations, including selections from works by Vesalius, Leonardo, Goya, Ingres, Michelangelo, others. 593 illustrations. 192pp. 7⅛ x 10¼.   20241-0 Pa. $9.95

CELTIC HAND STROKE-BY-STROKE (Irish Half-Uncial from "The Book of Kells"): An Arthur Baker Calligraphy Manual, Arthur Baker. Complete guide to creating each letter of the alphabet in distinctive Celtic manner. Covers hand position, strokes, pens, inks, paper, more. Illustrated. 48pp. 8¼ x 11.   24336-2 Pa. $3.95

EASY ORIGAMI, John Montroll. Charming collection of 32 projects (hat, cup, pelican, piano, swan, many more) specially designed for the novice origami hobbyist. Clearly illustrated easy-to-follow instructions insure that even beginning papercrafters will achieve successful results. 48pp. 8¼ x 11.   27298-2 Pa. $3.50

THE COMPLETE BOOK OF BIRDHOUSE CONSTRUCTION FOR WOOD-WORKERS, Scott D. Campbell. Detailed instructions, illustrations, tables. Also data on bird habitat and instinct patterns. Bibliography. 3 tables. 63 illustrations in 15 figures. 48pp. 5¼ x 8½.   24407-5 Pa. $2.50

BLOOMINGDALE'S ILLUSTRATED 1886 CATALOG: Fashions, Dry Goods and Housewares, Bloomingdale Brothers. Famed merchants' extremely rare catalog depicting about 1,700 products: clothing, housewares, firearms, dry goods, jewelry, more. Invaluable for dating, identifying vintage items. Also, copyright-free graphics for artists, designers. Co-published with Henry Ford Museum & Greenfield Village. 160pp. 8¼ x 11.   25780-0 Pa. $10.95

HISTORIC COSTUME IN PICTURES, Braun & Schneider. Over 1,450 costumed figures in clearly detailed engravings–from dawn of civilization to end of 19th century. Captions. Many folk costumes. 256pp. 8⅜ x 11¾.   23150-X Pa. $12.95

MY BONDAGE AND MY FREEDOM, Frederick Douglass. Born a slave, Douglass became outspoken force in antislavery movement. The best of Douglass' autobiographies. Graphic description of slave life. 464pp. 5⅜ x 8½. 22457-0 Pa. $8.95

FOLLOWING THE EQUATOR: A Journey Around the World, Mark Twain. Fascinating humorous account of 1897 voyage to Hawaii, Australia, India, New Zealand, etc. Ironic, bemused reports on peoples, customs, climate, flora and fauna, politics, much more. 197 illustrations. 720pp. 5⅜ x 8½. 26113-1 Pa. $15.95

THE PEOPLE CALLED SHAKERS, Edward D. Andrews. Definitive study of Shakers: origins, beliefs, practices, dances, social organization, furniture and crafts, etc. 33 illustrations. 351pp. 5⅜ x 8½. 21081-2 Pa. $8.95

THE MYTHS OF GREECE AND ROME, H. A. Guerber. A classic of mythology, generously illustrated, long prized for its simple, graphic, accurate retelling of the principal myths of Greece and Rome, and for its commentary on their origins and significance. With 64 illustrations by Michelangelo, Raphael, Titian, Rubens, Canova, Bernini and others. 480pp. 5⅜ x 8½. 27584-1 Pa. $9.95

PSYCHOLOGY OF MUSIC, Carl E. Seashore. Classic work discusses music as a medium from psychological viewpoint. Clear treatment of physical acoustics, auditory apparatus, sound perception, development of musical skills, nature of musical feeling, host of other topics. 88 figures. 408pp. 5⅜ x 8½. 21851-1 Pa. $11.95

THE PHILOSOPHY OF HISTORY, Georg W. Hegel. Great classic of Western thought develops concept that history is not chance but rational process, the evolution of freedom. 457pp. 5⅜ x 8½. 20112-0 Pa. $9.95

THE BOOK OF TEA, Kakuzo Okakura. Minor classic of the Orient: entertaining, charming explanation, interpretation of traditional Japanese culture in terms of tea ceremony. 94pp. 5⅜ x 8½. 20070-1 Pa. $3.95

LIFE IN ANCIENT EGYPT, Adolf Erman. Fullest, most thorough, detailed older account with much not in more recent books, domestic life, religion, magic, medicine, commerce, much more. Many illustrations reproduce tomb paintings, carvings, hieroglyphs, etc. 597pp. 5⅜ x 8½. 22632-8 Pa. $12.95

SUNDIALS, Their Theory and Construction, Albert Waugh. Far and away the best, most thorough coverage of ideas, mathematics concerned, types, construction, adjusting anywhere. Simple, nontechnical treatment allows even children to build several of these dials. Over 100 illustrations. 230pp. 5⅜ x 8½. 22947-5 Pa. $8.95

DYNAMICS OF FLUIDS IN POROUS MEDIA, Jacob Bear. For advanced students of ground water hydrology, soil mechanics and physics, drainage and irrigation engineering, and more. 335 illustrations. Exercises, with answers. 784pp. 6⅛ x 9¼. 65675-6 Pa. $19.95

SONGS OF EXPERIENCE: Facsimile Reproduction with 26 Plates in Full Color, William Blake. 26 full-color plates from a rare 1826 edition. Includes "The Tyger," "London," "Holy Thursday," and other poems. Printed text of poems. 48pp. 5¼ x 7. 24636-1 Pa. $4.95

OLD-TIME VIGNETTES IN FULL COLOR, Carol Belanger Grafton (ed.). Over 390 charming, often sentimental illustrations, selected from archives of Victorian graphics—pretty women posing, children playing, food, flowers, kittens and puppies, smiling cherubs, birds and butterflies, much more. All copyright-free. 48pp. 9¼ x 12¼. 27269-9 Pa. $7.95

PHOTOGRAPHIC SKETCHBOOK OF THE CIVIL WAR, Alexander Gardner. 100 photos taken on field during the Civil War. Famous shots of Manassas Harper's Ferry, Lincoln, Richmond, slave pens, etc. 244pp. 10⅝ x 8¼.   22731-6 Pa. $10.95

FIVE ACRES AND INDEPENDENCE, Maurice G. Kains. Great back-to-the-land classic explains basics of self-sufficient farming. The one book to get. 95 illustrations. 397pp. 5⅜ x 8½.   20974-1 Pa. $7.95

SONGS OF EASTERN BIRDS, Dr. Donald J. Borror. Songs and calls of 60 species most common to eastern U.S.: warblers, woodpeckers, flycatchers, thrushes, larks, many more in high-quality recording.   Cassette and manual 99912-2 $9.95

A MODERN HERBAL, Margaret Grieve. Much the fullest, most exact, most useful compilation of herbal material. Gigantic alphabetical encyclopedia, from aconite to zedoary, gives botanical information, medical properties, folklore, economic uses, much else. Indispensable to serious reader. 161 illustrations. 888pp. 6½ x 9¼. 2-vol. set. (USO)   Vol. I: 22798-7 Pa. $9.95
     Vol. II: 22799-5 Pa. $9.95

HIDDEN TREASURE MAZE BOOK, Dave Phillips. Solve 34 challenging mazes accompanied by heroic tales of adventure. Evil dragons, people-eating plants, blood-thirsty giants, many more dangerous adversaries lurk at every twist and turn. 34 mazes, stories, solutions. 48pp. 8¼ x 11.   24566-7 Pa. $2.95

LETTERS OF W. A. MOZART, Wolfgang A. Mozart. Remarkable letters show bawdy wit, humor, imagination, musical insights, contemporary musical world; includes some letters from Leopold Mozart. 276pp. 5⅜ x 8½.   22859-2 Pa. $7.95

BASIC PRINCIPLES OF CLASSICAL BALLET, Agrippina Vaganova. Great Russian theoretician, teacher explains methods for teaching classical ballet. 118 illus-trations. 175pp. 5⅜ x 8½.   22036-2 Pa. $5.95

THE JUMPING FROG, Mark Twain. Revenge edition. The original story of The Celebrated Jumping Frog of Calaveras County, a hapless French translation, and Twain's hilarious "retranslation" from the French. 12 illustrations. 66pp. 5⅜ x 8½.   22686-7 Pa. $3.95

BEST REMEMBERED POEMS, Martin Gardner (ed.). The 126 poems in this superb collection of 19th- and 20th-century British and American verse range from Shelley's "To a Skylark" to the impassioned "Renascence" of Edna St. Vincent Millay and to Edward Lear's whimsical "The Owl and the Pussycat." 224pp. 5⅜ x 8½.   27165-X Pa. $5.95

COMPLETE SONNETS, William Shakespeare. Over 150 exquisite poems deal with love, friendship, the tyranny of time, beauty's evanescence, death and other themes in language of remarkable power, precision and beauty. Glossary of archaic terms. 80pp. 5³⁄₁₆ x 8¼.   26686-9 Pa. $1.00

BODIES IN A BOOKSHOP, R. T. Campbell. Challenging mystery of blackmail and murder with ingenious plot and superbly drawn characters. In the best tradition of British suspense fiction. 192pp. 5⅜ x 8½.   24720-1 Pa. $6.95

THE INFLUENCE OF SEA POWER UPON HISTORY, 1660–1783, A. T. Mahan. Influential classic of naval history and tactics still used as text in war colleges. First paperback edition. 4 maps. 24 battle plans. 640pp. 5⅜ x 8½. 25509-3 Pa. $14.95

THE STORY OF THE TITANIC AS TOLD BY ITS SURVIVORS, Jack Winocour (ed.). What it was really like. Panic, despair, shocking inefficiency, and a little heroism. More thrilling than any fictional account. 26 illustrations. 320pp. 5⅜ x 8½. 20610-6 Pa. $8.95

FAIRY AND FOLK TALES OF THE IRISH PEASANTRY, William Butler Yeats (ed.). Treasury of 64 tales from the twilight world of Celtic myth and legend: "The Soul Cages," "The Kildare Pooka," "King O'Toole and his Goose," many more. Introduction and Notes by W. B. Yeats. 352pp. 5⅜ x 8½. 26941-8 Pa. $8.95

BUDDHIST MAHAYANA TEXTS, E. B. Cowell and Others (eds.). Superb, accurate translations of basic documents in Mahayana Buddhism, highly important in history of religions. The Buddha-karita of Asvaghosha, Larger Sukhavativyuha, more. 448pp. 5⅜ x 8½. 25552-2 Pa. $12.95

ONE TWO THREE . . . INFINITY: Facts and Speculations of Science, George Gamow. Great physicist's fascinating, readable overview of contemporary science: number theory, relativity, fourth dimension, entropy, genes, atomic structure, much more. 128 illustrations. Index. 352pp. 5⅜ x 8½. 25664-2 Pa. $8.95

ENGINEERING IN HISTORY, Richard Shelton Kirby, et al. Broad, nontechnical survey of history's major technological advances: birth of Greek science, industrial revolution, electricity and applied science, 20th-century automation, much more. 181 illustrations. ". . . excellent . . ."–*Isis.* Bibliography. vii + 530pp. 5⅜ x 8¼. 26412-2 Pa. $14.95

DALÍ ON MODERN ART: The Cuckolds of Antiquated Modern Art, Salvador Dalí. Influential painter skewers modern art and its practitioners. Outrageous evaluations of Picasso, Cézanne, Turner, more. 15 renderings of paintings discussed. 44 calligraphic decorations by Dalí. 96pp. 5⅜ x 8½. (USO) 29220-7 Pa. $4.95

ANTIQUE PLAYING CARDS: A Pictorial History, Henry René D'Allemagne. Over 900 elaborate, decorative images from rare playing cards (14th–20th centuries): Bacchus, death, dancing dogs, hunting scenes, royal coats of arms, players cheating, much more. 96pp. 9¼ x 12¼. 29265-7 Pa. $12.95

MAKING FURNITURE MASTERPIECES: 30 Projects with Measured Drawings, Franklin H. Gottshall. Step-by-step instructions, illustrations for constructing handsome, useful pieces, among them a Sheraton desk, Chippendale chair, Spanish desk, Queen Anne table and a William and Mary dressing mirror. 224pp. 8⅛ x 11¼. 29338-6 Pa. $13.95

THE FOSSIL BOOK: A Record of Prehistoric Life, Patricia V. Rich et al. Profusely illustrated definitive guide covers everything from single-celled organisms and dinosaurs to birds and mammals and the interplay between climate and man. Over 1,500 illustrations. 760pp. 7½ x 10⅛. 29371-8 Pa. $29.95

Prices subject to change without notice.

Available at your book dealer or write for free catalog to Dept. GI, Dover Publications, Inc., 31 East 2nd St., Mineola, N.Y. 11501. Dover publishes more than 500 books each year on science, elementary and advanced mathematics, biology, music, art, literary history, social sciences and other areas.